Veda as Vision

Vistas of Vedic Philosophy

Veda as Vision

Vistas of Vedic Philosophy

ShashiPrabha Kumar

DK PRINTWORLD
Publishers of Indian Traditions

Cataloging in Publication Data — DK
[Courtesy: D.K. Agencies (P) Ltd. <docinfo@dkagencies.com>]

Kumāra, Śaśiprabhā, 1951- **author**.
Veda as vision: vistas of Vedic philosophy / ShashiPrabha Kumar.
pages cm
Papers presented at various conferences and seminars in India and abroad over the last two decades.
"The present book is a sequel to an earlier one titled Veda as word ..." – Preface.
Includes bibliographical references and index.
ISBN 9788124613290 (HB)

1. Vedas – Criticism, interpretation, etc. 2. Hindu philosophy. I. Title.

LCC BL1112.26.K86 2025 | DDC 294.5921046 23

ISBN: 978-81-246-1329-0

First published in India in 2025

Printed and Published by:
D.K. Printworld (P) Ltd.
Regd. Office: "Vedaśrī", F-395, Sudarshan Park
ESI Hospital Metro Station, New Delhi - 110015
Phones: (011) 4172 2626, 98713 94815
e-mail: indology@dkprintworld.com
Web: www.dkprintworld.com

Foreword

Professor ShashiPrabha Kumar's *Veda as Vision* is the timely rain when devalorization threatens human existence itself. India of now is in a pilgrimage to the rejuvenation of the long-cherished values wherein we are divine (*amṛtā vayam* – *AV* 3.31.11). Reading through her pages renews our harmonization of the sacred and the profane. In the Vedic vision, it is implicit that life is the colour and fragrance of the Divine. The plenitude of life in the Vedic tradition is in contrast to the obscuration of the sinful origin of life. *Śvestāśvatara Upaniṣad* 2.12 says: *yogāgnimayaṁ śarīram* (body is a fire with *yoga*). Life in our tradition is *yajña* or vivacity, elan. This denotation of *yajña* can be inferred from its derivative in Avesta *yasna*, which has become *jaśna* (celebration) in New Persian. Professor Kumar summons us to energize the sentient deep in our being.

India has brought forth a New Education Policy, away from the Human Resource Development where humans were dehumanized as "resources" like petroleum and minerals. The esoteric mindscape of the Veda is the rise of humans (*udyānaṁ te puruṣa*) to their higher realms in the journey along time and space. Professor Kumar provides the sublime and secular dimensions of Vedic perceptions and their efflorescence in our lives. In the Vedic imperative *techne* has to live in the same shrine as wisdom. Professor Kumar lays before us the grand Vedic mindscape that integrates the transitory and transcendental into ever-evolving parameters. Value consciousness has to complement the value-neutrality of science. The very first chapter "Vedic Vision of

God, Man and Nature" reminds of Raynold Schwab's evocative observation in the Indian Renaissance:

> Western civilization has never matched the deepest metaphysical vision of the Indian civilization, a vision of the Ultimate which is both rational and intuitive.

Spirituality of Matter and Materiality of Spirit

The managers of culture have to mingle with the translogical creators of the quality of life in terms of rhythm and poetry, myth and legend. Therein lie the sap and sinews of culture, the throbbing substance of life and meta-life. *Bhakti* and *bhukti* in the new paradigm are the two shores for the waters to flow so that they do not slush in the shoreless.

Professor Kumar discusses the *apauruṣeya* nature of the Veda in its self-validity and the metaphysical relation between word and meaning. The prefix *a* in *apauruṣeya* is not a negative semanteme but connotes *trans* in the sense of transcendence. It is beyond material existence, the inner experience so that we are not cast into an unsystematic world. This concept in the thought of India was *philosophia perenris* whose two banks were *śruti* and *smr̥ti*. *Śruti* was 'continuity' and *smr̥ti* was 'change'. *Śruti* does not refer to hearing as such, but to glory or adoration, like *śravas* which refers to "fame, renown" in the *R̥gveda*. *Smr̥ti* is from the root √*smr̥* (to remember) something gone. Historically *smr̥ti* can be compared to Russian *smertnaya* (mortal). It is the sigmatic form of *mr̥ti* (dying) or the dying element. While the *śruti* (Vedas) enshrines glorious eternal values, *smr̥ti* is of the changing values.

The role of women to bring forth life and as creatrix of civilization is unique in the Veda as compared to world literature. The word *mā-tā* from the root √*mā* (to make, to produce, to give birth) is a kudos to feminity. The *R̥gveda* speaks of Sky the Father and Earth the Mother (*dyauṣpitā pr̥thivī mātā*). In its transmission to European languages Sky the Father became Zeus in Greek and Jupiter in Latin, and Earth the Mother was dropped. Femina gave humans the superpower of life vs the fury of elements of nature. She constructed a home for her child to come and thus became the founder of civilization, a veritable Goddess. India is the only country where Lakṣmī is the Goddess of Finance, Durgā that of Defence and Sarasvatī that of Education. In a Roman Catholic church Mary the "Mother of God (*Mater Dei*)" cannot be inside the sanctum and she stands in a pavilion outside.

Professor ShashiPrabha Kumar's presentation is a new paradigm: Greek *para* (beyond) + *digm* from the Greek root *deikanumi* (I see). It is the showing of the yonder. She elucidates how the Vedic precedents opened up the dynamics of speech (*vāc*) that have shed ever new horizons of perennial development. Let us join her in an odyssey across the harmony of the Divine, Nature and Life.

1 January 2024 **Lokesh Chandra**

Preface

THE present book is a sequel to an earlier one titled *Veda as Word* edited by the undersigned and published by D.K. Printworld in association with the Special Centre for Sanskrit Studies, JNU, New Delhi in 2006, which was in turn inspired by a national seminar on the theme "Veda as Knowledge" organized by Dr Kireet Joshi under the auspices of Maharshi Sandipani Rashtriya Vedavidya Pratishthan, Ujjain in collaboration with the Indian Council for Philosophical Research, New Delhi in the year 2004.

The book in hand is an effort to explore the inherent vision of the Vedas and expound the underlying philosophical ideas coupled with appropriate and relevant evidences culled out from the original sources. The fourteen articles contained in this book provide a few glimpses of the lofty vision enshrined in the Vedas, such as God, Man and Nature, Self, Body, Women, Language, Yajña and Bhakti.

The word *veda* signifies knowledge which is essentially holistic and universal. It is therefore that the Vedic knowledge encompassess all aspects of cosmic existence: gross or subtle, macro or micro, physical or mental, ritual or spiritual. The *Taittirīya Brāhmaṇa* aptly proclaims:

> *anantā vai vedāḥ* । – 3.10.11.4
>
> Vedas are infinite knowledge.

It is not without reason then that the vast range and the deep sense of the Vedic knowledge cannot be duly comprehended by an ordinary human being since it is held to be delivered by the Supreme Divine at the beginning of each creation for the benefit of whole humanity:

यथेमां वाचं कल्याणीमावदानि जनेभ्यः । – यजु॰ २६.२

yathemāṁ vācaṁ kalyāṇīmāvadāni janebhyaḥ । – *YV* 26.2

I am obliged to all those scholars who invited me for participating in the conference/seminars organized by them and assigned me topics for writing several papers compiled in this book. Since these articles were written at different periods of time and for different places, several repetitions were unavoidable, although an endeavour has been made to minimize them.

I am extremely grateful to Professor Lokesh Chandra for his kind message in the Foreword. His words of wisdom will definitely add value to the volume.

Sincere thanks are extended to the Chairman, Member Secretary and the distinguished members of Indian Council of Philosophical Research (ICPR) for agreeing and approving my request for publication of this volume. This will definitely help in disseminating Vedic wisdom among the scholars and students of philosophy and encourage further research in this area.

Shri Susheel K. Mittal of D.K. Printworld deserves credit for bringing out the book in a befitting manner.

I deem it a privilege to be born in a family who not only followed Vedic tradition but also facilitated my study of Vedas by sending me to an oriental institute, Kanya Gurukula Sasni, Hatharas in my formative years. It was there that I got a chance to enter the majestic portals of Vedic wisdom and encounter the flood light of Vedic vision. It was in fact due to the strong influence of Swami Dayananda Saraswati which enabled women and other deprived sections of society to study the Vedas and imbibe the elevating message envisioned in them. Therefore, I owe it to Maharshi Dayananda Saraswati (b.12 February 1824) and offer the book as a tribute to him on the occasion of his 200th birth anniversary:

> इदं नम ऋषिभ्यः पूर्वजेभ्यः पूर्वेभ्यः पथिकृद्भ्यः । – ऋग्० १०.१४.१५
>
> *idaṁ nama ṛṣibhyaḥ pūrvajebhyaḥ purvebhyaḥ pathikṛdbhyaḥ* ।
>
> – *Ṛ̥V* X.14.15

My sincere gratitude to all the former sages and seers who delved deeper into the secrets of the Vedas and transmitted their knowledge to posterity!

Buddha Pūrṇīmā, VS 2081 **ShashiPrabha Kumar**
4 June 2024

Contents

Abbreviations

AitaBrā	*Aitaeya Brāhmaṇa*
AitaUp	*Aitareya Upaniṣad*
AŚS	*Āpastamba Śrautasūtra*
ĀśvaGṛ	*Āśvalāyana Gṛhyasūtra*
AV	*Atharvaveda*
BraSū	*Brahmasūtra*
BṛUp	*Bṛhadārṇyaka Upaniṣad*
ChāUp	*Chāndogya Upaniṣad*
Gītā	*Śrīmad Bhagavadgītā*
GoBrā	*Gopatha Brāhmaṇa*
JaimiUp	*Jaminīya Upaniṣad*
JaiUpBrā	*Jaiminīya Upaniṣad Brāhmaṇa*
KaṭhUp	*Kaṭha Upaniṣad*
KauBrā	*Kauṣītaki Brāhmaṇa*
MbhŚP	*Mahābhārata*, Śānti Parva
MīSū	*Mīmāṁsāsūtra*
MS	*Manusmṛti*
MuUp	*Muṇḍaka Upaniṣad*
ṚV	*Ṛgveda*
SāmaBrā	*Sāmavidhāna Brāhmaṇa*
ŚānĀr	*Śāṅkhāyana Āraṇyaka*

ŚāṅBrā	*Śāṅkhāyana Brāhmaṇa*
ŚatBrā	*Śatapatha Brāhmaṇa*
SV	*Sāmaveda*
TĀ	*Taittirīya Āraṇyaka*
TaiBrā	*Taittirīya Brāhmaṇa*
TaitSaṁ	*Taittirīya Saṁhitā*
TaiUp	*Taittirīya Upaniṣad*
TāṇḍyaBrā	*Tāṇḍya Mahābrāhmaṇa*
YS	*Yogasūtra*
YV	*Yajurveda*

Introduction

THE present book is an anthology of fourteen papers written and presented by me at various conferences and seminars in India and abroad over the last two decades. A few of these have also been published in reputed journals and volumes. Details are being given at the end of respective chapters. It was felt that not many of these papers could be accessed easily. Therefore, it was suggested by my friends and students that all these papers on Vedas should be made available in a single book so that the integral vision of the Vedas is expressed in a coherent manner.

The Vedas are the ancient most sources of Indian knowledge tradition but are meant for the whole of humanity. They are not the texts of philosophy per se, but the subsequent development of Indian philosophical schools is essentially rooted in them as will be clear from the following pages. Propagation of Vedic vision is a dire need of the hour since India's New Education Policy is based on Vedic knowledge (vide statement of HRD Minister, 11 May 2020).

Vedic vision is not only holistic but also integrates all the levels – physical and spiritual, micro and macro, action and devotion, male and female, mortal and immortal, as well as information, knowledge and wisdom. Accordingly, papers incorporated in this volume are aimed at bringing out the inherent Vedic vision which is not limited to any spatio-temporal boundaries, but is broadly relevant for all times and climes. To elaborate:

The first paper "God, Man and Nature in Vedic Vision" expounds the three basic entities propounded in the Vedic world view. The traditional Indian notion of *sat*, *cit* and *ānanda* symbolizes these three principles enunciated in the Vedas albeit in the reverse order.

Self or consciousness is the primary concern of all philosophical enterprise across the schools of Indian philosophy – Hindu, Buddhist and Jaina. So, the second paper "Vedic View of Self" provides a foundation to the inner quest for an eternal principle leading to the fulfilment of this aspiration in the nature of self-realization according to the Vedic sources.

The third paper "Vedic Conception of Human Body" focuses upon the significance and exaltation of human body in Vedic view. Vedas depict the human body in different images to illustrate its microcosmic model in the universe. According to Vedic view, human body is not just a physical organism but a divine abode as all the divine powers have chosen to reside in it (vide *Aitareya Upaniṣad*). It is therefore termed *devapūḥ* (divine dwelling); the highest goal of immortality can be realized only through the human body. At the same time, it is just a means and not the end in itself; so the Vedic view is different from modern materialistic conception of human body.

The fourth paper "R̥gvedic View of Life" presents a lofty vision of life and is clearly based on preceding three papers. It narrates an inclusive world view as available in the *R̥gveda*, enunciates the inherent aim of human life along with the universal message of gender equality and collective unity. Besides, genuine concern and veneration for all the aspects of Nature like bipeds, quadrupeds as also forests and rivers is expressed through the principles of *yajña* and *r̥ta*.

The next paper is titled as "Mortality, Trans-Mortality and Immortality in Vedic Thought" and is a logical sequel to the fourth paper which charts the path for human life. Accordingly, mortality is given to us human beings while immortality is our ultimate aim. Since we all are progeny of the immortal, therefore we have to transcend mortality and reach out to our final destination of immortal bliss.

Today, the world we live in is distraught with exclusive fragmentation and restrictive demarcation at all fronts. But the Vedic vision propounds an underlying inclusiveness coupled with the inherent interconnectedness. The sixth paper in this volume explains "Vedic Vision of Inclusiveness and Interconnectedness" according to which each entity of the universe is permeated with a single and innermost principle of consciousness. In essence, there is a correspondence between the broad principles of outer world and the subtle processes of inner world in Vedic view. This needs to be kept in mind while dealing with distinct objects and different people of the society at large.

This brings us to the next chapter titled as "Vedas as a Foundation Source of Spirituality". Usually, the Vedas are understood to be centred on ritualism, but delving deeper into the philosophy of Vedas, it becomes evident that there is a certain current of spirituality in all the Vedic narratives. It has rightly been characterized as "Spirituality of Matter" and "Materiality of Spirit".

The eighth paper discusses different dimensions of the "Concept of Bhakti in Vedas" such as: *bhakti* as a moral principle, the nature of divine or deity and the devotee, as also the relationship between both of them, mental modes of the devotee, three tiers of prayer and several desires of the seeker. It goes without saying that the ultimate aim of *bhakti* is nothing less than immortality in Vedic view.

"Yajña in Vedic Tradition" is the ninth paper which describes the Vedic notion of *yajña* as a mode of worship and its philosophical implications. Five types of *yajña*s enjoined in

Vedic view are in fact one's obligations to other human beings as well as divine beings, animals, insects, etc. Significance of *mantras* ordained for chanting along with the offering in a *yajña* is discussed and the role of *yajña* in maintaining the environmental balance is also supported with the evidence from various experiments being carried out across the world.

The tenth paper "Vedic View of Language as Power" is based upon the efficacy of Vedic *mantras* as powerful sound vibrations. Vedas in the form of Śruti represent an oral tradition which emphasizes the importance of *vāk* (speech). *Akṣara, oṁ* and the three *vyāhṛtis* signify word-power which culminates in the chanting of Vedic *mantras*. Ideas like speech and mind express that in Vedic vision language as also of speech and breath is held to be an extraordinary feminine force.

Proper recitation of Vedic *mantras* and proper performance of Vedic *yajñas* require an adequate training which is encapsuled in the form of six Vedāṅgas (subsidiaries of Vedas). Śikṣā, the *first* of these, is the branch which focuses on proper recitation while the eleventh paper "Fundamentals of Vedic Education" explains the basic philosophy of education in Vedic view. Education in Vedic view is founded on the double track of training, i.e. a participatory pattern for both the seeker and the seer. It is not just imparting the formal training to the disciple but enkindling in him the urge to awaken a higher level of consciousness so that he can comprehend the underlying essence of everything around him.

"Vedic Vision of Cosmic Harmony" is the twelfth paper which explores and expounds the inherent synergy between *piṇḍa* (microcosm) and *brahmāṇḍa* (macrocosm) – inner and outer, subtle and gross, individual and universal. Several principles have been enunciated in Vedas to foster this feeling of positive bonding between dichotomous entities of the world for a peaceful living.

"Persona of Women in Vedas" discusses the gender issue from its most basic and original sources and propounds a principle of complete complementarity between male and female. Depiction of women in Vedic view is so profound and powerful that there is no parallel to it in the whole of world literature. Therefore, it is worth emulating and needs to be studied in detail.

The paper, "Concept of Veda-Apauruṣeyatva" deals with the long debate on this issue between Naiyāyikas and Mīmāṁsakas. The authenticity of Vedas is in fact dependent upon this idea of impersonal nature of knowledge which has been variously interpreted by different schools of Indian philosophy. Several theories related with this point such as the nature and source of *dharma*, eternity (or non-eternity) of Vedas, relation between word and meaning, and the self-validity of Vedas have been discussed in this paper.

Besides the above, an article titled "Vedic Studies in Germany" is appended at the end of the volume, as this will be of added interest to the readers of Vedas.

Guru Pūrṇimā VS 2080 **ShashiPrabha Kumar**
4 July 2023

1

Vedic Vision of God, Man and Nature

Precious or durable materials – gold, silver, bronze, marble, onyx or granite – have been used by most ancient peoples in an attempt to immortalize their achievements. Not so, however, with the ancient Aryans. They turned to what may seem the most volatile and insubstantial material of all the spoken word and out of this bubble of air fashioned a monument which more than thirty, perhaps forty, centuries later stands untouched by time or the elements. For the pyramids have been eroded by the desert wind, the marble broken by earthquakes and the gold stolen by robbers, while the Veda remains recited daily by an unbroken chain of generations, travelling like a great wave through the living substance of mind.

The Veda itself is the secret of the Veda. The foundation stone that India contributed to civilization, the Veda, is said to embody the regulations, the laws of the universe as "seen" by the gifted poets, prophets or seers, the *ṛṣi*s. Set by them in a special language to be joyfully proclaimed for future ages, it has come down to us through an elaborate oral tradition, consciously designed to prevent any distortion. Even today had we no written record available, it would still be possible to have access to the Veda as it existed when the text was fixed three or four thousand years ago! – Mee 1975: ix

* * *

> Whatever may be the date of Vedic hymns, whether 1500 or 5000 BCE, they have their own unique place and stand by themselves in the literature of the world. They tell us something of the early growth of the human mind of which we find no trace anywhere else. Whatever aesthetic judgements may be pronounced on them, in the eyes of the historian and the psychologist they will always retain their peculiar value, for superior to the oldest chronicles, for superior to the most ancient inscriptions, for every verse may every word in them, is an authentic document in the history of the greatest empire, the empire of the human mind, as established in India, in the second millennium BCE. – Müller 1971: 35

* * *

> The Vedas are still learnt by heart as they were long before the invasion of Alexander and could now be restored from the lips of religious teachers if every manuscript or printed copy of them were destroyed. – Macdonell 1971: 8

* * *

THE present chapter proposes to expound the Vedic conception of God, Man and Nature as available in the four Vedic Saṁhitās, namely *Ṛgveda*, *Yajurveda*, *Sāmaveda* and *Atharvaveda*.

I

The four books called Vedas (books of knowledge) have been orally transmitted from one generation to another in different parts of India for more than 5,000 years.

II

Apart from the antiquity and the uninterrupted oral tradition, the significance of Veda lies in its profound, positive and pristine world view wherein the trinity of principles, viz. God (*Īśvara*), Man (*jīva*) and Nature (*prakṛti*), is pronounced at various levels; but all the three entities are depicted in such an interconnected and intertwined manner that none of these can be stated to exist exclusively. The universal message and the eternal essence of the Vedic view is rooted in its holistic conception of God, Man and Nature which reflects to be "One in Many" as well as "Many in One" (Bose 1954: 24). To illustrate this unitive vision of the Vedas, it would be appropriate to quote two well-known verses from the *Ṛgveda* and the *Yajurveda* each which explicitly mention the above three eternal principles – God, Man and Nature – as follows:

> *dvā suparṇā sayujā sakhāyā samānaṁ vṛkṣaṁ pari ṣasvajāte* ।
> *tayoranyaḥ pippalaṁ svādvattyanaśnannanyo abhicākaśīti* ॥
> – *ṚV* I.164.20
>
> Two beautiful winged birds are co-habitating in a friendly manner on the same tree; one of them is eating the tasty *pippala* fruit while the other, that does not eat, overlooks all.

* * *

> *īśāvāsyamidaṁ sarvaṁ yatkiñca jagatyāṁ jagat* ।
> *tena tyaktena bhuñjithāḥ mā gṛdhaḥ kasya sviddhanam* ॥
> – *YV* 40.1
>
> All, whatever exists in this universe, is pervaded by God supreme. Enjoy it, knowing full well that it will have to be abandoned/renounced. Do not be greedy. To whom do the riches belong.

III

Accordingly, God (*Īśvara*) in Vedic view is the pure and perfect, Divine, Supreme Self who is not affected with the worldly afflictions. The human being (*jīva*) is the doer and enjoyer of fruits of his own actions while the third factor – matter (*prakṛti*) is the abode of all natural processes taking place. In fact, the traditional Indian conception of God or the Supreme Self as *saccidānanda* represents this trifurcation in a subtle way such as follows:

God	*Man*	*Nature*
Sat (Ever existent) *Cit* (Conscious) *Ānanda* (Blissful)	*Sat* and *cit*	*Sat* only

The Vedic view of God enunciates the divinity in various ways but the broadly underlying idea of One (*R̥V* VIII.58.2; *SV* 372), Supreme (*R̥V* X.121.1), Omnipotent (*R̥V* X.81.3), Omniscient (*R̥V* I.75.2, VI.14.2) and Omnipresent (*YV* 32.8) being is the most pervasive.

God has been depicted in several expressions and also described variously as father or mother (*R̥V* VIII.98.11, X.82.3), brother (*R̥V* X.7.3), friend (*R̥V* VIII.74.2), lover (*R̥V* VIII.84.1) and a guest (*R̥V* VI.15.1) in the Vedas but there is no suggestion of his physical appearance in any way. So, the one with many names (*R̥V* I.164.46); masculine and the feminine (*AV* X.8.27); abstract as well as manifest (*YV* 32.4) all have been well accommodated in the eclectic attitude regarding God reflected thoughout the Vedic elucidation. The divine presence has been narrated in the glory of the Nature and the harmony of the *r̥ta* (cosmic order). In other words:

> The divinity is to be apprehended in terms of moral and aesthetic values. Vedic worship is aniconic. It uses no symbol besides what is found in Vedic poetry and ritual. As no material image is used, the Vedic poet can easily identify one *deva* with another. – Bose 1966: 24

IV

This brings us to the Vedic conception of man. It goes without saying in this regard that the word "man" is used here as a gender neutral term and it simply denotes a person or a human being. According to Vedic view, we, the human beings, are the most blessed ones in the sense that we are not only born as the progeny of the divine (*R̥V* X.13.1) but also have the potential to awaken and enlighten our consciousness from high to higher and then the highest levels of existence (*R̥V* I.50.10; *YV* 35.14). But it must be mentioned here that the Vedic view emphasizes upon the inner transformation of man rather than any external or socialized sense as being proposed by some modern scholars (Mumford 1956: 24).

In other words, the Vedic view conceives of a human being in a progressive or ascent-oriented (*AV* VIII.1.6) model, initially as *jana* or merely a born being, then describes him as a *puruṣa* or an embodied consciousness while ultimately it proclaims him to be *manu* (a rational being) and bear the divine:

> ... *manurbhava janayā daivyaṁ janam* ॥ – *R̥V* X.53.6
>
> May you first strive to become a Man and then rise to the status of a an enlightened one, the Divine!

From this point of view, knowledge, freedom of will, responsibility and enjoyment of fruits are all assigned to a human being to enable him to strive for his sublime aspirations and accomplish his ultimate aim of cosmic peace through a perfect parity between his inner nature and the external world at large so that there is no distortion or disparity at various levels of existence. The Vedic vision of man as a moral agent is therefore duty-centric rather than the contemporary rights-oriented approach.

It is in this background that the Vedic prayers for fearlessness (*AV* XIX.15.6), goodwill (*YV* 34.1-6) and moral upliftment (Sharma 1991: 72-73) of human beings as well as care and concern for the Nature around him should be comprehended. The Vedas present an utmost expression of harmony between God and Man, Man and Man as well as Man and Nature. The charm of Vedic depiction lies in the intense emotional bonding amongst these three principles of the universe. Just as there are narrations of several relations conceived between God and Man, similarly we find many expressions of the inner bonding between Man and Man and also Man and Nature: Son, Mother, Father, Friend, Protector, Benefactor, etc.

V

The glory of Nature has been manifested in Vedic poetry with utmost devotion. The Veda inculcates the culture of caring and nurturing Nature not only in personified presence but also divinized magnificence.

Vedic vision of Nature is poetically rendered in various ways; different deities invoked in the Vedic verses are in fact several aspects of Nature. The Vedas visualize the beauty of Nature in diverse forms such as physical, psychical and spiritual. Almost all the aspects of Nature – earth, water, fire, air, storm, sky, rain, forests, mountains, rivers, animals, birds and reptiles have been eulogized in the Vedas, so much so that the Vedic wisdom itself has been stated to have originated in the lap of Mother Nature:

upahvare girīṇāṁ saṅgame ca nadīnāṁ ।
dhiyā vipro ajāyata ॥ – *YV* 26.15

> The all-wise Lord manifests himself to them, who pray in the valleys of mountains and at the confluence of streams.

In the Vedic world view, all life in the cosmos is interrelated and interwoven; the process of transmutation, cyclic degeneration and regeneration of natural resources is an underlying postulate. The Man–Nature interdependence is at the centre of Vedic vision enunciated through sacred incantations and articulated as rituals for repeated reminding of the need to sustain and foster the ecological balance of Nature.

It is not without reason then, that the feelings of mutual affinity (*AV* VII.52.1), universal friendship (*YV* 36.18), apology (*R̥V* VIII.45.34), grace (*SV* 1872) and gratitude (*R̥V* I.89.2; *AV* XII.1.62) are abundantly expressed in the Vedic verses in the most gracious manner. That is why the Vedic delineation has been held to be the earliest and the best form of poetry:

> Very many of the hymns are merely strings of formulae, but some, despite all the constraints which weigh upon them, show remarkable vigour and originality, and classical India never attained the intensity of expression of some of these old poems. – Renou 1957: 8

VI

Even beyond the form of Vedic poetry and the narration of above-mentioned three entities in an effective and spontaneous manner, it is the interconnectedness of the entities envisioned in Vedic view which points towards an inherent idea of cosmic order, coherence and compatibility, best expressed through the key concepts of *ṛta* and *satya*, *tapas* and *yajña* in Vedic philosophy.

The concept of *ṛta* is the most basic and foundational principle in Vedic view; it is so wide that it includes within its ambit the ritual, the natural as well as the moral order. The spirit of *ṛta* pervades and guides the cosmos from within, even the Supreme Being derives his sanction from the moral law so that there is perfect divine justice, manifested through all cosmic activities. From this point of view, the Vedic notion of *ṛta* anticipates the doctrine of *karma* because it implies that even in the case of individual actions, *ṛta* (eternal moral law) is responsible for the apportionment of reward and punishment. Various aspects of *ṛta* (Kane 1973: 2) inclusively signify that

> the three universal types of being, viz. God, soul and matter, (are) all bound by the universal spirit of *ṛta* in their respective fields of activity. – Singh 1984: 46

To put it more precisely, " … *ṛta* is the nucleus, the navel or the hub of all movements, of the wheel of life" (Mishra 2004: 38). The principle of *ṛta* signifies the sublime and inviolable regularity of the cosmos as also the inner harmony and moral order of a man's conduct. The Vedic idea of *ṛta* finds its manifestation in the moral principle of the individual, i.e. *satya*. *Ṛta* and *satya* are in fact the keywords of Vedic philosophy and represent twin aspects of the same notion; hence both are said to be born out of the same source, *tapas* (*R̥V* X.190.1).

Tapas is the spiritual fire blazing in the heart of man, which, being kindled, lifts him from the animal to the spiritual (divine) plane. *R̥ta* and *satya* as ends and *tapas* as the means form the foundation of Vedic philosophy and religion. It is, therefore, that according to the Veda, true worship is rendered when it is offered with the observation of *r̥ta* and *satya* and with *śraddhā* (faith) and *tapas* (*R̥V* IX.113.2).

In brief, *r̥ta* and *satya* stand for the Vedic view of interdependence between natural law and the moral law; both these laws have also been expressed by the word *dharman* (*R̥V* I.164.50, II.13.7). The Veda envisages that those who live in terms of *r̥ta* as moral form also participate in *r̥ta* as aesthetic form, since good life is made happy and beautiful by the bountiful Nature (*R̥V* I.90.6).

The holistic and harmonious view of Veda is contained in yet another key concept of *yajña* which symbolizes the subtle Vedic ideal of cosmic interdependence among God, Man and Nature. The secret of this principle of *yajña* lies in offering oneself for the other. Etymologically the term *yajña* signifies a spirit of cosmic harmony through sacrificing (Kumar 2005: 59-75) one's own limited interests for the world at large. The process of mutual re-enforcement and benign sacrifice operates at both the levels – microcosmic as well as macrocosmic – wherein the divine offers himself for creating the world (*R̥V* X.90.16); Nature offers itself for protecting and sustaining the life while it is the obligation of Man to cultivate his inner sense of casting off the petty pursuits so as to protect and restrengthen the external environment around him. In fact, the Veda has itself proclaimed *yajña* to be the navel of the universe (*R̥V* I.164.35). *Yajña* is the central thread binding together the souls of men with the divine on the one end and the natural forces on the other.

VII

What follows from the above brief delineation is that the Vedic view of God, Man and Nature is an inclusive one; it accepts and accommodates God, Man and Nature, all the three as eternal, independent entities but at the same time envisages a strong synthesis among these. In fact, the quintessence of Vedic philosophy lies in comprehending the clue that while the Divine is the supreme protector of *ṛta* and the Natural powers uphold their benign resources for sustaining the world, it is obligatory upon us, the human beings, to enhance our moral worth, inculcate a sense of righteousness and maintain the balance. It is therefore that the Vedas invariably exhort man to overcome evil and proceed further till the final goal of universal harmony is achieved; the ultimate stage of ecstasy is solicited herein through a self-disciplined, well ordained and harmonious way of life which is the perennially relevant message of the Vedas.

To conclude with a Vedic prayer wherein all the three eternal principles mentioned above are aspired to exist in complete concord:

> *ādityā rudrā vasavaḥ sunīthā dyavakṣāmā pṛthivī antarikṣam sajoṣaso yajñamavantu devā ūrdhvaṁ kṛṇvantvadhvarasya ketum* ।
> – *ṚV* III.8.8

> May the cosmic divine powers such as sun, wind and life-giving breath afford protection and may heaven and earth and other divine powers cherish our worshipful acts with a common consent. May they raise aloft the banner of our dedicated action of public good.

2

Vedic View of Self

VEDAS are held to be the most ancient and authentic storehouse of Indian philosophy and culture. It is not only their anthropological significance, or poetic appeal, but also the philosophical background and spiritual content which pervades throughout these fountainheads of knowledge, sustains them as a source of inspiration and strength for the whole of humanity, and makes them universal in character. Moreover, India and the Indian philosophy are known for their knowledge of the self (*ātmavidyā*), which is contained primarily in the Vedas and Upaniṣads.

I

The most striking feature of Vedic philosophy is its emphasis on the divinity of a human being and immortality of his self. The Vedas speak of an individual as a combination of the perishable material body and the imperishable inner spirit[1] which is the essential, immortal self. Mortality of a person is limited to his body and earthly existence only, since his self is immortal by nature. It is in this background that in the famous R̥gvedic verse addressed to Rudra Tryambaka, it is prayed that, "release us

---

1 *amartyo martyenā sayoniḥ* । – *R̥V* I.164.30, 38

from mortal life and not from immortality".[2] In another Ṛgvedic verse, human beings are addressed as "children of immortality, who inherit the celestial regions".[3]

From this point of view, human life is nothing but a pursuit of the divine, a quest for immortality while dwelling in the mortal frame of existence. Just at the beginning of this journey, a fundamental enquiry about one's own existence is the impelling factor which culminates in self-realization; this is the beginning as well as the end of *darśana* in India: from *ko 'ham* to *so 'ham* is the length and breadth of life according to this view. There is a very thin line between these two but a broad course of contemplation matched with austerities fills the gap. The Vedic view of life envisages that although human beings are tied up with death,[4] yet a mortal can transcend it and attain immortality by knowing the self. There is no other way to reach the ultimate goal.[5]

This immortal aspect or the spiritual essence of man has been expressed as *ātman* in the Vedas which is usually translated into English as the self or soul. So, the Vedic view of self is mainly the concept, connotation and concurrence of *ātman* in the four Vedic Saṁhitās.

It is to be clarified at the outset that the Vedic philosophy does not present any coherent and cogent conceptualization of *ātman* but it definitely provides supple and serious stock of ideas which may prove foundational in this respect. The following delineation is undertaken as a modest attempt in the same direction.

---

2 *mṛtyormukṣīya māmṛtāt* । – *ṚV* VII.59.12

3 *śṛṇvantu viśve amṛtasya putrā ā ye dhāmāni divyānī tasthuḥ* ॥ – *ṚV* X.13.1

4 *mṛtyubandhava ādityā manavḥ* । – *ṚV* VIII.18.22

5 *tameva viditvātimṛtyumeti nānyaḥ panthā vidyate 'yanāya* । – *YV* 31.18

II

The word *ātman* has been most frequently used in Indian philosophy and literature right from the *Ṛgveda* up to the modern times. In the *Ṛgveda* itself it occurs about thirty times (Narahari 1944: 43), about twenty-two times quite independently in different case-endings and eight times as a part of compounds like *ātmadā* and *ātmanvat*. Not only that, an abridged form *tman* of the word *ātman* is used about seventy-eight times (Narahari 1944: 5) in different case-endings in the *Ṛgveda*, used partly as a reflexive pronoun and partly as an adverb.

As far as the various meanings of the word *ātman* (Sharma 1972: 11-13) are concerned, even in the *Ṛgveda* it denotes as many as half a dozen meanings such as:

a. Wind (*ātman vātaḥ*)
b. Breath (*prāṇa*)
c. Oneself (*svayam*)
d. Body (*śarīra*)
e. Essence
f. Controller
g. Eternal and intelligent principle

Etymologically the word *ātman* has been derived from the following two roots:

a. √*at sātatyagamane* (to move constantly), and
b. √*ap vyāptau* (to pervade).

Accordingly, Yāska, the famous Vedic interpreter, has explained the word *ātman* in three ways;

that which

i. moves constantly,
ii. pervades everywhere, and
iii. appears pervaded or contained (by the material body).[6]

---

[6] *ātmā atatervā, āptervā, api vāpta iva syād yāvad vyāptibhūtaḥ* ।
– *Nirukta* 3.15

In other words, *ātman* is that pervasive principle which sustains its existence in all the stages of waking, dream, deep sleep, death, etc. According to Śaṅkara, "that everlasting principle which receives, which possesses and which enjoys the objects is eulogized as *ātman*".[7]

Interestingly, some Western scholars have derived the term *ātman* in a different manner. German scholar Schweitzer has tried to identify the word with the German word *Ātmen* and derive it from the root √*an* (= to breathe), while Georg Curtius and Grassmann have derived it from the root √*an* (√*vā*) (= to blow)(Schweitzer 1960: 39). Paul Deussen, however, does not seem to favour these derivations and says that it is a highly abstract word which is to be derived from the root *a* as seen in *aham* (I) and *ta* (perhaps from *tad* = this). Accordingly, it denotes "this I", the self which, in due course, is felt to be the final expression for the ultimate fact of existence arrived at by stripping away the various coverings which envelop the ultimate reality, the covering of the body, the covering of the mind, the covering of the intellect, etc. (Sharma 1972: 13).

In the later Vedic period, when the meaning of the word *ātman* evolved and attained new dimensions, the various senses attributed to the word were recorded in the Sanskrit lexicons[8] as follows:

a. Creature (*jīva*)
b. Nature or habit (*svabhāva*)
c. Effort (*yatna*)
d. Sight (*dr̥ṣṭi*)
e. Intellect (*buddhi*)
f. Ultimate reality (*Brahman*)

---

7 *yadāpnoti yadādatte yaccātti viṣayānayam* ।
yaccāsya santato bhāvastasmādātmetikīrtyate ॥
– quoted by Śaṅkara in his *Kaṭhopaniṣadbhāṣya* 2.1.1

8 *Vācaspatyam*, vol. 1, pp. 663-85; *Śabdakalpadrama*, vol. 1, p. 172.

g. Body (*deha*)
h. Mind (*manas*)
i. Exclusion of the others (*paravyāvartanam*)
j. Son (*putra*)
k. Fire (*agni*)
l. Air (*vāyu*).

In the light of the above, many scholars have tried to trace the evolution of the concept of *ātman* in Vedic philosophy. According to Keith, the word *ātman* might have originally implied *wind* from which sprang up the sense of breath; from breath developed the sense of "self" and subsequently it came to stand for the reflexive person (1925: 451-52). Further, it was taken to express such meanings as "body", "trunk", "the essential nature of a thing", "a principle distinct from the members of the body and body itself", "consciousness" (*vijñāna*) and finally the ultimate reality of the universe, which is expressed as *Brahman* in the later texts. In the words of S. Radhakrishnan:

> *Ātman* is the principle of man's life, the soul that pervades his being, his breath *prāṇa*, his intellect, *prajñā* and transcends them. *Ātman* is what remains when everything, that is not the self, is eliminated. – 1953: 73

III

The very notion of the self as an individual represents an embodied existence, hence body is stated to be the abode of *ātman*. Since the immortal soul of man lives in it, the mortal body is also expressed to enjoy a sort of reflected divinity. The *Atharvaveda* makes a detailed statement about the indwelling spirit, using the beautiful analogy of the lotus for the body of man:

> The nine-petalled lotus (that is the body of man) covered over by three bands in which lives the spirit with the *ātman*. That, verily, the *Brahman*-knowers know. Desireless, serene,

> immortal; self-existent, contented with the essence, lacking nothing is that one fears not death who has known: That *Ātman*, serene, unchanging, ever youthful.[9]

In another place, the *Atharvaveda*, praying for the health and efficiency of every limb, adds: "And may my soul (*ātmā*) remain unconquered".[10]

Various other expressions have also been given to denote the spiritual significance of human body, such as:

i. Divine dwelling (*devānām pū* – *AV* 10.2.31)
ii. Divine boat (*daivī nāva* – *AV* 7.6.3)
iii. Abode of the *Brahman* (*brahmapurī* – *AV* 10.2.2-30)
iv. Divine chariot (*devaratha* – *YV* 29.43.54)
v. Field-being (*kṣetra* – *R̥V* X.32.7; *AV* 11.1.22).

All these analogies are meant to signify that the body, although being physical and perishable, is not going to last for ever, yet it deserves due care and importance because it is here that the self finds its abode. The twin terms like *kṣetra–kṣetrajña, ratha–rathin, kṣara–akṣara* and *martya–amr̥ta* are actually intended to manifest the mutual connection between body and the soul. The same is beautifully conveyed in the verse I.164.38 of the *R̥gveda*:

> *apāṅ prāṅeti svadhayā gr̥bhito 'martyo martyenā sayoniḥ* ।
> *tā śaśvantā viṣūcīnā viyantā nyanyaṁ cikyurna ni cikyuranyam* ॥
>
> Rearwards and forwards goes one, held by Svadhā, becoming immortal, having the same origin as the mortal. These two, eternal, moving around, go in different directions. They understand the one: They do not understand the other.

---

9 *puṇḍarīkaṁ navadvāraṁ tribhir guṇebhirāvr̥tam* ।
tasmin yad yakṣam ātmanvat tad vai brahmavido viduḥ ॥ – *AV* 10.8.43

10 *ūrvorojo jaṅghāyorjavaḥ pādayoḥ pratiṣṭhā ariṣṭāni me sarvātmā nibhr̥ṣṭaḥ* । – *AV* 19.60.2

IV

It is also worth mentioning here that the embodied self is mostly understood to be an individual soul (*jīva*).

The term *jīva* occurs in the *Ṛgveda* in several senses such as life (V.44.5, V.78.9, X.57.5), living being in general (I.92.9, IV.51.5), children (X.18.4), etc. But it also occurs in the sense of individual soul or the ultimate reality in an individual (I.164.30). The same usage continued in later Vedic and post-Vedic literature so as the word *jīva* came to be denotative of the eternal principle in an individual. Thus, for example, Śaṅkara frequently uses this word in the sense of "ultimate reality in an individual". The same is sometimes called *jīvātmā* and sometimes only *jīva*, the later part being dropped. Jaina system of philosophy adopted this word to indicate "the intelligent and eternal principle in an individual" and *ajīva* as unconscious material (*pudgala*).[11]

This brings us to the question of individual soul vis-à-vis Supreme Soul. In fact, we do find a direct mention of duality in this respect in the famous verse of *Ṛgveda* I.164.20:

> *dvā suparṇā sayujā sakhāyā samānaṁ vṛkṣaṁ pariṣasvajāte* ।
> *tayoranyaḥ pippalaṁ svādvattiyanaśnannanyo abhi cākaśīti* ॥
>
> Two birds, friends, united to each other, resort to a common tree. Of the two, one eats the tasty berry the other without eating, looks on.

Here we are clearly led to the concept of *jīvātman* and *Paramātman*, the relative and the absolute self, an important idea of the post-Vedic philosophy.

It is interesting to note here that even this explicit statement of dual principles, which came to be expressed as the *jīva* and *Brahman* in Indian philosophy is variously interpreted by different scholars to suit their philosophical presuppositions. But

---

11 *tāvajjīvājīvākhye dve tattve staḥ tatra bodhātmako jīvaḥ abodhātmakastvajīvaḥ* । – *Sarva-Darśana-Saṁgraha,* Ārhatadarśanam

one thing is very certain in this regard that the Vedic philosophy, at many more places, does denote these two principles of individual as well as Supreme Self. In fact, in the verse quoted above, all the adjectives are used indiscriminately for both of these kinds of self which have been characterized as friends and dwelling on the same tree. In another Ṛgvedic *mantra,* we find description of *ajo bhāga* (*ṚV* X.16.4) or the unborn portion in the ephemeral body of man which goes on to suggest that there is some eternal principle in it too.

V

Another noteworthy feature of Vedic philosophy is that numerous synonyms (*Nirukta* 14.10) have been used to indicate the principle of self or soul which go on to prove the point stated above. All such terms, when studied in a proper perspective, provide sufficient material for thought and scholars from ancient times have elaborated upon these. On the basis of such studies, it can be said that out of all these the two prominently popular terms in Indian thought are *ātman* and *Brahman.* In the later Vedic literature, mainly the Upaniṣads, these words are used interchangeably, but in the Vedic Saṁhitās their connotations are diverse and nothing can be said in a definite manner except that the evolution of the thought-process must have affected some semantic changes in the course of development of words also.

VI

In the famous Puruṣa-Sūkta of the *Ṛgveda* (X.90.1-16), which is repeated in the *Yajurveda* (31.1), *Śatapatha Brāhmaṇa* (13.6.2.2) and *Taittirīya Āraṇyaka* (3.12.1), we find that the word *puruṣa* too denotes two levels of reality: individual as well as cosmic. This famous hymn presents a symbolic account of the manifestation of divinity through creation wherein the divine manifested only a part of him and *puruṣa* as individual being was the first manifestation of the ultimate on the relative plane. The etymology of the word *puruṣa* also signifies the embodied or limited self. But that is not to be taken as a complete picture, since the hymn opens with the introduction of an anthropomorphized form of the first principle of the universe which is described as having 1,000 heads, 1,000 eyes and 1,000 feet.[12] The implication of all this is that he (the cosmic *Puruṣa* or the Creator Lord) singly pervades all the creatures. He also covers the earth, i.e. all the world, from all sides and still stands 10 fingers beyond that.

In the opinion of a modern Vedic scholar, Earth (*bhūmi*) is to be read here as meaning the universe. *Puruṣa* is said here to be immanent everywhere and in everybody. By the term "he is furthermore wider by 10 fingers", it is apparently intended to mean that he is also transcendent. Thus, poetic imagination easily crosses the hurdle which theology is unable to deal with satisfactorily, viz. the simultaneous immanence and transcendence of the godhead (Sundarraj 1994: 495-96). In the words of Radhakrishnan, the reciprocity of the causes of birth implies here that *Puruṣa* (Supreme Reality) is "the begetter as well as the begotten" (1956, vol. 1: 156). All this clearly indicates that the Vedic view of self (*ātman*) was much influenced by this concept of *puruṣa* where the unity in diversity is discussed under the appellation *puruṣa.*

VII

Similarly, Indra, who is so frequently invoked in the Vedic Saṁhitās, conveys much more in this regard. Indra's description in the Vedas has been interpreted at two levels: Supreme and the individual. But at both these levels, Indra represents the spiritual essence or the eternal self which rules over the non-eternal forms of existence. In the transcendental sense, Indra is the one (*ekaḥ*), the single (*kevalaḥ*), the ultimate (*paraḥ*), the supreme (*paramaḥ*), the primal (*prathamaḥ*), the great (*mahān*). As a *deva* (manifested divinity), he is coexistent with *ṛta* and *satya,* and is the saviour (*trātā*), the rescuer (*pātā*), the purifier (*pāvaka*)

---

12 *Ṛgveda* X.90.1, tr. Ralph T.H. Griffith.

and the leader through the path of goodness (*sunītiḥ*). As a hero (*sūraḥ*), Indra is the destroyer of wicked powers (*vṛtrahā, ghnan vṛtrāṇi*), the conquerer unconquered (*jetā aparājitaḥ*), lord (*patiḥ*) and king, and ruler over his own divine dominion, made free from Vṛtra's or the enemy's aggression (*svarāṭ*), and, he is the Lord of the people (*gaṇapatiḥ*) (Bose 1966: 26).

But above and behind all these, Vedic Indra is in fact the self (*ātman*) who controls the sense organs (*indriya*s). He is called Indra because he tears them with his spiritual strength and stabilizes them.[13]

It is in this background that Indra is stated to be the Lord of *deva*s, this is precisely the secret of his sovereignty: just as the *ātman* is the Supreme Power in the universe, Indra is the greatest among the *deva*s (*ṚV* I.129.10, II.12.9; *AitaBrā* 7.16), he is Śatakratu (*ṚV* VI.45.25) (performer of hundred deeds) and Saptaraśmi (*ṚV* II.12.12) (master of seven rays); these seven rays are actually the seven *prāṇa*s (vital airs) in the human body, they are the seven *paridhi*s (limits) of the soul (*ṚV*).

Indra is said to be the controller of these seven *prāṇa*s, meaning thereby that one, who intends to realize the *ātman*, has to regulate the seven sense organs which have been so often mentioned in the Vedic verses. Indra is *vṛṣabha* (ibid. X.103.6) (strong bull), since he is capable of controlling them in one single stroke.

The bravery and valiance of Indra, as found in the Vedas, signify the urge of an indomitable will. In the exhortation of Indra to win his autonomy by defeating Vṛtra, there is also the exhortation to humans, to win spiritual sovereignty by fighting to win over the powers of evil:

> "Be heroic, brothers, following the example of Indra" – *imaṁ sajātā anu vīrayadhvan* (*ṚV* X.103.6) is the call of the Veda. Not

---

13 *kaścanāsminvā idamindriyaṁ pratyasthāditi tasyendrasyendratvam* ।
– *TaiBrā* 2.2.10.4

only that, Indra is the eternally young hero, years do not age him, nor do months and days wear out Indra (*R̥V* VI.24.7). The mystery of Indra's eternal youth can be revealed through the spiritual power of the self which does not wither away at any time. Indra's glory manifests the transcendental nature of the spirit, "not even 100 heavens or 100 earths or even 1,000 suns could match his being" (*R̥V* VIII.70.5). He is the model (*pratimāna*) for all the world (*R̥V* II.12.9). He is in fact the prototype (*pratirūpa*) of all forms.

> For each and every form he is the model, it is his form that is to be seen everywhere. Indra by his charm (*māyā*) moves in many forms truly, his bay steeds are yoked in a thousand times.
> – *R̥V* VI.47.18

Obviously, the delineation of Indra is in realty the development of the Vedic view of self both at the level of *ātman* as well as *Paramātman*: here, Vedic realism seems to be merging in transcendentalism and sowing the seeds of Vedānta (Bose 1966: 25-26).

It is interesting to quote Śaṅkarācārya here who, while commenting on the verse quoted in the *Br̥hadāraṇyaka Upaniṣad* (14.8), says:

> Why did he come in so many forms. Were name and form not manifested, the transcendent nature of *ātman* as pure intelligence would not have been known.[14]

VIII

Another important expression for *ātman* in the Vedas is *prāṇa*. It is derived from the root *ān*, to breathe and is therefore related to one of the derivations of the word *ātman*. It occurs at many places in the Vedas conveying the sense of "life breath" (*R̥V* I.66.1, 48.10, 101.5; III.53.21; X.59.6, 121.3, 189.2) as well as "the Ultimate Reality" (*AV* 11.4.1).

---

[14] Śaṅkara in his commentary on the verse (*R̥V* VI.47.18) quoted in *Br̥hadāraṇyaka Upaniṣad* 2.5.19.

Prāṇa is the life-force of human body, it is the inner lustre of that self-luminous spark called *ātman* (*YV* 3.7). In other words, *prāṇa* is *aṅgirasa,* the vitality pervading throughout the limbs of the human physique (*YV* 3.3). It is *prāṇa* that joins this mortal body with immortality: *amr̥tamu vai prāṇaḥ* (*ŚataBrā* 9.1.2.32). *Prāṇa* is the foundation of this body and it is known as *puruṣa* as well, since it lies in the body (*GoBrā* 1.39).

Prāṇa is the symbol of consciousness in Vedic philosophy; it is through this *śepa* (sign) that the greatest level of consciousness, *mahāprāṇa,* is realized. That is why *prāṇa* is narrated as Śunaḥśepa in Vedic texts since *aśva* and *śvāna* are not horse and dog but the appellations of *prāṇa* only (*ŚāṅBrā* 5.2; *KauBrā* 3.3). In fact, all conscious beings such as *puruṣa, gau, aśva, ajā* and *avi* which are conventionally interpreted as the names of human beings or animals are the symbols of *prāṇa* (Agrawala 1983: 84) in Vedic view.

Prāṇa is also equated with the seven *r̥ṣi*s (*AV* 10.2.27), who dwell in the divine light of the head, characterized as heaven. It means that the seven sense organs are connected and controlled by the self, the centre of consciousness within human body (*Br̥Up* 2.2.3-4). In fact, the Vedic *mantra*s, especially from the *Atharvaveda* extol the supremacy of *prāṇa* in very clear terms and propound that it is through the elevation of *prāṇa* that the mortal human beings can attain immortality. In fact, the twin divine physicians invoked as Aśvinīkumāras in the Vedic *mantra*s are none but the dual functioning of *prāṇa* and *apāna* only (*AV* 7.53.2).

IX

The Vedic view of self envisages that the same eternal principle which dwells within the non-eternal frame of the individual *piṇḍa* as *jīvātman* manifests itself as *Paramātman* at the cosmic level of *brahmāṇḍa.* There are many expressions available in the Vedic verses to denote this Supreme Self, but the first and foremost among such terms is *Brahman.* This word occurs at over 200 places in the *Ṛgveda* in various forms and in both the genders, masculine and neuter; it connotes several senses in different Vedic verses and the scholars have tried hard to interpret them (Sharma 1972: 15-18). However, the idea of *Brahman* as an expression of the Absolute Reality is derived from the etymology of the word itself and it continues throughout the development process of its conceptualization. From this point of view, *Brahman* signifies the Supreme Self, the essence of all that is intangible and eternal. Words like Viśvakarmā, Bṛhaspati, Prajāpati, Viṣṇu, Skambha, Ucchiṣṭa, Yama, Varuṇa, Agni and Āditya are different delineations of the same supreme power which creates, sustains and destroys the world.[15] *Oṁ, Eka, Īśa* and *Akṣara* are the characterizations of him only, the first and final principle of the universe. To quote:

> We have already traced in detail how this search was prosecuted through the period of the Brāhmaṇas, how Prajāpati was gradually displaced by *Brahman* and how, finally, the most definite expression for the object of man's search was found in the conception of *ātman. Ātman* is Indian expression for that we are accustomed to call "the first principle".
>
> – Deussen 1908: 85-86

In fact, the Vedic philosophy is so subtle and suggestive that there may be numerous interpretations of its abstruse symbolism and so the Vedic view of self defies logic in expressing the Supreme Reality in so many ways which might seem contradictory and confusing at times. But scholars have found that there are particular techniques of style to imply the divine all-pervasiveness. One of them is to use the prefixes *sam* and *vi,* having contrary meanings, the one signifying convergence and the other divergence:

---

15 Dayananda Saraswati, 2001a, *Satyārtha Prakāśa,* Samullāsa I, Īśvaranāma- Vyākhyā, pp. 06-19.

saṁ ca vi ca eti । – *YV* 32.8

Therein unites and therefrom emanates all.

* * *

vipaśyati … saṁ ca paśyati । – *ṚV* III.62.9

He sees all living beings separately and together.

He, the *purohita* (stationed at the front) is one who leads together (*samnaya*) and leads separately (*vinaya*). – *ṚV* II.24.9

Varuṇa is of our own land (*saṁ-deśya*) Varuṇa of a foreign land (*vi-deśya*). – *AV* 4.16.8

– Bose 1966: 295

X

On the basis of the above, it may be said that the Vedic view of self visualizes and seeks the divinity pervading the universe in its "unmanifested form". The beginning of this search is in the form of a question beautifully expressed in the Vedic *mantra*s like the following ones:

- … *kasmai devaya haviṣā vidhema* । – *ṚV* X.121.1, 9
- *ko addhā veda ka iha pravocat* । – *ṚV* X.129.6

This perennial pursuit was termed as *sampraśna* (great query):

yo devānāṁ nāmadha eka eva tam sampraśnaṁ bhuvanā yanti sarvā । – *Atharvaveda* 2.1.3

All the varieties of existence are in constant quest of this truth, the secret of their own spirit which is difficult to be grasped. Inadequacy of language compels us to capture the mystery beyond, in words like *yat* and *yo* which are so indefinite in nature but the profundity of the inner urge to reveal the mystery leads to the awareness of the essence as *sat* and the unification of all realities in that (*tat*):

venastatpaśyannihitam guhā sat yatra viśvam bhavatye-kanīḍam ॥ – *YV* 32.8

Vena beholds That being, hidden in the cave, in whom all find one single home.

The direct vision of the universal, divine presence finds a spontaneous expression in the following form of certainty which points towards the one and single reality wherein all forms of essence converge:

tadevāgnistadātiyastadu vāyustadu chandramāḥ tadeva śukraṁ tad brahma tā āpaḥ sa prajāpatiḥ ॥ – *YV* 32.1

Agni is that, Āditya is that, Vāyu is that, *candramā* is that, the bright is that, *Brahman* is that, waters are that, Prajāpati is that.

The immediate experience of this underlying unity of all forms of existence culminates in self-realization. The splendour of the self shines in such first person utterance as follows:

vedāhametaṁ puruṣaṁ mahāntamādityavarṇam tamasaḥ parastāt । – *YV* 31.18

I have known this Great *Puruṣa,* who is refulgent as the sun beyond darkness.

In short, the Vedic view of self seems to be a gradual transition from the awareness of a soul within our soul to the identification of our self with the Supreme Self as stated at the close of *Yajurveda*:

so asavaham: oṁ khaṁ brahma । – *YV* 40.17

That (*Puruṣa*) I am, *oṁ* the Supreme Being, the Eternal *Brahman.*

3

Vedic Conception of Human Body

THE chapter intends to expound and examine the conception of human body as available in Vedic sources, mainly the four Vedic Saṁhitās.

Vedas are held to be the earliest available literature of humankind and the most ancient sources of Indian philosophical thought; these texts are in fact esteemed as the perennial treasure house of knowledge in Indian tradition.[1] The profound Vedic vision has not only influenced the ways of thinking of Indian people, but has also percolated through their modes of living. Vedic view of life is an inclusive one wherein the idea of body and self, matter and spirit is well integrated. Accordingly, human body, though material and mortal, is taken to be a means for attaining the highest goal of immortality. It is, therefore, that in Vedic view, the human body is not just described from an outer, organic aspect, rather, it is presented in a holistic manner and therefore all its parts are desired to be nourished[2] and not to be neglected.

---

1 *bhūtam bhavyam bhaviśyacca sarvam vedātprasiddhyati* । – *MS* 12.97

2 *vāṅma āsannasoḥ prāṇaścakṣurakṣṇoḥ śrotram karṇayoḥ* ।
āpalitāḥ kesāḥ asonā dantā bahu bāhvorbalam ॥
ūrvorojo jaṅghāyorjavaḥ pādayoḥ ।
pratiṣṭhā ariṣṭāni me sarvātmānibhṛṣṭaḥ ॥ – *AV* 19.60.1-2

II

The rich and deep Vedic thought is expressed through a poetic rendering of the highest order. Therefore, the language of Vedic literature is extremely metaphorical. The area of Vedic philosophy is so vast and its concepts are so subtle that it is at times difficult to capture the exact sense of the terse Vedic statements, more so when they appear to be suggestive rather than being descriptive. Nonetheless, there is an internal persuasiveness of Vedic thought which permeates through the entire tradition of Indian philosophy. Although the Vedic philosophy is usually characterized in an exclusive manner, either as "spiritual" on the one hand or "ritual" on another hand, yet on closer study it is revealed that there is in fact a fine synthesis of both these aspects – the physical as well as the mental, the mundane as well as the sacred. Accordingly, the Vedic idea of human body is an integral one. It not only presents a depiction of the finite material frame but also envisages deeper layers of vital, mental, intellectual and spiritual aspects. So, it is all the more relevant in contemporary consumerist discourse where physical body is held to be just an anatomical form and indulgence in bodily pleasures is considered to be the be-all and end all of human life.

It is worth mentioning here that in Vedic view, the human body is extolled as an abode of the divine, immortal spirit; the mortal aspect of human body does in no way make it a despicable object, rather, it is stated to be the means for attainment of immortality, the ultimate aim of life. It is not without reason then that, good health and proper nourishment of physical body is desired for in several Vedic prayers,[3] but at the same time there are finer aspirations and higher goals to achieve in human life:

---

3 *tanupā agne 'si tanvam me pāhāyuredā agne 'syāyurme dehi varcodā agne 'si varco me dehi । agne yanme tanvā ūnam tanma āpṛṇa ।*

– *YV* 3.17

Beholding the uprising divine light beyond the mundane darkness, we by and by approach the spiritual one, the divine of divines.[4]

III

The first and foremost feature of human body according to Vedic philosophy is that it is held to be a micro model of the macrocosm; the complete ecosphere of the universe is represented in it and there is perfect parity between the two: *yathā piṇḍe tathā brahmāṇḍe*. In fact, it is held to be the most amazing creation of the divine. This feeling is expressed in a full hymn of the *Atharvaveda* comprising of thirty-three verses wherein several questions have been raised about the remarkable working of human body such as follow:

> By whom the two heels of humans were formed? By whom the flesh was put on? By whom the two ankles? By whom the beautiful fingers? By whom the orifices? By whom the two foot-soles and who gave him support in the middle?[5]
>
> Why did they make the two ankles below, and the two knee-joints above them? Separating the two shanks, where did they set them in and where the two joints of the two knees? Who has thought and planned it?[6]
>
> Who provided a human with two arms, so that he may act with vital strength. Which was the enlightened one who put two shoulders upon his trunk?[7]

---

4 *udvayam tamasaspari svaḥ paśyanta uttaram* ।
devam devatrā sūrya-maganmajyotiruttamam ॥ – *YV* 20.21

5 *kena pārśni abhṛte puruṣasya kena māṁsam sambhṛtam kena gulphau* ।
kenāṅgulīḥ peśanīḥ kena khani kenocchlaṅkhaṅkhau madhyataḥ kaḥ pratiṣṭham । – *AV* 10.2.1

6 *kasmannu gulphavadharavakṛṇvanasthīvantavuttarau pūruṣasya* ।
jaṅghe nirṛtya nya dadhuḥ kva svijjānunoḥ saṁdhī ka u tacasciketa ॥ – *AV* 10.2.2

7 *ko asya bāhū samabharadvīryam karavāditi* ।
ansau ko asya taddevaḥ kusindhe adhya dadhau ॥ – *AV* 10.2.5

> Which was that deity, who first having made a human skull, made the brain, the forehead and the occiput, and having piled up the pile between his two jaws, ascendant to heaven?[8]
>
> Who placed within him the semen, so that he may extend his line? Who has conducted the intellect into him? Who has put the singing (voice) and who the dancing in him?[9]

In view of the above, the human body is termed as a field (*kṣetra*) in Vedic verses for sowing and reaping the fruits of action by each individual; while the one who owns and knows this field, i.e. the self, is said to be the *kṣetravit* or *kṣetrapati*:

> One who knows not the true path inquires from one, who knows it; and directed by the skilful guide, he travels onward; this is, in truth, the blessing of instructions got from others and thereby one finds the straight path that leads directly forward.[10]
>
> May the divine refulgent Lord, the saviour, be for our happiness; may the radiant dawns be propitious to us. May the clouds be propitious for our people; may the sovereign Lord of universe bless us for happiness.[11]

Therefore, the Vedas exhort the human beings to stay undiseased in their own fields, i.e. bodies:

> Turn thou towards her together with the cattle; be opposite

---

[8] *mastiskamasya yatamo lalāṭam kakāṭikāmprathamo yaḥ kapālam* ı
citvā cityam hanvoḥ pūruṣasya divam ruroha katamaḥ sa devaḥ ıı
– *AV* 10.2.8

[9] *ko asminreto nyadadhattanturā tāyatāmiti* ı
medham ko asminnadhyauhatko bāṇaṁ ko nṛto dadhau ıı
– *AV* 10.2.17

[10] *akṣetravit kṣetravidaṁ hyaprāṭ sa praiti kṣetravidānuśiṣṭaḥ* ı
etadvai bhadram-anuśāsanasyota śrutiṁ vindatyañjasīnām ıı
– *ṚV* X.32.7

[11] *saṁ no devaḥ savitā trayamāṇaḥ saṁ no bhavantūṣaso vibhātīḥ* ı
saṁ naḥ parjanyo bhavatu prajābhyaḥ śaṁ naḥ kṣetrasya patirastu śambhuḥ ıı
– *AV* 19.10.10

> to her together with the divinities; let not curse attain thee, nor wicked craft (*abhicāra*) bear rule (*vi-rāj*) in thine own field (*kṣetra*), free from disease.[12]

Moreover, the human body is held to be sacred in Vedic view since it is the abode of various deities and is therefore stated to be the divine city, Devapurī, i.e. Ayodhyā:

> With eight circles and nine gates or portals impregnable is the castle of the enlightened ones. Therein lies the golden chest, conductor to the world of bliss-encompassed by brilliant light.[13]

It needs to be noted here that the human body is characterized as *ayodhyā* a divine city where there are eight circles (*cakra*s) and nine doors (*dvāra*s) for safeguarding the golden treasure (of bliss or consciousness) which is covered with light (of knowledge). (*aṣṭā-cakrā* = eight basic building materials of body, see *TĀ* 1.27.2-3) (*tvak* = skin; *asrak* = blood; *māṁsa* = flesh; *meda* = fat; *asthi* = bone; *majjā* = marrow; *śukra* = semen and *oja* = glow); (*nava-dvārā* = nine portals – seven in head: two eyes, two ears, two nostrils, one mouth opening and two below for extricating urine and faeces). All of these stay together in human body in a harmonious manner, there is no battle or struggle among them since each one is living and working in its own sphere. Obviously, this model of harmony which is operating within the human body at a micro level is universal and needs to be adopted at the macro level in all spheres of life – be it familial, social or cosmic. The integral relationship between the parts and the whole is in fact a Vedic paradigm for universal accord and cosmic concord, which is manifested through the most intimately enjoyed personal experience of human body.

---

12 *abhyāvartasva paśubhiḥ sahainām pratyanenām devatābhiḥ sahaidhī* ।
mā tvā prāpaccchapatho mābhicāraḥ sve kṣetre anamīvā vi rāja ॥
– *AV* 11.1.22

13 *aṣṭācakrā navadvārā devānām pūrayodhyā* ।
tasyām hiraṇyayaḥ koṣaḥ svargo jyotisāvṛtaḥ ॥ – *AV* 10.2.31

The remarkable sanctity of human body is revealed through a parable in the *Aitareya Upaniṣad* which goes on like this:

> God first created the divine forces like Agni, Vāyu and Āditya in the beginning; these divine forces requested God to provide them with a beautiful abode so that they could enjoy the experiences of life. God first created the body of a cow and showed them to the divine forces but they did not like it and disapproved of the same. Thereafter God created the body of a horse but the divine forces did not like it too. Finally the lord brought the human body and they all shouted happily: This is perfect, this is good. Then he asked all the divine forces to enter different parts of the human body.
>
> Fire becoming speech entered the mouth. Air becoming breath entered the nostrils. Sun becoming sight entered the eyes. Directions becoming sound entered the hearing organ. Herbs and plants becoming hair entered the skin. Moon becoming mind entered the heart. Death becoming exhalation (*apāna*) entered the navel. Water becoming semen entered the generative organ.[14]

On the basis of this narrative, it goes without saying that in Vedic view, human body is held to be the best among the bodies of all living beings.

Interestingly, the *Jaiminīya Upaniṣad Brāhmaṇa* also expresses the same view and mentions that the fire-God entered the human body in the form of speech (*vāk*), the moon-God entered

[14] *tābhyo gāmānayattā abruvanna vai no 'yamalamiti tābhyo 'śvamānayattā abruvanna vai no 'yamalamiti* ॥
tābhyaḥ puruṣamānayattā abruvan sukr̥taṁ bateti puruṣo vāva sukr̥tam । *tā abravīdyathā 'yatanam praviśateti* ॥ – *AitaUp* 1.2.2-4

agnirvāgbhūtvā mukhaṁ prāviśadvāyuḥ prāṇo bhūtvā nāsike prāviśadādityaścakṣurbhūtvākṣiṇī prāviśaddiśaḥ śrotraṁ bhūtvā karṇau prāviśannoṣadhivanaspatayo lomāni bhūtvā tvacaṁ prāviśaṁścandramā mano bhūtvā hr̥dayaṁ prāviśanmr̥tyurapāno bhūtvā nābhiṁ prāviśadāpo reto bhūtvā śiśnaṁ prāviśan ।।

it in the form of mind (*manas*), sun-God in the form of eye (*cakṣu*), directions (*diśaḥ*) in the form of ear (*śrotra*) and the air (*vāyu*) in the form of nose (*prāṇa*). Therefore, the human body is stated to be a divine assembly.[15]

The human body is not only an abode of different deities, but also a dwelling for the seers. Several Vedic verses expound that there are seven seers who actually signify the five sense organs besides the mind and the intellect within the human body and vigilantly guard it from inside against all odds that might be prevailing outside:

> Seven seers have been posted in the body. Seven guard it all the time with constant alertness. Seven pervading ones reach the world of sleeping and there keep awake the two life bestowers, that never sleep and that stand by to protect good people.[16]

The *Śatapatha Brāhmaṇa* explains these seven seers within the human body and narrates that both the ears are in fact sages Gautama and Bharadvāja, both the nostrils are sages Vasiṣṭha and Kaśyapa, both the eyes are sages Viśvāmitra and Jamadagni and mouth is Sage Atri.[17]

The *Atharvaveda* also echoes the above depiction as follows:

> This is a bowl with opening on the sideways and bottom upward; glory of all form is deposited in it. Therein sit

---

15 *esā daivī pari sad, daivī sabhā, daivī saṁsat* । – *JaiUp* 2.11.12-13

16 *sapta ṛṣayaḥ pratihitāḥ śarīre sapta rakṣanti sadamapramādam* । *saptāpaḥ svapato lokamīyustatra jāgṛto asvapnajau satrasadau ca devau* ॥ – *YV* 34.55

17 *imaveva gotamabharadvājau ayameva gotamo 'yam bharadvāja imaveva viśvāmitrajamadagnī ayameva viśvāmitro 'yam jamadagnirimāveva vasaṣṭhikaśyapāvayameva vasiṣṭho 'yam kaśyapo vagevatrirvaca hyannamadyate 'ttirha vai namaitadyadatririti sarvasyatta bhavati sarvamasyannam bhavatiya evam veda* । – *ŚatBrā* 14.5.2.6

> together the seven seers, who have become the protectors of this great one.[18]

All these elucidations imply that the human body is a holy habitat for the seers and so it deserves to be maintained with piety and reverence.

IV

Various appellations are available in Vedic verses to denote the human body such as:

i. *śarīram* – *R̥V* (Kh.) 12.1; *AV* 5.30.13, 11.8.11, 19, 25, 34; *BrUp* 4.4.16

ii. *kāyaḥ* – *YV* 20.4

iii. *gātram* – *AV* 18.4.52

iv. *tanus* – *R̥V* X.4.6; *AV* 4.25.5, 14.1.38

v. *śavaḥ* – *R̥V* X.8.5, IV.8.8, VIII.12.26, VIII.24.2; *AV* 20.56.01

vi. *vapuḥ* – *R̥V* III.39.3, 55.9; *YV* 30.14; *AV* 6.72.1

vii. *kṣetra* – *AV* 11.1.22, 19.10.10.

Obviously, these terms convey the rich litany for human body presented in Vedic view.

At the same time it is also denoted from these delineations that in Vedic philosophy human body is neither treated as "cultural artefacts", fabricated both in the writing and reading of "body texts" in the Derridian[19] (Fox 1997) sense nor as an anatomical object of postmodern discourse as discussed by Michel Foucault.[20] On the contrary, human body is conceived to

---

18 *tiryagbilaścamasa ūrdhvabudhnastasminyaśo nihitaṁ viśvarūpam* ।
tadāsata r̥ṣayaḥ sapta sākam ye asya gopā mahato babhūvuḥ ॥
– *AV* 10.8.9

19 Fox, Nick J., 1997, "Is There Life After Death?: Texts, Frames and Differends" In *Foucault, Health and Medicine*, ed. Alan Petersen and Robin Bunton, 31-50, London: Routledge.

20 For details, see Lupton 1994.

be a sacred substratum in Vedic view rather than just a physical frame. Even the famous Puruṣa Sūkta of the *R̥gveda* (*R̥V* X.90) which has been quoted by a contemporary scholar as the only evidence to demonstrate the Vedic image of human body as "The Body of Sacrifice"(Wujastyk 2009) cannot be explained just at the ritual level, since there are profound spiritual concepts contained within it.

Even at the very basic level, there are several Vedic verses wherein health and strength of human body is aspired so that the pursuit of goodness may be accomplished.[21] It means that the human body is not something just physical to be despised due to its being filled with filthy material inside but it is much more and a rare divine gift bestowed on humankind as a pious means for performing noble deeds and attaining the ultimate end of life. Therefore, the human body is neither to be outrightly deplored nor to be simply adored as the ultimate end in itself; it is not an instrument for indulging in sensual pleasures, but the only means for acquiring higher goals in life:

> Oh my child! you are mounted on a new chariot, which is wheel-less and single-poled, but it turns everywhere (and on all sides). You have fashioned it mentally; you stand thereon though you know not the mystery of it.[22]

V

To put it more precisely, the human body and its parts are neither to be satiated nor to be suppressed but to be sublimated in Vedic view. Accordingly, the human body is described as a sacred altar wherein a constant *yajña* is continuing; the same has been metaphorically expressed as follows:

---

21 *bhadraṁ karṇebhīḥ śr̥ṇuyāma devā bhadraṁ paśyemākṣabhiryajatrāḥ* ।
sthirairaṅgais-tuṣṭuvāṁśas-tanūbhir-vyaśema devahitaṁ yad-āyuḥ ॥

– *R̥V* I.89.8

22 *yaṁ kumāra navaṁ rathamacakraṁ manasākr̥ṇoḥ* ।
ekesaṁ viśvataḥ prāñcam apaśyannadhi tiṣṭhasi ॥ – *AV* X.135.3

> Bones are the wooden sticks in this *yajña*, his mind is the chief priest (Brahmā), vital air is the singing priest (*udgātā*), *apāna* air is the presentor (*prastotā*), *vyāna* air is the receiver (*pratihartā*), speech is the offering priest (*hotā*), eye is the officiating priest (*adhvaryu*), *prajāpati* is the member, other organs are the reciting priests (*hotrāśāṁsinaḥ*) helping sacrificers while self is the main sacrificer (*yajamāna*).[23]

The Vedic depiction also characterizes human body as a chariot (*ratha*). In a R̥gvedic verse, it is stated that the human body is a chariot of Indra, which contains four yokes and three whips, this chariot is started every morning after cleaning and refreshing and is driven by goodwill and pure intellect.[24] Elsewhere, the *R̥gveda* raises a query about the birth of this body in the form of a chariot and provides an answer as well:

> Who gives birth to this youth? Who has driven the chariot off? Who can tell us how it takes a subsequent body?[25]
>
> How does the subsequent body come into existence after the previous one? Before that the causal matter is held outstretched; and subsequently, the form comes out of it.[26]
>
> This is the dwelling of the Self, the Yama, which is called the

---

[23] *puruṣo vaiyajñastasya ... mana eva brahma, prāṇa udgātā, apānaḥ-prastotā, vyānaḥ pratihartā, vāghotā, cakṣuradhvaryuḥ, prajāpatiḥ sadasyaḥ aṅgāni hotrāśāṁsinaḥ, ātmā yajamānaḥ* ।
– *Gopatha Brāhmaṇa* 2.5.4

[24] *prātā ratho navo yoji sasniścaturyugas trikaśaḥ saptaraśmiḥ* ।
daśāritro manuṣyaḥ svarṣāḥ sa iṣṭibhir matibhī raṁhyo 'bhūt ॥
– *R̥V* II.18.1

[25] *kaḥ kumāram ajanayad rathaṁ ko nir avartayat* ।
kaḥ svit tad adya no brūyād anudeyī yathābhavat ॥ – *R̥V* X.135.5

[26] *yathābhavad anudeyī tato agram ajāyata* ।
purastād budhna ātataḥ paścān nirayaṇaṁ kr̥tam ॥ – *R̥V* X.135.6

fabric of gods (the organs of senses); this pipe is sounded for his gratification and he is propitiated by hymns.[27]

The *Yajurveda* also describes human body in the form of a chariot in which the soul as a charioteer is driving the horses (sense organs), whereas, its desires and mind are motivating the reins of the chariot.[28]

The above metaphor used for the human body being a chariot is beautifully revealed in the following well-known verses of the *Kaṭhopaniṣad*:

> Know the (individual) self as the master of the chariot and the body as the chariot. Know the intellect as the charioteer, and the mind as verily the bridle.[29]
>
> They call the organs the horses; the organs having been imagined as horses, (know) the objects as the roads. The discriminating people call that Self the enjoyer when it is associated with body, organs and mind.[30]

VI

Besides the above delineations in Vedic view, the human body is elucidated as a divine boat (*daivī nau*) as well. According to this narration, this divine boat is an impeccable creation which does neither overflow nor drip from anywhere and is provided to us sinless mortals for crossing over to reach the goal of well-being:

---

27 *idaṁ yamasya sādanaṁ devamānaṁ yad ucyate* ।
iyam asya dhamyate nāḷīr ayaṁ gīrbhiḥ pariṣkṛtah ॥ – *ṚV* X.135.7

28 *rathe tiṣṭhannayati vājinaḥ puro yatra yatra kāmayate susārathiḥ abhīsūnām mahimānampanāyata manaḥ paścādanu yacchanti rasmayaḥ* ॥ – *YV* 29.43

29 *ātmānaṁ rathinaṁ viddhi śarīraṁ rathameva tu* ।
buddhiṁ tu sārathiṁ viddhi manaḥ pragrahameva ca ॥ – *KaṭhUp* 1.3.3

30 *indriyāṇi hayānāhurviṣayāṁsteṣu gocarān* ।
ātmendriyamanoyuktaṁ bhoktetyāhurmanīṣiṇaḥ ॥ – *KaṭhUp* 1.3.4

> For our weal, may the sinless, embark upon the divine boat, the creative power (*aditi*) fitted with good oars, unleaking, well-protecting like earth, unblemished like sky, full of comforts, and conducting wisely.[31]

Evidently, the subtle suggestion in the above depiction is that we, the travellers in this divine boat should be pure-hearted, only then it can lead us to the highest goal. Life is a long and arduous journey, and it can be successfully completed if the mode of this journey is adequately equipped and flawlessly working. So, the human body needs to be looked after carefully and maintained well.

Last but not the least, the human body is also equated with a divine lute (*daivī vīṇā*) which resonates with soul-stirring music provided that the players of such a lute are dexterous enough:

> Thereafter, this becomes a divine lute this human lute becomes an image of that.[32]

Obviously, the music emanating from this divine lute is suggestive of the explicit speech which only the human beings can speak. Just as an expert lute-player attracts everyone through his music, a person, who speaks well, can accomplish all his tasks through his effective speech. So, the human beings, as indwellers of their consecrated bodies should strive for a melodious symphony within their finite frame; this would in turn lead to attainment of infinite bliss.

---

31 *sutrāmāṇaṁ pr̥thivīṁ dyām anehasaṁ suśarmāṇam aditiṁ supraṇītim* ।
daivīṁ nāvaṁ svaritrām anāgasam asravantīm āruhemā svastaye ॥
– *R̥V* X.63.10

32 *atha iyam daivi vma bhavati* । *tadanu kr̥tirasau mānuṣī vīṇā bhavati* ॥
tadyathā iyamakuśalena vādayitrā vīnā 'rabdhā na tatkr̥tsanam vīṇā-rtha sādhyatyevameva akuśalena vaktrā vāgārabdhā na tatkr̥tsanam vāgartha sādhayati । *tadyathā haivevam kuśalena vādayitrā vīṇārabdhā kr̥tsnam vīṇārtha sādahyatyevameva kuśalena vaktrā vāgārabdhā kr̥tsanam vāgārtha sādhayati* ॥
– *ŚāṅĀr* 8.9-10

VII

What follows from the above brief discussion is that in Vedic view, the human body is held to be a sanctum sanctorum and so it deserves to be exalted. But it needs to be reiterated that this significance and sacredness of human body in Vedic view does not in any way convey that the body in itself is the ultimate end in itself. On the other hand, the human body is sanctified in Vedic conception because it is the rarest means for realizing the ultimate end which cannot be attained through lesser or ignoble ways. In other words, the highest aim of human life is the attainment of immortality according to Vedic philosophy, this can be accomplished only through the finite mortal frame and so human body has to be hallowed.

To sum up, it may be remarked that the Vedic conception of human body is an integral one since it does not define it just as a limited physical organism or a material form which demarcates and differentiates humanity through caste, colour or creed but elevates it to the subtle conceptual level signifying of a purest and rarest bounty, equally bestowed upon all the human beings for fulfilment of the utmost aim of life, i.e. the immortality, since all of them are proclaimed to be the progeny of the divine.[33]

---

33 *yuje vāṁ brahma pūrvyaṁ namobhir vi śloka etu pathyeva sūreḥ* । *śr̥ṇvantu viśve amr̥tasya putrā ā ye dhāmāni divyāni tasthuḥ* ॥ – *R̥V* X.13.1

4

Ṛgvedic View of Life

THE *Ṛgveda* is the oldest available document in the library of the mankind. It presents a pronouncedly rich source of knowledge which is yet to be paralleled. The poetic vision, the linguistic rigour, the historic antiquity and the philosophic profundity of the *Ṛgveda* have all been widely studied and richly acclaimed. But what fascinates one at once is the simple and strong, elevating and ennobling view of life which emerges from a cursory reading of the *Ṛgveda*. It is this universal message of the *Ṛgveda* which is perennially relevant for humanity and holds the primary concern of this paper, i.e. the nature, aim and way of life as propounded in the *Ṛgveda*.

I

The *Ṛgveda* proclaims and addresses all the human beings of the world as progeny of the divine and implores them to be humane and divinize their posterity as well. Accordingly, human life in the Ṛgvedic vision is not just an ordinary occasion, but a rare opportunity to accomplish the ultimate aim of life that is no less than the goal of immortality, which can be achieved through a well-ordained view of life envisioned in various Ṛgvedic hymns.

The Ṛgvedic view of life is not limited or fragmented, it is an inclusive, universal and transtemporal vision in which the reality is neither dissected into isolated observations, nor the individual differences are ignored; rather, they are integrated into a simple, unified and liveable insight which is reflected at various levels – subtle and gross, one and many, sacred and profane. The same can accordingly be comprehended from the point of view of an individual person and his progress to perfection, as also in relation to one's spouse, the family, the society and the world at large.

II

As stated above, according to the Ṛgvedic world view, emergence of life is not just accidental at the individual level, it is in fact a divine process and a unique occasion for unravelling the deeper mystery of life and for continuation of the cosmic cycle. Therefore, the birth of a child is itself a celebration of life in Vedic view and is determined by well-defined rules and rites enjoined in the Gṛhyasūtras. It is in this human birth that the mortal beings get an opportunity to attain immortality, although they are all eternally tied to death:

> *mṛtyubandhava … manavaḥ* । – *ṚV* VIII.18.22
>
> Humans have death as their lifelong companion.

It is noteworthy here that since the mortal body is an abode of the immortal spirit, the Vedas proclaim that the body needs to be nourished and strengthened at first, only then other aspects of life can be fruitfully enjoyed. This basic view of a holistic, healthy and harmonious life is expressed in several Ṛgvedic verses such as:

> *imā brahmendra tubhyaṁ śaṁsi dā nṛbhyo nṛṇāṁ śūra śavaḥ* ।
> – *ṚV* X.148.4
>
> Oh Resplendent Lord! these prayers have been addressed to you, Grant Oh hero! strength to these humans.

* * *

yo agniṁ tanvo dame devaṁ martaḥ saparyati ।
tasmā id dīdayad vasu ॥ – *ṚV* VIII.44.15

Whosoever mortal worships the divine fire within his body for the attainment of wealth and riches, to him it gives all of these.

* * *

pavitraṁ te vitataṁ brahmaṇaspate
prabhur gātrāṇi paryeṣi viśvataḥ ।
ataptatanūr na tadāmo aśnute śṛtāsa
id vahantas tat sam āśata ॥ – *ṚV* IX.83.1

Oh Lord of divine enlightenment! your processes of purification are widely stretched out (in cosmos); You are the sovereign, who rules over the entire creation from all sides; You never get tired (become hot) in your work; Your divine bliss is not obtainable to those who are unripened. Only the mature ones receive the graces from you.

Moreover, completeness of age, which is devoid of diseases and sins, is the ideal of Ṛgvedic seers:

śatam in nu śarado anti devā yatrā
naś cakrā jarasaṁ tanūnām ।
putrāso yatra pitaro bhavanti mā
no madhyā rīriṣatāyurgantoḥ ॥ – *ṚV* I.89.9

Hundred autumns are assigned to us by God in the midst of our passing existence subject to old age and decay. We, who are sons today shall be fathers tomorrow and therefore, may we have no afflictions or infirmities in the midst of our lifespan!

III

The most immediate form of individual growth is seen through marriage in Ṛgvedic vision. This is very well reflected in the Ṛgvedic verses on marriage ceremony where friendship is solicited and oneness of hearts is sought between the husband and wife.

ihaiva staṁ mā vi yauṣṭaṁ viśvamāyurvyaśnutam ।
krīḷantau putrairnaptṛbhir modamānau sve gṛhe ॥
– *ṚV* X.85.42

May you both (husband and wife) stay here, not be separated, And may live full life that is bestowed upon you. Playing with your children and grandchildren, Enjoying in your own home!

* * *

samañjantu viśve devāḥ samāpo hṛdayāni nau ।
saṁ mātariśvā saṁ dhātā sam u deṣṭrī dadhātu nau ॥
– *ṚV* X.85.47

May the universal *deva*s and *āpas* join our hearts together;
So may Mātariśvan, Dhātrī and Dveṣṭrī unite us both!

Another expression to this congruent principle is available in the male–female parity which is so well established in the *Ṛgveda* that it needs a lot of elaboration. But the same can be substantiated through various epithets used in several other hymns for designating a woman (Kumar 1999a: 32-33). In fact, the message of the *Ṛgveda* in this regard is that the foundation for social solidarity and universal concord is laid in a happy family where both the partners live and work in complete coordination rather than the aggressive competition or constant confrontation of modern times.

The *Ṛgveda* not only depicts a perfect parity between the two but also goes a step further and declares that it is the wife who symbolizes the house:

jāyed astaṁ maghavantsedu yonis
tad it tvā yuktā harayo vahantu ।
yadā kadā ca sunavāma somam
agniṣṭvā dūto dhanvātyaccha ॥ – *ṚV* III.53.4

May the wife, Oh bounteous One! be provided with a dwelling, so that she gives birth to your child. Let the horses be harnessed to your chariot and convey you there. We prepare the herbal juices proper to the season. May the fire divine come as messenger before you.

It is in this background that the bride is even addressed as the *samrājñī* (illuminant/empress) of the house:

> *samrājñī śvaśure bhava samrājñī śvaśrvāṁ bhava* ı
> *nanāndari samrājñī bhava samrājñī adhi devṛṣu* ıı
> – *ṚV* X.85.46
>
> Be a queen to thy father-in-law, a queen to thy mother-in-law, A queen to thy husband's sister, and a queen to thy husband's brothers.

No wonder that a dialogue in the *Ṛgveda* carried on by the wife of the sacrificer, the *yajamāna* himself and Prajāpati (the genius of procreation) exhibits the delicacy of the relationship between husband and the wife and also underlines the sacredness of the act of procreation (*ṚV* X.184.1-3): Human birth is stated to be a symbolic culmination of the cosmic birth of all living things; therefore, Agni, the life-germ of all creatures and the power that fecundates waters, is invoked for bestowing children to the couple:

> *agne śukreṇa śociṣo ru prathayase bṛhat* ı
> *abhikrandan vṛṣāyase vi vo made garbhaṁ dadhāsi jāmiṣu vivakṣase* ıı
> – *ṚV* X.21.8
>
> Oh Fire divine! your glory spreads far and wide by your radiant lustre; In your exhilaration, you pour rainwater and impregnate herbs and plants.

IV

The union of two individuals through marriage results in a family, where again collective endeavour is aspired and coordination among different members with varying types of temperaments is enunciated as follows:

> *kārur ahaṁ tato bhiṣag upalaprakṣiṇī nanā* ı
> *nānādhiyo vasūyavo 'nu gā iva tasthimendrāyendo pari srava* ıı
> – *ṚV* IX.112.3

I am a singer, Dad is a physician, Mummy throws the corn upon the grinding stone; Having various occupations, and seeking riches, We remain (in peace and harmony) in the family, like cattle in a common stall. May you flow, Oh elixir of bliss!, for the sake of the aspirant self! Flow Indu, flow on for Indra.

It is through the idea of a loving family that the *Ṛgveda* presents a comprehensive paradigm of social organization wherein the inborn natural inequalities are to be minimized and people live like brothers:

ajyeṣṭhāso akaniṣṭhāsa ete saṁ bhrātaro
vāvṛdhuḥ saubhagāya ।
yuvā pitā svapā rudra eṣāṁ sudughā
pṛśniḥ sudinā marudbhyaḥ ॥ – *ṚV* V.60.5

Like brothers, of whom no one is elder, no one younger, they grow up together for their mutual prosperity. Their father, the cosmic source of vitality, is ever-youthful, doer of good deeds, and mother, the midspace, who is easy to be milked, make their days favourable for their growth.

Another one of such verses is worth quoting here:

... pumān pumāṁsaṁ paripātu viśvataḥ ॥ – *ṚV* VI.75.14

One human being should look after the other human being by all means.

There is another prayer in the *Ṛgveda* for forgiveness of sins against all human beings:

aryamyaṁ varuṇa mitryaṁ vā
sakhāyaṁ vā sadam id bhrātaraṁ vā ।
veśaṁ vā nityaṁ varuṇāraṇaṁ vā
yat sīmāgaścakṛmā śiśrathastat ॥ – *ṚV* V.85.7

The person who loves us is a friend, a comrade for ever, brother, a neighbour who is always with us and even the stranger.

This brings us to the point of interdependence of life according to the *Ṛgveda*. The Ṛgvedic model of life is not exclusive and compartmentalized, rather it is inclusive and integral wherein human beings and all elements of nature are depicted as complementary to each other. The emotional bonding between human beings and various forms of Nature is expressed in several prayers of the *Ṛgveda* according to which collective cooperation among all groups of people is solicited and benign bounties of Nature are invoked. In fact, the Ṛgvedic hymns evidence a strong desire to embrace the whole of reality and encompass the complete cosmic creation. So, human life is seen here as an inclusive enterprise in which all the concrete particulars of the universe are well accommodated.

In this way, the *Ṛgveda* envisages a roadmap for peace and harmony charted through an individual's heart, since it is in the mind of humans that all seeds of discọrd and dissonance are sown. In other words, it is only when a human being is at peace with oneself, that he or she can find peace elsewhere. It is therefore that the prayers for self-improvisation, self-enrichment and self-proclamation are abundantly available in the *Ṛgveda*.

Ṛgvedic view of life is metaphorically expressed as a rocky river which we all have to swim across by carrying all that is good and leaving all that is ignoble:

aśmanvatī rīyate saṁ rabhadhvam
uttiṣṭhata pra taratā sakhāyaḥ ।
atrā jahāma ye asann aśevāḥ śivān
vayam uttaremābhi vājān ॥ – *ṚV* X.53.8

The rocky stream flows on, hold you all together, Quit you like heroes and cross over, my friends! Leave here all those that are evil. Let us cross to powers which are noble.

VI

The Ṛgvedic idea of a meaningful life implies an ascent-oriented, dynamic model following which each one of the human beings should and can attain the fullest glory already inherent within oneself. It is in this background that the Ṛgvedic prayers for overall enjoyment in life like the following ones can actually be comprehended:

... viśvāhā vayaṁ sumanasyamānāḥ ॥ – *Ṛ*V VI.75.8

So let us here, daily, be joyous!

* * *

viśvadānīṁ sumanasaḥ syāma paśyema nu sūryamuccarantam ।
– *Ṛ*V VI.52.5

May we at all seasons be possessed of healthy minds, and may we behold the rising sun.

It is only when a person is contented and happy within that his aspirations for a full and long life for himself as also for all of his fellow-beings make complete sense:

taccakṣur devahitaṁ śukram uccarat ।
paśyema śaradaḥ śataṁ jīvema śaradaḥ śatam ॥ – *Ṛ*V VII.66.16

That God-ordained bright eye of the universe (Sun) rises, may we behold it for a full hundred autumns, and may we live a hundred autumns.

* * *

... devā na āyuḥ pra tirantu jīvase ॥ – *Ṛ*V I.89.2

May the gods lengthen our life!

* * *

... bhadraṁ jīvanto jaraṇāmaśīmahi ॥ – *Ṛ*V X.37.6

May we attain old age by living life in a noble way!

* * *

bhadraṁ karṇebhiḥ śṛṇuyāma devā
bhadraṁ paśyemākṣabhiryajatrāḥ ।
sthirairaṅgaistuṣṭuvāṁsas-
tanūbhirvyaśema devahitaṁ yadāyuḥ ॥ – *Ṛ*V I.89.8

Oh learned people! may we with our ears listen to what is beneficial. Oh noble persons! worthy of sacred deeds, may we see with our eyes that is desirable. May we, engaged in your praises, enjoy with firm limbs and sound bodies; a full term of life dedicated to God.

In fact, when life is seen from such a positive and profound point of view, only then one can feel the constant flow of sweetness in and around oneself:

madhu vātā ṛtāyate madhu kṣaranti sindhavaḥ ।
mādhvīr naḥ santvoṣadhīḥ ॥

madhu naktam utoṣaso madhumat pārthivaṁ rajaḥ ।
madhu dyaurastu naḥ pitā ॥

madhumānno vanaspatirmadhumāṁ astu sūryaḥ ।
mādhvīrgāvo bhavantu naḥ ॥ – *ṚV* I.90.6-8

Sweet blows the breeze for him, who lives by Law, rivers for him pour sweets. So may the plants be sweet to us! Pleasant be our nights, pleasant dawns, and pleasant the dust of the earth! Pleasant for us the Father Heaven! May the lordly forest tree give us pleasure! Pleasant be the Sun! And pleasant the rays of light!

VII

The Ṛgvedic hymns abound in depicting due care, concern, reverence and veneration for all the aspects of Nature pervading the earth, the heaven and the mid-region.

In this context, the Ṛgvedic prayers for peace in all aspects of the world like the following ones are also notable:

katarā pūrvā katarāparāyoḥ kathā jāte kavayaḥ ko vi veda ।
viśvaṃ tmanā bibhṛto yaddha nāma vi vartete ahanī cakriyeva ॥
- *ṚV* I.185.1

Which of these is older, and which later? How were they born? Who knows it, you sages? These of themselves support all things existing. The twins uphold, though motionless and footless, a widespread having feet and moving.

* * *

bhūriṁ dve acarantī carantaṁ
padvantaṁ garbhamapadī dadhāte ॥ – *R̥V* I.185.2
nityaṃ na sūnuṁ pitrorūpasthe
dyāvā rakṣataṁ pr̥thivī no abhvāt ॥

May we be close to both the Worlds, who suffer no pain, parents of gods, who aid with favour. Wide, vast and manifold, whose bounds are distant, these reverent, I address at this our worship; the blessed pair, victorious, all sustaining. Protect us, Heaven and Earth, from fearful danger.

* * *

aneho dātramaditer anarvaṁ huve
svarvadavadhaṁ namasvat ।
tad rodasi janayataṁ jaritre
dyāvā rakṣataṁ pr̥thivī no abhvāt ॥ – *R̥V* I.185.3

These Heaven and Earth, bestow prosperity on all sustainers of the region. Holy ones and wise; two bowls of noble kind: between these, the god, the effulgent sun, travels by fixed decree. Widely capacious pair, mighty, that never fail, the Father and the Mother keep all creatures safe.

* * *

atapyamāne avasāvantī anu
ṣyāma rodasī devaputre ।
ubhe devānām ubhayebhirahnāṁ
dyāvā rakṣataṁ pr̥thivī no abhvāt ॥ 4 ॥ – *R̥V* I.185.4

Son of these parents, he the priest with power to cleanse, sage, sanctifies the world with his surpassing power.

A reference must also be made to the following:

dyaurme pitā janitā nābhiratra
bandhurme mātā pr̥thivī mahīyam । – *R̥V* I.164.33

The heaven (or the sun) is my parent and progenitor; the navel (of the earth) is my kinsman; the spacious earth is my mother.

Here a special mention needs to be made of another hymn (*Ṛ̥V* X.146) addressed to the goddess of forest, Araṇyānī:

> The Forest Queen, the tutelary Goddess of the forest and wilderness, which has a message to us in the context of the large-scale deforestation that is taking place all over the world. In a prophetic vein the poet asks the question why the Goddess of the wood has moved away from the village; is this not a comment on the present-day situation in which the steady expansion of urban life and the growth of consumerism lead to the diminution of the forest and ecological imbalance? The poet observes that the Forest-Goddess never kills anyone and that no one attacks a person under her protection. Also, the hymn praises her for being a kind, hospitable hostess, offering abundant, natural food, even though she does not fit.
>
> – Balasubramaniam 1996: 94

The *Ṛ̥gveda* presents plenty of prayers addressed to various aspects of Nature such as the earth, the sky, the sun, the moon, the rivers, the rain, the dawn and the night. So, it has rightly been called a Nature-Poetry: several modes of Nature-worship in the *Ṛ̥gveda* have been enunciated such as prayer, laudation, propitiation and sacrifice (Chaubey 1970: 128-33).

VIII

Life according to the *Ṛ̥gveda* is not only meant for fulfilling individual aspirations, but also caring for and nurturing other aspects of life. This is sought to be obtained through the Vedic principle of *yajña*, i.e. sacrificing one's best for the world at large. The concept of *yajña* is so central in Ṛ̥gvedic thought that one cannot understand the complete picture of life without an overt or covert reference to it.

> If one had to choose a single word to express the quintessence of the Vedic Revelation, the word *yajña* (sacrifice) would perhaps be the most adequate. – Panikkar 2001: 347

More importantly, this principle of *yajña* is not just an external act to be performed by a particular individual in a spatio-temporally limited sense. This involves a much deeper and subtle idea which is linked with the *piṇḍa* and *brahmāṇḍa*, i.e. the microcosm as well as the macrocosm. So, the Vedic ritual is a combination of visible and the invisible, atomic and the cosmic, darkness and the light, matter and the spirit, human and the divine (Kumar 2005c: 62).

From this angle, *yajña* (ritual act) is a step towards spiritual discipline, social solidarity and cosmic harmony.

> The Vedas regard the universe as a seamless garment in which all living beings have their appropriate places. Their interdependency is emphasized, the welfare of one being determined by the welfare of all. – Moore 2008: 218

It is through this spirit of ceaseless cooperative activity of both inanimate nature and living beings as also of the creator God that the wheel of creation is kept moving – *yajña* signifies this spirit of harmony through sacrifice. In the famous Puruṣa Sūkta of the *Ṛgveda*, this principle of congruity between the individual *puruṣa* with the cosmic *puruṣa* is metaphorically interwoven within the ritual of creation. There is a question posed in one of the significant hymns of the *Ṛgveda* as follows:

> *pṛcchāmi tvā param antaṁ pṛthivyāḥ*
> *pṛcchāmi yatra bhuvanasya nābhiḥ* ।
> *pṛcchāmi tvā vṛṣṇo aśvasya retaḥ*
> *pṛcchāmi vācaḥ paramaṁ vyoma* ॥ – *ṚV* I.164.34

> I ask you, what is the uttermost end of the earth? I ask you, what is the navel of the world? I ask you, what is the fecundating power of the rain-shedding steed; I ask you, what is the supreme space of (holy) speech?

Thereafter, a clear answer to the above question is provided in the next verse of the *Ṛgveda* itself:

iyaṁ vediḥ paro antaḥ pṛthivyā
ayaṁ yajño bhuvanasya nābhiḥ ।
ayaṁ somo vṛṣṇo aśvasya reto
brahmāyaṁ vācaḥ paramaṁ vyoma ॥ – *ṚV* I.164.35

The altar is the uttermost end of the earth; this sacrifice is the navel of the world. The herb offering is the fecundating power (semen) of this rain-shedding steed. This Lord is the supreme space of (holy) speech.

Obviously, this speaks of the centrality of *yajña* in the philosophy of *Ṛgveda*.

IX

Ṛta is another Ṛgvedic idea which has perfect coincidence with *yajña*, so much so that some scholars have even suggested to take these two terms as synonyms (Aguilar 1976: 27-28). According to the *Ṛgveda*, there is a constant and rhythmic regularity in the cosmic cycle; the same is manifested through the concepts of *ṛta* as well as *ṛtu* (Sundarraj 1994: 233-36) which set the pace for a well-ordained life.

The concept of *ṛta* is very wide in its connotation, since it includes within it the ritual, the natural and the moral order, all at the same time. The supremacy of *ṛta* in Ṛgvedic world view is manifested in various ways such as:

- All the *deva*s are born out of *ṛta*. *Ṛta* is the first and foremost of the divine origins. – *ṚV* VII.66.13
- All the *deva*s reside in *ṛta*. – *ṚV* X.85.1
- They follow the path of *ṛta*. – *ṚV* III.5.3 and VII.56.12
- They know and preserve the path of *ṛta*. – *ṚV* I.147.1 and IX.73.8
- They rule over the world with the help of *ṛta*. – *ṚV* I.163.5
- For human beings, *ṛta* is the source of happiness. – *ṚV* IV.23.8 and IX.73.1

- In the families or houses of noble persons, streams of *ṛta* keep flowing. – *ṚV* V.12.2 and IX.97.23
- Those, who perform bad deeds, cannot cross the path of *ṛta*. – *ṚV* IX.73.6
- *Ṛta* reigns supreme everywhere – in the sun, in the mountain, in the sacrifices and in truth. – *ṚV* IV.40.5

The Ṛgvedic notion of *ṛta* finds its manifestation in the moral principle of the individual; it is due to the power of *ṛta* that nothing in this universe can act arbitrarily:

> We have in connection with *ṛta* a purely complete system of ethics, a kind of counsel of Perfection. – Bloomfield 1972: 125

It is owing to the power and prominence of *ṛta*, coupled with *satya* and rooted in *tapas*, that the seed for all other noble and sublime feelings is sown in the hearts of human beings. Both the levels of subtle as well as gross are governed by the same moral order which expresses itself in various binary concepts of the Vedic world view such as *ṛta–anṛta*, *satya–asatya*, *śiva–aśiva*, *bhadra–durita*, *sukṛta–duṣkṛta* and *jyoti–tamas*.

X

What follows from the above delineation is that the *Ṛgveda* not only urges upon human beings to stay united and interconnected with other human beings and all elements of the universe but also inspires them to enkindle their inner stream of consciousness and ascend higher and higher (*ṚV* I.50.10) so as to reach up to the level of ultimate bliss of immortality:

> *yatra jyotirajasraṁ yasminloke svarhitam* ।
> *tasminmāṁ dhehi pavamānāmṛte loke akṣita indrāyendo*
> *parisrava* ॥ – *ṚV* IX.113.7
>
> Oh Lord of divine love! place me in that immortal undecaying world, where the light is perpetual and where the blissful, everlasting luster keeps shining all the times. May you, Oh elixir! flow for the self.

More importantly, the Ṛgvedic view of life is not limited to any caste or creed, class or clime; it is a complete, cohesive and universal pursuit for individual perfection as well as a paradigm for cosmic concord. Therefore, it may be said:

> The *Ṛgveda* is a glorious song of praise to the gods, the cosmic powers at work in Nature and in Man. Its hymns record the struggles, the battles, the victories, the wonder, the fears, the hopes and the wisdom of the Ancient Path Makers. Glory be to them! – Mee 1975: Intro.

A prayer to Indra beautifully sums up the Ṛgvedic view of life and the aspirations of Vedic people:

indra śreṣṭhāni draviṇāni dhehi cittiṁ
dakṣasya subhagatvam asme ।
poṣaṁ rayīṇāṁ ariṣṭiṁ tanūnāṁ
svādmānaṁ vācaḥ sudinatvam ahnām ॥ – *ṚV* II.21.6

Bestow on us, Indra, the best of treasures: The efficient mind and great brilliance. The increase of wealth, the health of bodies. The sweetness of speech and the fairness of days!

In brief, the Ṛgvedic view epitomizes a life which aims for overall accomplishment rather than just material achievement and utmost fulfilment rather than partial attainment. Needless to say that this can only be made possible through total upliftment of the human spirit to a level where nothing except an aspiration for boundless bliss and immortality is expressed as follows:

yatrānandāśca modāśca mudaḥ pramuda āsate ।
kāmasya yatrāptāḥ kāmāstatra māmamṛtaṁ kṛdhīndrāyendo
pari srava ॥ – *ṚV* IX.113.11

Make me immortal in that realm. Where beatitude and transports of delight and joy and cheer. Where the highest desires have been filled. For Indra flow thou on, Indu!

To conclude, in the words of the *Ṛgveda* itself, let us all pray and wish for a lofty vision which may lead us to universal welfare and cosmic harmony.

5

Mortality, Transmortality and Immortality in Vedic Thought

THE present chapter aims at expounding and examining some salient features of Vedic thought with special reference to the concept of mortality (*mṛtyu*) vis-à-vis transmortality (*atimṛtyu*) and immortality (*amṛta*).

Apparently, the three terms denote three separate ideas but actually they are so closely intertwined in Vedic philosophy that it is difficult to understand any one of them in an exclusive and isolated manner. Hence, there will be an effort to bring out the inherent essence of these concepts which are so vitally concerned to humanity across time and clime.

II

The Vedic view exhorts human beings as *amṛtasya putrāḥ* (sons of immortality) (*ṚV* X.13.1) and propounds that although mortality is given to human beings, there is a possibility to transcend it via transmortality which is a midway sojourn between the two extreme ends of mortality and immortality. In other words, mortality belongs to the body, while immortality is the nature of soul and anyone can attain it, provided one has realized it as the ultimate goal of life and has acquired the requisite eligibility: transmortality or the capability to transcend death. This technique of transcendence is nothing short of a certain kind of knowledge, a knowledge of the Supreme.

In brief, the Vedic conception of immortality as the highest aim of human life delineates a dominantly optimistic spirit which not only craves to crush death and live a fully accomplished life of hundred years, but also aspires to cross over the bondage of mortality.

The Vedas represent a balanced, optimistic and spirited view of life and death. Accordingly, mortality is unavoidable for humanity while immortality is sought after; transmortality is the *via media* through which a mortal being can fulfil this aspiration. In fact, there are two visible approaches to death – according to one view, if death is the be-all and end-all of life, then what is the joy in living. Therefore, life itself should be rejected as a meaningless existence. In contrast to this pessimistic view, there is another view which holds that when death is inexorable and final, then one should enjoy life to the brim and not bother about anything else. Obviously, both these views are extremes and one-sided only, hence none of these two can satisfy the eternally pertinent quest of humanity which not only seeks a solace from mortality but also aspires to attain immortality.

The uniqueness of Vedic view lies in the fact that on the one hand it does not deny death and accepts it as an eternal, divine norm:

> *nakirasya praminanti vratāni* | – *AV* 18.1.5
>
> None can deny His ordinances.

But on the other hand and more significantly so, it propounds that there is no reason to be disappointed, since there is a possibility of overcoming death and attaining an eternal state of perfect bliss. Therefore, during one's lifetime, one should live with full enthusiasm:

ārohaṇamākramaṇaṁ jīvato jīvato 'yanam । – *AV* 5.30.7

Ascent and aggression (against evil or disease) is the way of each and every living being.

III

It is in the above background that the Vedas represent an ascendent human will to live as well as to reflect a natural acceptance of death. There are several prayers in the Vedas which convey a universally relevant, strong message of hope for humanity such as:

śataṁ jīvantu śaradaḥ purūcīrantar-
mṛtyuṁ dadhatāṁ parvatena । – *ṚV* X.18.4

May the living creatures live for 100 bounteous autumns, May they keep death far away from them, hidden behind the ridge.

* * *

śatāyuṣaṁ kṛṇuhi cīyamānaḥ । – *YV* 13.41

Oh Lord! flourishing here, may you grant me life of 100 years!

Mortality is the inevitable fact of life and the unavoidable fate of animate beings; all the bipeds and quadrupeds are under the control of death, but the Veda assures that the lord of life himself will bear one up, so there is no need to be afraid of death. The universal human aspiration to avoid death is expressed in the Veda with a positive goal to be obtained:

mṛtyurīśe dvipadāṁ mṛtyurīśe catuṣpadām ।
tasmāt tvaṁ mṛtyorgopaterudbharāmi sa mā bibheḥ ॥
– *AV* 8.2.23

Death rules over bipeds, death rules over quadrupeds, from that death, the master of the earth, I (the Lord of Life) bear you up. Now, do not be afraid.

Obviously, the fear of death is the greatest fear for human beings, but the optimistic vision of the Vedas provides a bright ray of hope by proclaiming that the mortals can attain immortality:

... martāsaḥ santo amṛtatvamānaśuḥ । – *ṚV* I.110.4

They (Ṛbhus, the wise ones), though mortals, attained immortality.

Although the Vedas do not overlook the fact that human beings, like other creatures, are born mortal and they have death as their lifelong companion.

pra sū na āyurjīvase tiretana । – *ṚV* VIII.18.22

Graciously lengthen our life so that we may live.

Yet it is aspired that one should live an entire, unimpaired and accomplished life. There are several prayers in the Vedas which not only indicate a strong will to life but also reflect an intense desire to avoid death. A few to mention are:

yadagne martyastvaṁ syāmahaṁ mitramaho amartyaḥ ।
– *ṚV* VIII 19.25

O Adorable Lord, shining with friendly radiance and worshipped with oblations, may I, though a mortal, become immortal as you are.

* * *

paraṁ mṛtyo anu parehi panthāṁ
yaste sva itaro devayānāt ।
cakṣuṣmate śṛṇvate te bravīmi mā
naḥ prajāṁ rīriṣo mota vīrān ॥ – *ṚV* X.18.1

Depart Oh death! go from here and pursue your own path which is distinct from the path of gods or enlightened ones. Oh death! I pray to you, who has eyes to see and ears to hear, not to injure our offsprings and heroes.

* * *

āyuṣāyuḥkṛtāṁ jīvāyuṣmān jīva mā mṛtāḥ ।
prāṇenātmanvatāṁ jīva mā mṛtyorudagā vaśam ॥ – *AV* 19.27.8

Live your life with a full lifespan provided by the life-givers. Live a long life, do not die! Live with the life of the spirited ones. Do not submit to death.

mā tantuśchedi vayato dhiyaṁ me mā
mātrā śāryapasaḥ pura ṛtoḥ || – *ṚV* II.28.5

Oh Venerable one! cut not the thread of my life, engaged in weaving the thread of my life and may not the measure of my work be shattered before the season!

IV

Since the Vedic sages have set a standard age of one hundred years with a hale and hearty body and sound mind as an optimum period for life, hence there are insistent invocations for longevity as well:

śataminnu śarado anti devā yatrā
naścakrā jarasaṁ tanūnām |
putrāso yatra pitaro bhavanti mā
no madhyā rīriṣatāyur gantoḥ || – *ṚV* I.89.9

Verily a hundred autumns lie before us, gods! Within which you cause decay of our bodies; Within which the sons become fathers, do not break in the middle the course of our fleeting life.

* * *

paśyema śaradaḥ śatam |
jīvema śaradaḥ śatam |
budhyema śaradaḥ śatam |
rohema śaradaḥ śatam |
pūṣema śaradaḥ śatam |
bhavema śaradaḥ śatam |
bhūyema śaradaḥ śatam |
bhūyasīḥ śaradaḥ śatāt | – *AV* 19.67.1-8

May we see through hundred autumns! May we live through hundred autumns! May we know through hundred autumns! May we rise through hundred autumns! May we prosper through hundred autumns! May we remain established hundred autumns! May we grow through hundred autumns! Even more than hundred autumns!

It is also noteworthy here that although the dominant will to live longer is radiantly expressed in the Vedic verses, it is not just dragging on the existence of body; rather, it is a living with all the bodily organs in the fittest condition and the head held high. In other words, the Vedic view propounds that one should not only live a long life but also have perpetual physical vigour and perfect mental alertness:

vāṅ ma āsannasoḥ prāṇaścakṣur akṣṇoḥ śrotraṁ karṇayoḥ
apalitāḥ keśā aśoṇā dantā bahu bāhvorbalam ।
ūrvorojo jaṅghāyorjavaḥ pādayoḥ
pratiṣṭhā ariṣṭāni me sarvātmānibhṛṣṭaḥ ॥ – *AV* 19.60.1-2

May I have voice in my mouth, breath in my nostrils; sight in my eyes, hearing in my ears; hair that has not turned grey, teeth that have not decayed, and great strength in my arms. May I have power in my thighs, swiftness in my legs, steadfastness in my feet. May all my members be uninjured and my soul unimpaired.

Besides, there are several prayers in the Vedas which not only reflect the human will to live a full term of life for enabling one to complete his work (as quoted above, *ṚV* II.28.5) but also a sick man's will to life which is sought to be aroused by the following exhortation:

ayaṁ lokaḥ priyatamaḥ devānāmaparājitaḥ ।
yasmai tvamiha mṛtyave diṣaḥ puruṣa jajñiṣe ।
sa ca tvāmanu hvayāmasi mā purā jaraso mṛthāḥ । – *AV* 5.30.17

This world, the unconquered one, is the most beloved of all the enlightened ones. Oh human! we call you back from the death, destined for which you were born here. We call you back. May you not die before reaching old age.

V

Rudra is depicted to be the God of Death in Vedic verses. In the well-known *Śatarudrīya* chapter of the *Yajurveda*, homage is paid to death in hundred forms of Rudra wherein two aspects of him are presented: the benign as well as the terrible. This is, in a way, suggestive of the fact that Rudra represents both life as well as death. It is, therefore, aspired that the fierce form of Rudra be pleased and the benevolent aspect of him bestow grace upon all:

avatatya dhanuṣṭvaṁ sahastrākṣa śateṣudhe ।
niśīrya śalyānāṁ mukhā śivo naḥ sumanā bhava ॥ – *YV* 16.13

Having unbent thy bow, and dulled the points of thy arrows, Thou, thousand-eyed, hundred-quivered, be benevolent and gracious to us!

Yama, the son of Vivasvān Āditya is also described as the deity of death in the Vedas and strangely enough, it is suggested that he was the first one to have chosen to die and desert mortal life for an immortal abode:

yamo no gātuṁ prathamo viveda
naiṣā gavyūtirapabhartavā u ।
yatrā naḥ pūrve pitaraḥ pareyurenā
jajñānāḥ pathyā anu svāḥ ॥ – *R̥V* X.14.2

Yama was the first to find us our abode, a place that can never be taken away, where our ancient fathers have departed, all who are born, go there by that path, treading their own.

VI

The Vedic view vindicates that death or mortality is, in fact, the divine statute, no one, even though he had hundred selves, can outlive the statute of *devas*:

na devānāmati vrataṁ śatātmā cana jīvati ।
taṭhā yujā vi vā vr̥te ॥ – *R̥V* X.33.9

One cannot live indefinitely, since it is not so designed by the *devas*.

Keeping in view the inescapable fact that the human being is destined to die, the Vedic vision approaches death from two angles: one being the physical and material which has briefly been dealt with above and the other which propounds that death is just an end of the body (*dehānta*). Hence, till such a time that one is living, one should live with full zeal and in a positive, sanguine way. In fact, the funeral hymn of the *R̥gveda* asserts that the death of one member of the society should not take away the joy of living from others, since the loss of someone's life shall be compensated by a new life:

yathāhānyanupūrvaṁ bhavanti
yatha r̥tava r̥tubhiryanti sādhu ।
yathā na pūrvamaparo jahātyevā
dhātarāyūṁṣi kalpayaiṣām ॥ – *R̥V* X.18.5

> As days follow days, one after another, as seasons follow seasons in order, as the successor does not fail the predecessor, similarly, the Ordainer, from the lives of these (will create new lives).

It means that even at the physical level, continuity of life from one person to another is a significant source for transcending mortality according to Vedic thought:

devebhyo hi prathamaṁ yajñiyebhyo
'mr̥tatvaṁ suvasi bhāgamuttamam ।
ādiddāmānaṁ savitarvyūrṇuṣe
'nūcīnā jīvitā mānuṣebhyaḥ ॥ – *R̥V* IV.54.2

> For holy *deva*s thou hadst at first produced immortality, the noblest of all portions, then, as a gift to men, Oh Sāvitrī, thou openedst, mortal existence, life succeeding life.

From the conceptual point of view, the Vedic idea of death proclaims that the innermost, indomitable spirit of human beings is immortal, while the body, of course, is mortal. It is an undeniable fact that, essentially the physical body can never attain immortality; it has to decay and decease. Nevertheless, the Veda says that the body should not die before its full life, rather it should die after living a full life and drop off like a ripe cucumber from its stem, while the spirit immortal should reach out to the immortal:

tryambakaṁ yajāmahe sugandhiṁ puṣṭivardhanam ।
urvārukamiva bandhanāt mṛtyormukṣīya māmṛtāt ॥
– *Ṛ̥V* VII.59.12

To Tryambaka our offerings, to the fragrance-bearer, the increaser of nourishment. May he release me, like the cucumber (is released) from its stem, from mortal life, not from immortality.

VII

This promise of lifting a mortal being up to the level of immortality, where the fear of death cannot affect him, is the foremost contribution of Vedic philosophy. According to the Vedas, both immortality and mortality are a shadow of the divine:

yasya chāyāmṛtaṁ yasya mṛtyuḥ ... ॥ – *Ṛ̥V* X.121.2

Immortality and mortality are the shadow of Him alone.

The same feeling is echoed in the following verse which elucidates that even the natural forces like Savitā are governed by divine norms and act as observers under the cosmic order of darkness and effulgence, of mortality and immortality:

ā kṛṣṇena rajasā vartamāno niveśayannamṛtaṁ martyaṁ ca ।
hiraṇyayena savitā rathenā devo yāti bhuvanāni paśyan ॥
– *Ṛ̥V* I.35.2

The refulgent sun, springing through the obscure regions, arousing both the mortal as well as immortal, beholding the several worlds, comes as if mounted on a golden chariot.

Since a person is not just the body, but also the soul, hence death is only the giving up of physical mortality while the soul remains immortal. It is therefore that one, who has realized this truth and known the *ātman* as ageless, deathless, has no fear of death:

akāmo dhīro amṛtaḥ svayambhū
rasena tṛptaḥ na kutaścanonaḥ ।
tameva vidvān na bibhāya mṛtyor
ātmānaṁ dhīramajaraṁ yuvānam ॥ – *AV* 10.8.44

The Supreme is free from desire, self-possessed, immortal, self-existing, contented with bliss and lacking nothing in any respect; it is only by knowing Him, who is the self-possessed, Undecaying and ever young self, that one does not have any fear of death.

VIII

The journey for the ultimate goal of immortality begins at the level of mortality only; it is here that the indwelling spirit can be realized, hence the mortal body is not something to be despised or denounced. Rather, it being the limited abode of the unlimited immortal consciousness has to be worshipped like a divine region. It is with this idea that the *Atharvaveda* states:

ūrdhvo nu sṛṣṭāstiryaṅ nu sṛṣ āḥ
sarvā diśaḥ puruṣa ā babhūva ।
puraṁ yo brahmaṇo veda
yasyāḥ puruṣa ucyatye ॥ – *AV* 10.2.28

Whether created vertically or created horizontally, all the quarters are pervaded by the cosmic being. He, who knows the castle of the Lord Supreme, is called *puruṣa* due to this.

IX

In fact, the relationship between mortality and immortality is so close that both of them have been described as dwelling in the same abode:

anacchaye turagātu jīvamejadbhuvaṁ madhya ā pastyānām ।
jīvo mṛtasya carati svadhābhiramartyo martyendā sayoniḥ ॥
– *AV* 9.10.8

The soul, endowed with life-breath and fast speed, goes out and the dead body is left behind in the dwelling. The immortal soul, hitherto living in the mortal body, keeps on moving from life to life by its own nature.

Therefore, it is implied in the Vedic thought that the secret of transmortality has to be unravelled within one's own existence where the mortal and the immortal inhere inseparably:

apāṅ prāṇeti svadhayā gr̥bhīto 'martyo martyenā sayoniḥ ।
ta śaśvantā viṣūcīnā viyantānyanyaṁ cikyurna cikyuranyam ॥
– *AV* 9.10.16

The immortal soul, associated with the mortal body, ceaselessly moves the lower (inferior) or the upper (superior) bodies according to its own actions. They both go always together, and everywhere together; (we the humans) have comprehended the one (whilst in the physical body) but have not comprehended the other (the soul free from body).

X

As mentioned above, the bridge between the extreme ends of mortality and immortality is the knowledge of the Supreme. It is only after knowing the real nature of the Absolute that the mortal being can attain immortality. As stated above, mortality is "given" to the human beings while immortality is their ultimate "goal", but the wide gap between these two opposite ends of the same stream has to be crossed through the "gateway" of knowledge; there is no other way out:

tameva viditvātimr̥tyumeti nānyaḥ panthā vidyate 'yanāya ॥
– *YV* 31.18

By knowing Him alone, one transcends death, there is no other way to go.

The term *atimr̥tyumeti* (*mr̥tyum atyeti*, i.e. transcending death) used in the above Vedic verse is a vital clue for transmortality; this is the only means for attaining immortality. No mortal can attain immortality unless he transcends death and death can only be transcended by realizing the essential truth that it is the body which dies while the indwelling spirit or soul is beyond death:

> *iyaṁ kalyāṇyajarā martyasyāmṛtā gṛhe* ।
> *yasmai kṛtā śaye sa yaścakāra jajāra saḥ* ॥ – *AV* 10.8.26
>
> This auspicious one (female) is not affected by age; an immortal in the home of a mortal. For whom she was made, he sleeps and he who made her, has grown old.

Hence, there should not be any doubt about the fact that not only death can be transcended but also that the goal of immortality can be attained, as is evidenced by the following Vedic statements such as:

> *yatra devā amṛtamānaśānāstṛtīye dhāmannadhyairayanta* ।
> – *YV* 32.10
>
> Where the enlightened ones reside in the third abode enjoying immortality.

* * *

> *yatrānandāśca modāśca mudaḥ pramuda āsate* ।
> *kāmasya yatrāptāḥ kāmāḥ tatra māmamṛtaṁ kṛdhi* … ॥
> – *ṚV* IX.113.11
>
> Make me immortal in that realm, where there is lasting happiness, pleasure and supreme joy and where the wishes of the wisher have been completely fulfilled.

* * *

> *yatrānukāmaṁ caraṇaṁ trināke tridive divaḥ* ।
> *lokā yatra jyotiṣmantastatra māmamṛtaṁ kṛdhi* … ॥
> – *ṚV* IX.113.9
>
> Make me immortal in that realm, in the third sphere, in the third heaven, where worlds are brightened with radiance!

* * *

XI

What follows from the above is that although human beings are born mortal, there is an essential inner quest which perpetually propels them to rise higher and further higher so as to reach the eternal, immortal aspect of their existence. From this point of view, mortality and immortality are two sides of the same truth, inseparably interconnected. It is not without reason then that the twin terms *mṛtyu* and *amṛta* have repeatedly occurred together in the Vedic verses (*ṚV* VII.59.12, X.13.4; *AV* 10.7.15).

In the words of Veda itself, although the body has to die ultimately, when employed in the pursuit of immortality, this mortal body does not remain a cause of bondage; rather, it acts as a well-structured boat for crossing over the ocean of world:

sutrāmāṇaṁ pṛthivīṁ dyāmanehasaṁ
suśarmāṇamaditiṁ supraṇītim ।
daivīṁ nāvaṁ svaritrāmanāgasama-
sravantīmāruhemā svastaye ॥ – *AV* 7.6.3

May we, the sinless, embark upon this divine boat for our weal, which is fitted with good oars, unleaking and well protected like earth, unblemished like sky, full of comforts and conducting wisely.

In brief, there lies beneath this finite, physical body, an essence which is endless, pure and perfect; that is verily the source as well as the treasure of immortal bliss. Anyone, who has realized this truth, can transcend death and attain immortality:

avidyayā mṛtyuṁ tīrtvā vidyayāmṛtamaśnute । – *YV* 40.13

One (who pursues worldly knowledge and the Spiritual one side by side) overcomes death by worldly knowledge and gains immortality through the spiritual one.

To conclude, a Vedic prayer for immortality is worth quoting:

vivasvān no amṛtatve dadhātu
paraitu mṛtyuramṛtatvaṁ na aitu ।

imān rakṣatu puruṣān ā jarimṇo
moṣveṣāṁ asavo yamaṁ guh ‖ – *AV* 18.3.62

May Vivasvān set us all in Immortality; let what is mortal, go away from us and what is immortal come to us. Let (him) defend all these persons until old age; let not their life-breaths go to Yama.

6

Vedic Vision of Inclusiveness and Interconnectedness

VEDAS are the most ancient texts of humanity, but they propound the most novel vision for cosmic harmony and global peace. The present chapter aims to highlight two basic concepts of Vedic philosophy which are foundational for the attainment of peace in modern world, viz. "inclusiveness", viewed from the metaphysical aspect, and "interconnectedness", seen from the empirical point of view.

II

The Vedic philosophy presents a complete, comprehensive and holistic world view according to which all life in the cosmos is intertwined and interwoven, the process of interrelation works at all levels of existence. Nothing is exclusive in this universe in the sense that nothing stands in isolation, even the highest principle of consciousness, i.e. the all-pervading Absolute is permeated in all the beings of the world:

venastatpaśyannihitaṁ guhā sad yatra
viśvaṁ bhavatyekanīḍam ।
tasminnidaṁ saṁ ca vi caiti sarvaṁ
sa otaḥ protaśca vibhūḥ prajāsu ॥ – *YV* 32.8

The loving sage beholds that mysterious Existence wherein the universe comes to be one nest. Therein unites and therefrom issues the whole; the Lord is warp and woof in created beings.

In other words, each entity of the cosmos is pulsating with the one innermost, subtle principle of consciousness:

eka evāgnirbahudhā samiddha ekaḥ
sūryo viśvamanu prabhūtaḥ ।
ekaivoṣāḥ sarvamidaṁ vi bhātyekaṁ
vā idaṁ vi babhūva sarvam ॥ – *R̥V* VIII.58.2

One is Agni kindled in many a spot, one is Sūrya shining over all, one is Uṣas illumining all this that which is one has become this All.

* * *

ejad dhruvaṁ patyate viśvamekaṁ । – *R̥V* III.54.8

All moving and stationery beings rest upon one base.

But, it must be clarified here that this does not convey monotheism in the technical sense of the term, rather, it suggests that there is an inner impersonal essence beneath each personal existence:

āviḥ sannihitaṁ guhā jarannāma mahatpadam ।
tatredaṁ sarvamarpitamejat prāṇāt pratiṣṭhitam ॥ – *AV* 10.8.6

Though manifest, it lies concealed, as if, in a cave, an ancient name and a great place. Therein is well established all this, that which moves and that which breathes.

The great Absolute is like the thread in a garland, the string which holds all the beads together:

vedāhaṁ sūtraṁ vitataṁ yasminnotā imā prajāḥ ।
sūtraṁ sūtrasyāhaṁ vedātho yat brāhmaṇaṁ mahat ॥
– *AV* 10.8.38

I have realized the widespread thread, into which these creatures have been woven, and I have realized the thread of the thread and also that, which is the great Lord supreme.

All the beings of the world are strewn in the same thread which pervades all and is the first principle of the universe:

> *parītya bhūtāni parītya lokān parītya sarvāḥ pradiśo diśaśca* ।
> *upasthāya prathamajāmṛtasyātmanātmānamabhi saṁviveśa* ॥
> – *YV* 32.11

> Having pervaded all the creatures, encompassing all the worlds, all the quarters and mid-quarters, and approaching the first born (daughter) of Eternity. He entered directly by his self in himself.

The one, innermost, all-pervading principle in which every object of the universe, living or non-living, finds a substratum of existence is variously described in various hymns of the Vedas. For example, Prajāpati in the *Ṛgveda*, Skambha in the *Atharvaveda*, Tadeva in the *Yajurveda* and Viśvadeva in the *Sāmaveda*:

> *prajāpate na tvadetānyanyo viśvā jātāni pari tā babhūva* ।
> – *ṚV* X.121.10

> Oh Lord of people! there is none other than you who has given existence to all these beings.

* * *

> *skambha idaṁ sarvamātmanvadyat prāṇannimiṣacca yat* ।
> – *AV* 10.8.2

> All this which has soul and which breathes and winks, verily is in the Skambha itself.

* * *

> *eṣo ha devaḥ pradiśo 'nu sarvāḥ pūrvo*
> *ha jātaḥ sa u garbhe antaḥ* ।
> *sa eva jātaḥ sa janisyamāṇaḥ* ।
> *pratyañjanāstiṣṭhati sarvatomukhaḥ* ॥ – *YV* 32.4

Surely, this *deva* pervades all the regions, he was born before everything, yet he is in the womb, still he is what has been born, also he is what shall be born, having faces all around, he stands facing each and every person.

* * *

sameta viśvā ojasā patiṁ divo ya eka idbhūratithirjanānām ।
sa pūrvyo nūtanamājigīṣaṁ taṁ vartanīranu vāvṛta eka it ॥
– *SV* 372

May all of you come and join us in praising that Lord who on account of his strength is the Lord of celestial region and who alone is honoured by everyone as if, He is the Chief Guest. He verily blesses all the new projects of public service and He is in truth the only one (as our reliance).

The Supreme Consciousness, which is at the foundation of the universe is also termed as Kāla (*kalayitā*) or creator in the Vedas. But it is a unique feature of Vedic philosophy that the creator himself is held to be a part of creation and the created, while all created beings and objects are dependent on Him; He is *Brahman* and Parameṣṭhī:

teneṣitaṁ tena jātaṁ tadu tasmin pratiṣṭhitam ।
kālo ha brahma bhūtvā bibharti parameṣṭhinam ॥ – *AV* 19.53.9

Urged by Him, created by Him, all that is set, surely, within Him. Time, becoming the Divine supreme, sustains the Lord seated in the highest abode.

The entire cosmos is just a manifestation of Him, who was this, who became this and who is witnessing this world as well:

pari dyāvāpṛthivī sadya itvā pari lokān pari diśaḥ pari svaḥ ।
ṛtasya tantuṁ vitataṁ vidhṛtya tadapaśyattadabhavattadāsīt ॥
– *YV* 32.12

Quickly going around the earth and heaven, around the worlds, around the quarters and around the realm of light, and having woven the well-spread threads of truth, He sees it, becomes it, and still is it.

The above truth is explicitly stated in the following, famous statement of *Yajurveda*:

īśāvāsyamidaṁ sarvaṁ yatkiñca jagatyāṁ jagat । – *YV* 40.1

All, whatsoever exists in this universe, is pervaded by God supreme.

The same sense is expressed in *Taittirīya Upaniṣad* too:

> *tatsṛṣṭvā tadevānuprāviśat* । – 2.6
>
> The Supreme *Brahman*, after creating the world, entered into that only.

What follows from the above Vedic statements is that the created or manifested physical world is not uncaused or accidental, but ordained and controlled by an underlying ultimate principle, the innermost spirit which is self-dependent:

> *ātmā devānāṁ bhuvanasya garbho*
> *yathāvaśaṁ carati deva eṣaḥ* । – *Ṛ̥V* X.168.4
>
> It is the life-force of the divine powers, it is the germ of the world and moves according to its own will.

III

It is worth mentioning here that different terms used in the Vedas for denoting several deities are in fact the names of same, single, Supreme Spirit which rests at the heart of the universe, manifests itself in various forms, sustains the whole created world and rules over it too:

> *rūpaṁ rūpaṁ pratirūpo babhūva*
> *tadasya rūpaṁ praticakṣaṇāya* ।
> *indro māyābhiḥ pururūpa īyate*
> *yuktā hyasya harayaḥ śatā daśa* ॥ – *Ṛ̥V* VI.47.18
>
> In every figure of his creation, the resplendent Lord has been the model. This is the only form for us to look on. He moves multiforms by his designs since His motivations, yoked to the Universe, are thousands in number.

* * *

> *hiraṇyagarbhaḥ samavartatāgre bhūtasya jātaḥ patireka āsīt* ।
> – *Ṛ̥V* X.121.1
>
> The sustainer Lord of illuminant celestial cosmos has been present from the very beginning; He has ever been the sole Lord of all created beings.

In the cosmic vision of the Vedas, which is the most secular, universal and therefore sacred, all forms of life share a common bond, all animate beings and inanimate things are manifestations of one and the same principle. But it must be clarified that this is not the monism of traditional type, since each being or thing of the cosmos has its own, individual existence and purpose in the integral world view of the Vedas. It is not that oneness alone matters in the universe, as will be clear from the following verses:

yadejati patati yacca tiṣṭhati prāṇa-
prāṇannimiṣacca yadabhuvat ।
taddādhāra pṛthvīṁ viśva-
rūpāṁ tatsaṁbhūya bhavatyekameva ॥ – *AV* 10.8.11

That which moves, flies or stands, and which breathes or breathes not, which winks and which has come into being, that one of universal forms sustains the earth. Being assembled, that becomes one only.

* * *

ānīdavātaṁ svadhayā tadekaṁ
tasmāddhānyanna paraḥ kiñcanāsa ॥ – *ṚV* X.129.2

That breathless one breathed upon as if by its own automation. Apart from that one, there was nothing else whatever.

* * *

yaḥ prāṇato nimiṣato mahitvaika
idrājā jagato babhūva ।
ya īśe asya dvipadaścatuṣpadaḥ
kasmai devāya haviṣā vidhema ॥ – *ṚV* X.121.3

He, by his greatness, has verily become the sole king of breathing and seeing world; He rules over this aggregate of bipeds and quadrupeds. Whom else, besides that bestower of happiness, can we offer all our devotion?

* * *

virāḍ vāg virāṭ pṛthvī virāḍ
antarikṣaṁ virāṭ prajāpatiḥ ।
virāṇmṛtyuḥ sādhyānāmadhirājo
babhūva tasya bhūtaṁ bhavyaṁ vaśe ॥ – *AV* 9.10.24

Virāj is speech, Virāj the wide earth. Virāj, the midspace, and Virāj is the Lord of creatures. Virāj is death, the overlord of *sādhyas* (souls seeking perfection). He has full control over what was and what will be. May he put what was and what will be, under my control.

* * *

trīṇi padā vi cakrame viṣṇurgopā adābhyaḥ ।
ato dharmāṇi dhārayan ॥ – *ṚV* I.22.18

The omnipresent God, the preserver of the indomitable, created three regions, the earth, mid-region and the celestial. He sustains and preserves the sanctity of all vital functions that keep life ticking.

* * *

suparṇaṁ viprāḥ kavayo vacobhirekaṁ
santaṁ bahudhā kalpayanti । – *ṚV* X.114.5

The beautiful winged bird (the deity) who is one, the wise poets imagine him with their words in various ways.

* * *

savitā paścātāt savitā purastāt savitottarāttāt savitādharattāt ।
savitā naḥ suvatu sarvatātiṁ savitā no rāsatāṁ dīrghamāyuḥ ॥
– *ṚV* X.36.14

The divine creator from westward, the divine creator from eastward, the divine creator from northward, the divine creator from southward. May the divine creator send us all bliss, may the divine creator grant us long life.

* * *

baṇmahān asi sūrya baḍāditya mahān asi ।
mahaste sato mahimā panasyate 'ddhā deva mahān asi ॥
– *YV* 33.39

Verily, you are great, Oh Radiant Sun! Verily you are great. Oh eternal! the greatness of the great one we adore. Verily you are great, Oh Supreme God!

IV

It needs to be emphasized that the Vedic view of inclusiveness does not deny individuality to different beings or objects; rather, it suggests a symphony of sorts, where each entity of the cosmos is in harmony with the greater, divine principle. It is not uniformity or oneness, where identities have to merge themselves but a unique "diversity in unity" wherein all forms of existence have full freedom to blossom in their own way, but share a spiritual bond at the deeper level which nourishes them. It is not to be imposed from outside, but inherently woven in their existence. The most striking feature of this philosophy is that it does not restrict itself to any class, creed or group, but encompasses the whole cosmos in its stride. The various appellations of the divine principle are also not personal nouns or individual names of any particular deity, they are, in fact, different depictions of the same, Supreme Principle. So, it is a globalization of a different kind which seeks spiritual unity rather than physical uniformity. The real import of Vedic statements like the following ones which proclaim that the whole world is like one nest or a village can be grasped only when this subtle background of Vedic view is comprehended:

yatra viśvaṁ bhavatyekanīḍaṁ । – *YV* 32.8

Where the whole universe becomes, (as if) one nest.

* * *

... viśvaṁ puṣṭaṁ grāme 'śminnanāturam । – *R̥V* I.114.1

May the whole universe become a strong, disease-free village!

* * *

mahatsadhasthaṁ mahātī babhūvitha । – *AV* 12.1.18

Thou hast become great, a great station (Oh Earth!).

V

The unitive vision of Vedas finds expression in several other forms also such as:

a. *Dualism* of binary principles is a basic concept which underlies the whole Vedic philosophy. The bond between *bhūta–bhavya, agni–soma, dyāvā–pr̥thivī, rayi–prāṇa, r̥ta-satya* and *yoṣā–vr̥ṣā* is so strong as well as deep-rooted in the Vedic view that one cannot explain one without referring to the other.

b. *Complementarity* of opposites is another conceptual device which is very foundational and widely available in the Vedas. The pairs of antonym terms like *anr̥ta–r̥ta, mr̥tyu–amr̥ta, tama–jyoti, asat–sat, vāmana–virāṭ, avidyā–vidyā* are so frequently used in Vedic verses that it is essential to grasp the symbolism underlying these ideas for a proper understanding of Vedic view.

c. *Parallelism* between gross and subtle or macrocosmic and microcosmic is also a very significant concept of Vedic interpretation. It is therefore stated in the following well-known Vedic dictum:

   yathā piṇḍe tathā brahmāṇḍe ।

   There is similarity at the level of an individual unit and the cosmos as a collective whole.

Accordingly, there is a correspondence between the broad principles of the outer world and the subtle processes of the inner world in Vedic view. Hence, the atomic as well as the most pervasive are twin ends of the same string. The Vedic statements like the following ones, which apparently seem to be paradoxical, are in fact suggesting the same symbolic relation between the two aspects of one and the same principle:

tadejati tannaijati tadu dūre tadu antike ।
tadantarasya sarvasya tadu sarvasyāsya bāhyataḥ ॥ – *YV* 40.5

It moves, but still it moves not. It is far away, even then it is very close. It is within all, it encompasses all this universe on the outer side as well.

* * *

bālādekamaṇīyaskamutaikaṁ naiva dṛśyate ।
tataḥ pariṣvajīyasī devatā sā mama priyā ॥ – *AV* 10.8.25

That is one, that is finer even than a hair, also there is one, that is not visible at all (that is visible as if nothing). The deity, that embraces them firmly, is dear to me.

VI

Moreover, the integral approach of Vedic philosophy is revealed in repeated assertions to the effect that all objects of the world are interrelated at the empirical level also. This relationship is again to be observed from two angles: *interconnectedness* and *intraconnectedness*. It means that on the one hand, all beings are connected with other living and non-living beings of the world and on the other hand, they are also connected with the members of their own species. For example, the Vedas propound in clear terms that there is interdependence between human beings and other forms of Nature; in fact, among all the elements of creation:

dyaurme pitā janitā nābhiratra bandhurme
mātā pṛthivī mahīyam । – *ṚV* I.164.33

The heaven is my parent and progenitor, the navel is my kinsman, the spacious earth is my mother.

* * *

samo asmabhyaṁ dvipade catuṣpade ca paśave anamīvā iṣaskarat । – *ṚV* III.62.14

May that stream of bliss grant to us and to our biped and quadruped animals, wholesome food.

Not only this, the emotional bonding of human beings with other living beings and various forms of Nature is also sought as follows:

śāntā dyauḥ sāntā pr̥thivī śāntamidamurvantarikṣam śāntā udanvatīrāpaḥ śāntā naḥ santvoṣadhīḥ । – *AV* 19.9.1

May heaven be peace-giving, earth be peace-giving and peace-giving be this vast midspace; may peace-giving be the waters of oceans and peace-giving be the herbs to us all.

Significantly, this interconnectedness among various elements of Nature is a distinct characteristic of Vedic philosophy which has percolated in the post-Vedic literature also.

VII

The Vedic vision of interconnectedness among various aspects of the universe is best exemplified in the concept of *yajña*. The natural, the physical and the spiritual all these layers of existence are deeply rooted in the principle of *yajña* from the cosmic point of view: (Kumar 2005c: 59-75)

The universe is created, sustained and even dissolved through the basic principle of *yajña*, i.e. through the combination and separation of two basic elements *agni* and *soma* representing twin aspects of the cosmos: solar energy and all other products sustaining on it. This is the formula of synthesis, a blending of the natural with the physical and the rising of the material up to the spiritual. The sky and the heaven, the solar and the earthly, the bodily and the psychic are combined through a process of sacrificing one for the other. The *yajña* is stated to be the best of acts, since it is based on the wider principle of synergy through sacrifice:

īśe tvorjje tvā vāyavasthā devo vaḥ
savitā prārpayatu śreṣṭhatamāya karmaṇe । – *YV* 1.1

We invoke you Oh Lord! for food, we invoke you for vigour, you are the vital breath. May the creator Lord depute you. Oh sacrificers! to the noblest accomplishments!

* * *

yajño babhūva sa ā babhūva
sa prajajñe sa nu vāvr̥dhe ।
punaḥ devānāmadhipatirbabhūva
so asmāsu draviṇamādadhātu ॥ – *AV* 7.5.2

The Lord of creatures (sacrifice) came into being. He came to be here all around. He was born and again he grew in vigour. He became the overlord of the bounties of Nature. May he bestow riches on us in abundance.

In fact, the universe cannot sustain or function without this feeling of mutual cooperation. This is the secret of balance of nature at the cosmic level (*brahmāṇḍa*) where the offerings are being made every moment for the divine powers and they are worshipped. The coordination of the humans with them is made possible and the sacrifice is completed with a feeling of giving up oneself for the world at large. From the individual (*piṇḍa*) point of view, *yajña* is an internal process wherein all the forces residing in the human body are sacrificing their best for the presiding deity within. In this way, Vedic *yajña* symbolizes the widest principle of the universe through mutual interconnectedness.

VIII

As far as the intraconnectedness of human beings is concerned, the Vedas hold that the whole world should be tied with the bond of brotherhood and friendship, since all the human beings are the progeny of the divine (*R̥V* X.13.1).

The Vedas distinguish themselves from all other literatures of the world by this inclusive view of humanity without any distinction; a clarion call is given to all human beings to become humane and bear divine progeny:

… *manurbhava janayā daivyaṁ janam* । – *R̥V* X.53.6

May you first strive to become HUMAN and then rise to the status of an enlightened one, the DIVINE.

The humankind should have universal friendship with each and every being:

> *mitrasya mā cakṣuṣā sarvāṇi bhūtāni samīkṣantām mitrasyāhaṁ cakṣuṣā sarvāṇi bhūtāni samīkṣe mitrasya cakṣuṣā samīkṣāmahe* ।
> – *YV* 36.18

> May all beings look on me with the eye of a friend. May I look on all beings with the eye of a friend; May we look on one another with the eye of a friend!

It is only when we be friendly with everybody that all the quarters of this world will become friendly to us:

> ... *pumān pumāṁsaṁ pari pātu viśvataḥ* । – *ṚV* VI.75.14

> One person should protect the other by all means.

What better idea of humanism can be thought of? Not only this, the Vedic idea of a world free from fear suggests that the humanity can meaningfully survive and strive further if there is genuine goodwill and mutual trust:

> *abhayaṁ mitrādabhayamamitrādabhayaṁ*
> *jñātādabhayaṁ parokṣāt* ।
> *abhayaṁ naktamabhayaṁ divā naḥ sarvā*
> *āśā mama mitraṁ bhavantu* ॥ – *AV* 19.15.6

> May the midspace make us free from fear. Free from fear may both these heaven and earth be (for us). May there be no fear to us from behind, from the front, from above as well as from below.

* * *

> *abhayaṁ naḥ karatyantarikṣamabhayaṁ*
> *dyāvāpṛthivī ubhe ime* ।
> *abhayaṁ paścādabhayaṁ purastāduttarād-*
> *adharādabhayaṁ no astu* ॥ – *AV* 19.15.5

> May there be no fear from a friend, no fear from a foe, no fear from the one known to us; no fear from the unknown one.

May there be no fear at night, no fear in the day for us. May all the regions be friendly to me.

IX

Although it is natural for any group of people that they will have amongst them the differences of mental, physical or financial status, yet the Vedas exhort human beings to live peacefully and affectionately:

jyāyasvantaścittino mā viyauṣṭa saṁ
rādhayataḥ sadhurāścarantaḥ ।
anyo anyasmai valgu vadanta eta
sadhrīcīnānvaḥ samanasaskṛṇomi ॥ – *AV* 3.30.5

You should not be separated – growing old and thinking wisely, thrive together, moving under a common yoke, speak sweetly to one another, I will make you have one aim and be of one mind. The two hands are alike but they do not perform the same work. Two cows calving at the same time.

Those, who are capable of helping others, should invariably do so, since the course of life is long and the circumstances keep changing like the wheels of a chariot:

pṛṇīyādinnādhamānāya tavyān
drāghīyāṁsamanu paśyeta panthām ।
o hi vartante rathyeva cakrānya
manyamupa tiṣṭhanta rāyaḥ ॥ – *ṚV* X.117.5

It is expected of every rich man to satisfy the poor implorer; Let the rich person have a distant vision (for a rich of today may not remain rich tomorrow). Remember that riches revolve from one man to another. As revolve the wheels of a chariot.

Not only this, the Veda goes a step further and directs that the human beings should live in complete concord, without being jealous of each other and there should be perfect union of hearts and minds amongst them:

sahṛdayaṁ sāmmanasyamavidveṣaṁ kṛṇomi vaḥ ।
anyo anyamabhi haryata vatsaṁ jātamivāghnyā ॥
– *AV* 3.30.1

The union of hearts and minds and freedom from hate I will bring you. Love one another as the cow loves the calf that she has borne!

Another such message of the Vedas worth quoting here is that the water-storage as well as share of food amongst family members should be common so that they stay united and gather round the sacrificial fire like spokes around the navel of a wheel:

samānī prapā saha vo annabhāgaḥ samāne yoktre saha vo yunajmi ।
samyañco 'gniṁ saparyatārā nābhimivābhitaḥ ॥ – *AV* 3.30.6

Common be your water-storage, common your share of food, I bind you together to a common yoke. United, gather round the sacrificial fire like spokes around the navel of a wheel.

In this way, the family concord, the social harmony and the union of hearts and accord of aims are solicited for a well integrated world in the Vedas. It must be noted here that it is not just the imposed grouping of people but the real, emotional bonding which is being aspired in the Vedic verses:

samānī va ākūtiḥ samānā hṛdayāni vaḥ ।
samānamastu vo mano yathā vaḥ susahāsati ॥
– *ṚV* X.191.4

Let your aims be common and your hearts of one accord, and all of you be of one mind, so you may live well together.

The use of term *susaha* (coming together in a noble way) is to be particularly marked here, since the Vedic view is positing a model of social coordination and a secret of united social life.

akṣaṇvantaḥ karṇavantaḥ sakhāyo
manojaveṣvasamā babhūvuḥ ।
ādaghnāsa upakaṣāsa u tve hṛdā iva
snātvā u tve dadṛśre ॥ – *ṚV* X.71.7

There are friends possessing eyes and others possessing ears; and yet they are unequal in mental apprehension.

* * *

samau ciddhastau na samaṁ viviṣṭaḥ
saṁ mātarā cinna samaṁ duhāte ।
samayościnna samā vīryāṇi jñātī
cit santau na samaṁ pṛṇītaḥ ॥ – *ṚV* X.117.9

The two hands are alike but they do not perform the same work. Two cows calving at the same time do not yield the same milk, both twins have not the same strength, two persons of the same family do not display equal liberality.

X

The Vedas do not show any sign of discrimination among human beings except that of a qualitative difference between good and bad which is a universal and eternal fact. Hence, the terms *ārya* or *deva* and *dāsa* or *dasyu* should not be taken to mean any separate classes of humans, they should rather be interpreted as the ones representing good and evil respectively. The battle between these two forces is constant, no doubt, but the Vedas implore upon humanity to fight for good and resist the evil so that the rule of noble may prevail:

indraṁ vardhanto apturaḥ kṛṇvanto viśvamāryam ।
apaghnanto arāvṇaḥ ॥ – *ṚV* IX.63.5

May the active be glorifying God/Self, Ennobling the whole world, Driving away the lawless/evil.

This may be substantiated with several examples. To quote A.C. Bose:

We find the antithesis between *ārya* and *dāsa* or *dasyu* in the Vedas: but the antithesis is stated as one between enlightenment and ignorance, goodness and wickedness, lawful life and lawlessness ... on the other hand, it is stated that the enemy, whether our king or a foreigner, should be valiantly opposed (*R̥V* VI.75.19).

The evil-doer from the ranks of the forward-marching people must be eliminated (*R̥V* X.53.8)

It is also said that God is the God of *dāsa as* well as of *ārya*: *yasyāyaṁ viśva āryo dāsaḥ śevadhipa ariḥ* । – Lord God of glory is He to whom both *ārya* and *dāsa* belong (*R̥V* VIII.51.9)

There is a prayer for the forgiveness of sins against the foreigner (*R̥V* V.85.7). – 1954: 33-34

XI

As regards the Vedic idea of intraconnectedness among human beings it must be mentioned that there is a perfect parity between male and female.

In *Atharvaveda* the physical union of husband and wife is depicted in a metaphorical manner and lifted to a spiritual level:

amo 'hamasmi sā tvaṁ sāmāhamasmyr̥ktvaṁ
dyauraham pr̥thvī tvam ।
tāviva saṁbhavāva prajāmājanayāvahai ॥ – *AV* 14.2.71

I am song, thou art verse; I am Heaven, thou art earth, we two together shall live here becoming parents of children.

The Vedas propound complete equality and complementarity between man and woman which has been followed in the later Vedic tradition of *ardhanārīśvara* and the marriage ritual. The various epithets used in the Vedas to denote a woman (Kumar 1999a: 32-33) are sufficient evidence to prove the respectable status a woman enjoyed in the Vedic society. So much so, she has been addressed to be a queen of the household.

Not only this, her intellectual capabilities are also recognized well in the Vedas; soon after the marriage, she is invited to address the *vidatha* a religious assembly in which it was the ambition of sages to speak eloquently:

pūṣā tveto nayatu hastagṛhyāśvinā tvā pra vahatāṁrathena ।
gṛhān gaccha gṛhapatnī yathāso vaśinī tvaṁ vidathamā vadāsi ॥
– *ṚV* X.85.26

Go to the house, the household's mistress, ruler of the home, thou wilt address the assembly. May Pūṣan lead thee from here by the hand! May Āśvins convey thee in their chariot.

* * *

sikṣā stotṛbhyo māti dhagbhago bṛhadvadema vidathe suvīrāḥ ॥
– *ṚV* II.11.21

May we sing your glory loudly at this sacred assembly and be blessed with worthy descendants.

It goes without saying that the foundation for social concord and universal harmony is laid in the happy family where both the partners live and work in coordination rather than the aggressive competition and confrontation prevalent in modern age. This basic truth had since been realized by the Vedic seers, hence the depiction of family union and conjugal love therein is unparalleled.

XII

The Vedas not only urge upon the humankind to stay united and interconnected with other elements of the universe but also inspire and awaken their inner stream of consciousness so that *jīva*s may rise up to the level of *deva*s and enjoy the ultimate bliss of immortality. Throughout the Vedic lore, there is an ascendant idea of getting up, growing, rising and transcending – this is what one may call Vedic dynamism. Many of the verses call upon humanity to ascend higher and still higher, such as:

ucchrayasva mahate saubhagāya । – *ṚV* III.8.2

Go up high for great auspiciousness.

The same spirit of ascending is reflected in the following aspirations of earthly beings who wish to transcend darkness and reach out to the highest light of spiritual glory:

udvayaṁ tamasaspari jyotiṣpaśyanta uttaram ।
devaṁ devatrā sūryamaganma jyotiruttamam ॥ – *Ṛ̥V* I.50.10

Looking at the transcendent light beyond the darkness, we have come to Sūrya, God among gods, the Light that is most excellent.

In another verse, the above desire is echoed as follows:

divaṁ ca roha pr̥thivīṁ ca roha ।
rāṣṭraṁ ca roha draviṇaṁ ca roha ॥ – *AV* 13.1.34

May you ascend to the heaven, and may you ascend on the earth, and may you ascend to the kingship and may you ascend to the wealth.

* * *

śukro 'si bhrājo 'si svarasi jyotirasi ।
āpnuhi śreyānsamatisaṁkrāma ॥ – *AV* 2.11.5

You are bright, you are blazing, you are the light, you are the illuminator. Attain superiority, surpass your equals.

XIII

On the basis of the above brief delineation, it may be stated that the Vedic view is an inclusive one, where each and every tiny particle of the cosmos is accepted as an individual object and nothing is negated or rejected but there is an underlying principle of interconnectedness which makes everything of the universe related to each other and to the Ultimate Reality as well. The integral vision of the Vedas is eternally relevant to humanity, since it propounds a basic principle of life and goes even up to the extent of those beings or things which are very minute and hence invisible:

yāṁśca paśyāmi yāṁśca na teṣu mā sumatiṁ kr̥dhi । – *AV* 17.1.7

Among those whom I see and those, whom I do not see, may you cultivate friendship for me.

In fact, this feeling of care and concern for all the aspects of creation is all that is vital for any sustainable society. The Vedas not only exhort the human beings to rise and grow themselves but also urge upon them to feel and fend for other aspects of life and world. We have to adopt this mindset and adapt it to our modern lifestyle so as to respect, appreciate and tend to the divine spirit in everything around us. This should not be taken as exclusive monism or pluralism, rather, a holistic view of the reality which is so beautifully expressed in *Atharvaveda* as follows:

> *pūrṇāt pūrṇamudañcati pūrṇaṁ pūrṇena sicyate* ।
> *uto tadadya vidyāma yatastatpariṣicyate* ॥ – *AV* 10.8.29
>
> From the full it takes out the full, the full is impregnated with the full. May we know today that, wherefrom that is impregnated.

7

Vedas as the Foundation-source of Spirituality

I

THE Vedas have been held in the highest esteem in Indian tradition not only because of their well-established antiquity, but also due to their universal significance as a reservoir of profound pristine knowledge orally transmitted from one generation to another.[1] Usually it is believed that the Vedic view pertains to the ritualistic aspect of life only, but a closer analysis reveals that the Vedas contain a much deeper message which is in fact the fountainhead of spiritual wisdom. In the words of Sri Aurobindo:

> Since our earliest ages, the Veda has been, in the invincible tradition of our race, the bedrock of all our creeds; in this our Goddess of veiled and ancient speech, we have always persisted in seeing the fruitful mother of all our Indian

---

1 "Never through the ups and downs of life during millenniums has the value of the Vedas as supreme spiritual documents been ignored, not even when, in later ages, the meaning was not fully grasped by all. It is this unshakable faith that made possible the unbroken continuity of the oral tradition of texts." – Bose 1966: 293

> spirituality; for it is nothing but the simple truth, evident whenever we look below the surface and beyond the details, that every creed, sect, school of philosophy which has had any roots in our Indian temperament or any vitality of survival in our Indian surroundings has been in its secret nature; if not in its open feature, a child of the eternal Vedic inspiration. All the outbursts of religious life have helped to maintain or renew through the course of several millenniums, the vitality of our race, the eternal richness and fruitfulness of our ancient culture. The fineness and profound sincerity of our undying spiritual attainment and endeavour, were derived, if we trace them to their remote source from the word or the substance of the Vedas. – 1985: 152, 168

II

Spirituality in Indian parlance is recognized as an orientation towards the innermost spirit, which in turn leads to realization of the utmost truth. The idea of spirituality is usually expressed through the Sanskrit term *adhyātma*, literally connoting "pertaining to *ātman*", it is, in fact,

> the name for the integrative function by which to unify the various aspects of existence. In this respect it is cognate to and paired with *ādhibhūta*, implying unification on the objective side and *ādhidaiva*, meaning integration *in divinis*. *Adhyātma* is used for integrating the various aspects of subjectivity which is, again, simply existence contemplated from the inwardized vantage point of the self. *Adhyātma* functions like a symbol pointing beyond itself, opening up levels of reality which remain undisclosed with a corresponding opening up of levels of the human mind beyond the discursive and the sense-bound. – Sivaraman 1995: xxii

The integrative role of spirit as suggested above, under the term *adhyātma* was long recognized by the earliest Vedic etymologist Yāska (fifth century BCE) who says explicitly:

mahābhāgyād-devatāyā eka ātmā bahudhā stūyate; ekasya ātmano anye devāḥ pratyaṅgāni bhavanti; itaretara-janmāno bhavanti; itaretaraprakṛtayaḥ; karmajanmānaḥ, ātmajanmānaḥ ... ātmā sarvaṁ devasya । – *Nirukta* 7.4

It is because of His great divisibility that they apply many names to him, one after another. The other gods come to be submembers of the one spirit (*ekasya ātmanā*) ... their becoming is a birth from one another, they are of one another's nature; they originate in function; the spirit is their origin. Spirit is even their chariot, their horse, their weapon, their arrows. Spirit is their whole of what God is – *ātmā sarvam devasya.*

Accordingly, the Sanskrit word *ātman* is the closest equivalent to spirit in its Western connotation, i.e. German *ātman,* to breathe, and Greek *auto* a sense of self-reference. The word *ātman* has been variously derived by Sanskrit writers (*Amarakoṣa* 3.3.109). One of the Sanskrit texts says that *ātman* is so called because it obtains all experiences (*āpnoti*), takes (*ādatte*) all things to itself and is beyond all objects (*atti viṣayān*), and because its existence is continuous and all-pervading (*yaccāsya santato bhāvaḥ*).[2]

What follows from the above is that in Indian tradition, spirituality signifies an inclination towards the realization of *ātman* and any activity directed towards the same end comes under spiritual activity. But it needs to be mentioned here that spirituality in this specific sense also integrates different approaches regarding the concept of *ātman* including I-consciousness and *Brahman*, the *jīva* and the *Īśvara*, the empirical as well as the transcendental, the negative and the affirmative. Several shades of queries towards this principle of *ātman* are included under the *adhyātma-vidyā*, the knowledge for discovery of the spirit in its ultimate essence.

---

2 *yadāpnoti yadādatte yaccātti viṣayān bahūn* ।
yaccāsya santato bhāvastasmādātmeti kathyate ॥
– *Lakṣaṇasaṁgraha*, p. 33

This brings us to the point of *summum bonum* of life or the highest goal of life, which is again cherished as spiritual in the sense of liberation or "freedom of the spirit" from bondage of ignorance. It incorporates both the aspects of the journey, i.e. the means as well as the end. Hence, no clear-cut distinctions like ethical or spiritual are made in Indian thought in this regard. It is, therefore, quite in the fitness of things to keep this idea of a broad vision of Indian spirituality in mind before we proceed further. The same has been very aptly remarked as follows:

> Spiritual activity is the activity of *ātman*-realization, which is translated generally as self-realization. … Thus, the spiritual is not anti-ethical but supra-ethical, not anti-aesthetic but supra-aesthetic, beyond the stage at which the ethical, the aesthetic, etc. are transcended. – Raju 1982: 195

III

As regards the issue of Vedas being the fountain-source of Indian spirituality, a reference must be made to the following statement of a contemporary scholar:

> The spiritual vision of the Vedas has inspired and set the pattern for much of later Indian theological and philosophical thought. It bespeaks a clear sense of reality and outlook and a *Weltanschauung* through its most vivid imageries and colourful symbols, covering in its encyclopaedic scope every aspect of human existence, the material, mental and spiritual in fully integrated way. In this integration, or harmony, indeed lies its true *spirituality.* – Pandey 1995: 5

The Vedas proclaim in clear terms that each entity of the cosmos is pulsating with the one, innermost spirit which is manifesting itself in various forms and permeating in all beings of the world (*R̥V* VIII.58.2).

The Great Spirit is like the thread in a garland, the string which holds all the beads together (*AV* X.8.38)

Evidently, the Vedic metaphor of a string in the garland is well reflected in the oft-quoted verse of *Bhagavadgītā*:

mayi sarvamidaṁ protaṁ sūtre maṇigṇā iva । – VII.7

All this is woven upon me like rows of gems upon string.

In other words, in the Vedic world view, all beings of the universe are connected in a single string which permeates all and is the primal principle of the world (*YV* 32.11).

The one immanent spirit wherein every object of the universe finds a support for sustenance is differently depicted in several hymns of the four Vedas such as follow:

yaḥ prāṇato nimiṣato mahitvaika idrājā jagato babhūva ।
ya īśe asya dvipadaścatuṣpadaḥ kasmai devāya haviṣā vidhema । – *R̥V* X.121.3

He by his greatness, has verily become the sole king of breathing and seeing world; He rules over this aggregate of bipeds and quadrupeds. Whom else, beside that giver of happiness, can we offer all our devotion?

* * *

nāma nāmnā johhavīti purā sūryāt puroṣasaḥ ।
yadajaḥ prathamaṁ sambabhūva saḥ tatsvarājyamiyāya
yasmānnānyat-paramasti bhūtam । – *AV* 10.7.31

A person calls the one deity by the other's name before sunrise and before dawn. When at first the Unborn sprang into being he won his own dominion beyond which nothing higher has been in existence.

* * *

yasyāmidaṁ viśvaṁ bhuvanamāviveśa tasyāṁ no devaḥ savitā dharma sāviṣat – *YV* 9.5

On this earth, where all this life has been accomodated, may the Creator God provide shelter to us all.

* * *

svādiṣṭhayā madiṣṭhayā pavasva soma dhārayā
indrāya pātave sutaḥ । – *SV* 467

Oh elixir of divine love! May you flow in the sweetest and most exhilarating stream, expressed for the acceptance of the aspirant the resplendent self.

IV

However, it needs to be clarified that the Vedic idea of One Supreme Being cannot be taken as monism in the technical sense since the Vedas also speak of duality (*R̥V* I.164.20) of principles and clearly mention plurality of beings as well (*R̥V* X.90.10). There are dual deities such as Dyāvāpr̥thivī, Aśvinau, Agnisoma, Mitrāvaruṇā, etc. as well as collectivity of divine forces like Maruts, Viśvedevās and several human beings including the *r̥ṣis*. The Vedic view, therefore, unfolds itself in a very subtle and complex form which cannot and should not be taken literally in the sense in which this simplified version is being presented. There are many layers and shades of relationship between the One Supreme Being, many gods and all human beings which are reflected in several Vedic hymns. The Veda itself says in numerous statements that the way this One appears and manifests itself as many is a great mystery:

ko dadarśa prathamaṁ jāyamānamasthanvantaṁ yadanasthā bibharti ।
bhūmyā asurasr̥gātmā kva svit ko vidvāṁsamupagāt praṣṭumetat ॥ – *R̥V* I.164.4

Who hath beheld him as he sprang to being, seen how the boneless one supports the bony?

* * *

acikitvāñcikituṣaścidatra kavīn pr̥cchāmi vidmane na vidvān ।
vi yastastambha ṣaḷimā rajāṁsyajasya rūpe kimapi svidekam ॥
– *R̥V* I.164.6

> What was that one who in the Unborn's image hath established and fixed firm these six regions of the world?

So, spirituality of the Vedas is much more deep and inscrutable than the compartmentalized theorizations of later times; it has rightly been characterized as "One in many" and "Many in One". The same has also been interpreted as "Vedic Exemplarism", i.e. the relation between the one and the many:

> This is as much as to say that Exemplarism, in the last analysis, is the traditional doctrine of the relation, cognitive and causal, between the one and the many: the nature of which relation is implied in Vedic Sanskrit by the expressions *viśvam ekam* (*ṚV* III.54.8), "the many that are one, the one that is manifold" (Plotinus, "integral multiplicaty"), *viśvam satyam* (*ṚV* II.24.12), "the manifold truth" and *viśvam … garbham* (*ṚV* X.121.7), "the germ of all" and more fully enunciated in *ŚB* X.5.2.16, "As to this they say", "Is he then one or many?" One should answer, "One and Many". For inasmuch as He is That, He is one; and inasmuch as He is multiply distributed (*bahudhā vyaviṣṭiḥ*) in his children, He is many, i.e. as the Person in the mirror (*ādarśe puruṣaḥ*), Who is born in his children in likeness" (*pratirūpaḥ prajāyāmājayate*, *KauṣUp* IV.11). – Coomaraswamy 2000: 357

V

Vedic spirituality is moulded in a different manner due to the fact that the Vedas are held to be divine/impersonal (*apauruṣeya*) in their origin, it is therefore that they are perfect and eternal. The supreme sanctity of the Veda is derived from the fact that it has the potency to denote even that which is not to be known from any other source of knowledge.[3] The authority of the Vedas is actually rooted in the theory of *veda-apauruṣeyatva* (for details see Kumar 2006b: 235-51) which is differently interpreted by various

---

3 *pratyakṣeṇāṇumityā vā yastūpāyo na vidyate* ।
etaṁ vidanti vedena tasmād vedasya vedatā ॥
– Sāyaṇa, in his introduction *Aitareyabrāhmaṇabhāṣyam*

scholars of Indian philosophy, but all of them unanimously accept its unquestionable authenticity. Even the so-called *nāstika* schools of Indian thought have developed in opposition to the Vedic view. Hence, they also owe their allegiance to the Veda in some way or the other. In the words of Sāyaṇācārya, the great commentator on the Vedas, "God created the whole universe out of the knowledge of Vedas: *yo vedebhyo 'khilam jagat nirmame*" (*Ṛgbhāṣyabhūmikā* 2). It means that Vedic knowledge existed even before the creation. Hence,

> the authority of the Vedas does not depend upon anything external. They themselves are authority, being the knowledge of God. And, as we shall see later, their truth is verifiable by any spiritual aspirant in transcendental consciousness.
>
> – Prabhavananda 1962: 25-26

The spiritually enlightened beings who have been in fact the chosen channels for giving expression to Vedic knowledge and who could directly perceive reality are termed as *ṛṣi*s in Vedic tradition.[4] They are the ones who have directly experienced the Vedic idea of truth and have a unified vision of reality. It is their elevated consciousness that the mystery of cosmic harmony unfolds at a deeper level of their being and understanding. The Vedic *ṛṣi*s are not only the ones through whom the Vedic knowledge is revealed as a universal vision that pervades among all aspects of reality: gods, human beings and elements of nature but also transmitters of the revealed truth, in a free-flowing manner, without any limitation or distortion. In this sense they are not just ordinary human beings, rather they are the extraordinarily gifted ones. So, the *Ṛgveda* describes the *ṛṣi* as poet, seer and knower of *ṛta*:

ऋतं चिकित्व ऋतमिच्चिकिद्धृतस्य धारा अनु तृन्धि पूर्वीः ।
नाहं यातुं सहसा न द्वयेन ऋतं सपाम्यरुषस्य वृष्णः ॥ — ऋग्वेद, ५.१२.२

---

4 *sākṣātkṛtadharmāṇa ṛṣayo babhūvuḥ* । – *Nirukta* 1.20

ṛtaṁ cikitva ṛtam iccikiddhyṛtasya dhārā anu tṛndhi pūrvīḥ ।
nāhaṁ yātuṁ sahasā na dvayena ṛtam sapāmyaruṣasya vṛṣṇaḥ ॥ – *ṚV* 5.12.2

O Lord! you who know the purpose of our truthful prayers, may you listen to our words and send forth full streams of eternal order. I do not use my might for the purpose of violence, and for duplicity in matters of truth and untruth. I faithfully follow the Lord of the eternal law.

Several epithets used in the Vedas for denoting the Vedic poets such as *jaritṛ* (singer), *kārin* (maker), *kāru* (artist in words), *ṛṣi* (seer), *kavi* (poet), *vipra* (inspired one), *dhīra* (intellectually endowed), *manīṣī* (mentally powerful) and *vedhas* (wise one) are indicative of the spiritual genius with which the *ṛṣi*s are endowed. The *Ṛgveda* describes the seers as *satyavācaḥ*,[5] whose words are true and speaks of hymns and God-loved words: *vācobhir devajuṣṭaiḥ*.[6] It is the purity of thought and freshness of insight that lead the Vedic poet to the vision of Ultimate Reality and it is only then that the Vedic hymns are revealed to him. It is for this reason that the *ṛṣi*s have been called "world-builders (*bhūtakṛt*): the world-building *ṛṣi*s who chanted the sacred words" (*AV* XII.1.39). These "world-builders" often speak like self-chosen representatives of humanity, looking back to the remote past and forward to the distant future (Bose 1951: 6). The poet-seers had earlier prepared themselves for this divine favour through practising *tapas* (spiritual austerities) and later gave this sacred speech to people at large out of their love for humanity:

---

5 *uto hi vāṁ pūrvyā āvividra ṛtāvarī rodasī satyavācaḥ* ।
naraścid vāṁ samithe śūrasātau vavandire pṛthivi vevidānāḥ ॥
– *ṚV* 3.54.4

6 *sūktebhirvo vacobhirdevajuṣṭairindrā nvagnī avase huvadhyai* ।
ukthebhirhi ṣmā kavayaḥ suyajñāḥ āvivāsanto maruto yajanti ॥
– *ṚV* 5.45.4

bṛhaspate prathamaṁ vāco agraṁ yat prairata nāmadheyaṁ dadhānāḥ । yad eṣāṁ śreṣṭhaṁ yad aripramāsītpreṇā tad eṣāṁ nihitaṁ guhāviḥ ॥ – *ṚV* X.71.1

When, lord of our prayer, the first of speech and the foremost the sages uttered, giving the unnamed a name which was their best and their most stainless, then They with love revealed the divine secret in their souls.

* * *

saktum iva titaunā punanto yatra dhīrā manasā vācam akrata । *atrā sakhāyaḥ sakhyāni jānate bhadraiṣām lakṣmīr nihitādhi vāci* ॥ – *ṚV* X.71.2

Where the sages formed the speech with the mind straining it, as they strain flour with the sieve, therein have friends discovered bounds of friendship whose holy beauty lies hidden in that speech.

* * *

aśvinā sāragheṇa mā madhunāṅktaṁ śubhaspatī ।
yathā bhargasvatīṁ vācmāvadāni janā anu ॥
– *AV* 6.69.2, 9.1.19

Dear Aśvins, Lords of Light! fill me with honey. So that I may speak the glorious word to the masses of mankind.

* * *

yathemāṁ vācaṁ kalyāṇīmāvadāni janebhyaḥ
brahmarājanyābhyāṁ śūdrāya cāryāya ca svāya cāraṇāya ca ।
priyo devānāṁ dakṣiṇāyai dāturiha bhūyāsamayaṁ
me kāmaḥ samṛdhyatāmupa mādo namatu ॥ – *YV* 26.2

May I address this auspicious speech to all the people. Intellectuals and administrators, workers and producers of wealth, our kinsmen and the strangers. May kinsmen and the favourite of the learned ones, and of him, who gives liberal guerdon may such and such wish of mine be fulfilled. May I get affection of so and so.

In these verses, the *ṛṣi* prays for sweet speech so that he may impart the sacred words to the whole society. This clearly indicates that in Vedic view, spiritual knowledge is universal. It is, therefore, that

> the truths revealed through the words of Veda are not secrets to be carefully kept from the public. The sage who knows them feels called upon to declare them to his fellowmen, irrespective of their social or cultural status. – Bose 1954: 154

VI

There is another distinctive feature of Vedic spirituality which finds expression in several hymns and that is the inclusiveness of Vedic view. Usually, it is held that spirituality and materialism are mutually exclusive but in Vedic vision both of these are integrated in such a way that it incorporates all aspects of the universe and rejects nothing. This unique feature of Vedic view has rightly been characterized as "Spirituality of Matter and Materiality of Spirit" (Balasubramaniam 1996: 90-109). It is in this background that the separation and struggle between the external and the internal, mundane and the divine, many and the one, darkness and light, evil and good has been sought to converge herein in a symphony of sorts. This perfect parity between the different orders has been explained through the Vedic principle of *ṛta* and is in fact the foundation of Natural Law as well as Moral Law. Even the *ṛṣi*s are described as people who praise *ṛta* and think straight.[7]

Ṛta is universal in the sense that it operates at all the levels, i.e. gods, humans and Nature. According to the *Ṛgveda*, the whole world shines forth in the light of *ṛta*,[8] and those who follow

---

[7] *ṛtaṁ śaṁsanta ṛju dīdhyānā divasputrāso asurasya vīrāḥ* ।
vipraṁ padamaṅgiraso dadhānā yajñasya dhāma prathamaṁ mananta ॥
– *Ṛ*V X.67.2

[8] *ṛtasya dṛḷhā dharuṇāni santi purūṇi candrā vapuṣe vapūṁṣi* ।
ṛtena dīrgham iṣaṇanta pṛkṣa ṛtena gāva ṛtam ā viveśuḥ ॥

the path of ṛta are bestowed upon with the benign bounties of Nature:

madhu vāta ṛtāyate madhu kṣaranti sindhavaḥ ।
– *ṚV* I.90.6

Sweet blows the breeze for one, Who lives by *ṛta*. Rivers pour for him sweets.

It is worth mentioning here that even the multiplicity of gods invoked in various hymns of the Veda is widely interpreted as natural phenomena and the harmonious relation of human beings with Nature is based on the concept of *ṛta*. It is this universal order, which lifts one from the given natural level and leads gradually to the ethical and then spiritual level.

In fact, the notion of *ṛta* holds the balance between spirit and matter. It is due to this cosmic law that human beings and nature are both tied in an inseparable bond. Nature is the nourishing force for all forms of life and so it is adored and admired throughout the Vedic verses. The Vedic hymns are full of love, respect and gratitude to different forms of nature. Several gods invoked in Vedic verses such as Savitṛ, Uṣas, Agni and Parjanya are also symbolized through Nature. There are many hymns in the Vedas which eulogize both earth and heaven together not only as phenomena of Nature but also as cosmic divinities.[9] The Vedic hymn addressed to Mother Earth (*AV* 12.1) presents a beautiful picture of diverse aspects of cosmic bounty while another hymn addressed to the presiding deity of the forest (*ṚV* X.146.1-6) is a touching message to humanity for being careful in the context of ecological imbalances prevalent today. This affectionate bonding of human beings and other aspects of the universe depicted in the Vedas needs to be emulated in contemporary climate of growing alienation from Nature.

– *ṚV* IV.23.9

[9] *ṚV* 1.160.1-5, 1.185.1-11.

VII

Yajña is the core concept of Vedic philosophy which indicates inherent relationship among various forms of cosmic existence and points to the foundation of Vedic spirituality. It is not just a mechanical ritual, rather, it is the underlying essential principle of individual growth, social solidarity and cosmic harmony (for details, see Kumar 2005c: 59-75). In the Puruṣasūkta of *Ṛgveda*, there is a reference to *puruṣa* (the individual being) as well as a supreme *Puruṣa* (cosmic being) interwoven metaphorically in the ritual of creation. This is, in fact, the central theme of Vedic spirituality according to which the *puruṣa* or the divine sacrifices himself for the glory of creation; this is the first and the noblest virtue according to Veda, which is characterized as *dharma* (*ṚV* X.90.16). Just as *ṛta* is externally maintaining the natural order of the cosmos, similarly *yajña* is operating from within the universe so as to sustain the cosmic cycle:

> *apa prāca indra viśvāṁ amitrānapāpāco abhibhūte nudasva* ।
> *apodīco apa śūrādharāca urau yathā tava śarman madema* ॥
> – *ṚV* X.131.1

> The *yajña* is drawn out with threads on every side and spread out by Nature's cosmic sacrifice for years hundred and one. Our fathers who have preceded us, weave it forward and backward, thus they worship (the creator Lord) when the world is woven.

Another verse in the *Ṛgveda* says that the *yajña*, in which a spiritually awakened mind is attuned, attains to harmony and reaches up to the divine, in a congenial coalescence of the world, since God himself is the immanent Lord of the world.[10]

VIII

This universal harmony which is accomplished through the

[10] *yuñjate mana uta yuñjate dhiyo viprā viprasya bṛhato vipaścitaḥ* ।
vi hotrā dadhe vayunāvideka inmahī devasya savituḥ pariṣṭutiḥ ॥
– *ṚV* V.81.1

Vedic principles of *ṛta* and *yajña*, leads one to the balance between material and spiritual, external as well as internal. This holistic attitude in turn enables us to perceive the manifestation of divine spirit in all the natural processes happening around us and enkindle the spark of divinity already present in us. Obviously, this harmonious state of mind is conducive to one's happiness, which is no less than the expression of spirituality within the mortal abode of immortal spirit; it signifies spiritual unfolding within the material frame (*AV* 10.8.44).

From this point of view, human life seems to be a journey from the body to the spirit, from finitude to infinity and from mortality to immortality. It is not without reason then that the Vedas repeatedly pronounce the value of human life as an opportunity to realize the true essence of oneself, which is hidden deep within each one of us. As already stated, all the human beings are addressed in the *Ṛgveda* as the progeny of the divine (*ṚV* X.31.1) and there is a call to raise divinely oriented generations in future (*ṚV* X.53.6). It is in this context that the Supreme Divine principle manifests himself in diverse forms (*ṚV* VI.47.18).

In short, this diversity of beings indicates to gods on the one hand and to human beings on the other hand. While several gods are symbols of different forces of the Supreme, human beings are no less important in the Vedic conception. Again, there are two levels of human beings: the *ṛṣis* who have actualized their latent capabilities of mind and intellect to the infinite level and the ordinary human beings who have a great potential which still awaits to be aroused and awakened. Although they have a finite mortal existence, yet are capable of and called for, ascending higher and higher in their search of light,[11] happiness and fulfilment of their aspirations.

---

[11] *ā roha tamaso jyotiḥ* । – *AV* 8.1.8

IX

The most significant message of Vedic spirituality is its inherent faith in the potential strength of humanity to accomplish the cherished goal of overcoming its limitations and reaching out to the eternal source of divine spiritual bliss. This strong optimism of Vedic spirituality inspires human beings to transcend mortality and attain immortality, which is expressed in the following verses:

> *yatra jyotir ajasraṁ yasmiṅl loke svarhitam* ।
> *tasmin māṁ dhehi pavamānāmṛte loke akṣita indrāyendo pari srava* ॥ – *Ṛ̥V* IX.113.7
>
> Where eternal lusture glows, the realm in which the light divine is set, place me, purifier, in that deathless imperishable world. For Indra, flow thou on, Indu!

* * *

> *yatra kāmā nikāmāśca yatra bradhnasya viṣṭapam* ।
> *svadhā ca yatra tṛptiśca tatra māmamṛtaṁ kṛdhīndrāyendo pari srava* ॥ – *Ṛ̥V* IX.113.10
>
> Make me immortal in that realm where beatitude and joy and cheer and transports of delight abound, where the highest desires have been filled. For Indra, flow thou on, Indu!

X

On the basis of above brief delineation, it may be stated that the Vedic vision of spirituality is so wide in its intent and so deep in its content that it is not exactly possible to capture all the shades of it in a small paper of this size. However, it is undoubtedly clear that it has percolated in all aspects of later Indian tradition in some way or the other. It is the vigour of Vedic vision that has reflected in several branches of learning and various ways of living in India for the past several centuries. The most significant reason for this universal appeal of the Vedic view is that the

Vedas are distinctive from all other literatures of the world due to the fact that the message enshrined in them is not restricted for any particular religion, caste, colour or creed; in fact, it is meant not only for the whole humankind but also for all living beings.[12] It goes even further to include all levels of existence: visible and invisible, gross and subtle, matter and spirit.[13] So, the Vedic view is very wide in its approach and is cosmic in its scope; it requires to be explored deeply and expounded extensively. Still it is hoped that the sketchy outline presented above succeeds in signifying a bit of the infinite depth as well as enormous width of the universal Vedic vision.

To conclude, in the words of Veda itself:

yasya bhūmiḥ pramāntarikṣamutodaraṁ ।
divaṁ yaścakre mūrdhānaṁ tasmai jyeṣṭhāya brahmaṇe namaḥ ॥ – *AV* 10.7.32

Homage to supreme *Brahman* of whom the earth is the base, the mid-region the middle, and who has made sky his head.

* * *

yasya sūryaścakṣus candramāśca punarṇavaḥ ।
agniṁ yaścakra āsyaṁ tasmai jyeṣṭhāya brahmaṇe namaḥ ॥ – *AV* 10.7.33

Homage to supreme *Brahman* of whom the sun is the eye on that becomes new again and again, and who has made Agni his mouth.

12 *śaṁ no astu dvipade śaṁ catuṣpade* । – *YV* 36.8

13 *yāṁśca paśyāmi yāṁśca na teṣu mā sumatiṁ kṛdhi* ॥ – *AV* 17.1.7

8

Concept of Bhakti in the Vedas

THE word *veda* literally connotes knowledge and it is usually held that the Vedas follow the path of knowledge and do not have much to offer in the field of *bhakti*. This view is also supported by the fact that the term *bhakti* is not explicitly mentioned in the Vedas (Kaviraj 2009: 183). But, on a closer study, it becomes clear that besides and beneath the shell of Vedic ritualism, there is ample material in the Vedas which reflects *bhakti* in its various aspects.

Etymologically, *bhakti* is the loving faith in God and surrender to him. It means either "the highest form of *bhakti* is affection fixed on God" or *bhakti* is the highest affection fixed on God (Kumar 2005: 128). It is also explained as the state of mind having the Supreme Being as its object (Bhattacharya 1990: 35). According to Nārada, *bhakti* consists in intensive love directed towards God,[1] it is blissful in character and on its fruition the devotee attains perfection and immortality, being thoroughly satisfied.

The concept of *bhakti* (celestial love) is in fact foundational and underlying in all the Vedic prayers. The triple manifestation of Vedic Saṁhitās known as *trayī* denotes three types of verses,

---

1 *sā parānuraktirīśvare* । – *Shandilya Bhaktisūtras* 1.1.2

viz. *Ṛk*, *Yaju* and *Sāma*.[2] The etymological derivation of these three terms signifies that all of them imply prayers to the Divine expressed in following ways:

ṛg arcanī – *Nirukta* 1.8

yajuḥ yajateḥ – *Nirukta* 7.12

gītiṣu sāmākhya – *MīSū* 2.1.36

> The *Ṛk* verses are meant for eulogizing, *Yaju* verses are employed in the sacrificial act while *Sāma* verses are for singing/chanting.

II

The very basic idea of *bhakti* presupposes that there is a deity or a personal god being addressed or adored, and a *bhakta* who is the devotee. The idea of *bhakti* as available in the Vedas expresses supreme celestial love between an impersonal God and the many *ṛṣis*/*jīva*s as devotees. From this point of view, prayer is the essential expression of *bhakti* and almost all the Vedic verses are evidently prayers, so it goes without saying that the inherent sources of *bhakti* are abundantly available in the Vedic philosophy. But it must be emphasized that the God described or suggested in Vedic verses is not a personal one while there are various names and several epithets used for addressing Him.

Therefore, the Vedic view of *bhakti* first needs to be explored from this angle, i.e. the nature of God. The Vedic concept in this regard is unique in the sense that the devotee first seeks to know the deity to be worshipped. In other words:

---

2 • *yasmādṛco apātakṣanyajuryasmādapākaṣan* ।
sāmāni yasya lomānyatharvāṅgiraso mukhaṁ ।
skaṁbhaṁ taṁ brūhi katamaḥ svideva saḥ ॥ – *AV* 10.7.20

• *evaṁ vā are mahato bhūtasya niḥśvasitametadyadṛgvedo yajurvedaḥ sāmavedo 'tharvāñgirasaḥ* । – *ŚatBrā* 14.5.4.10

> It is typical of Vedic worship that the worshipper seeks the knowledge of the object to be worshipped. His devotion is not blind, but is based on enlightenment. – Bose 1999: 80

It is only after his quest for knowing the deity is fulfilled that the devotee can have full faith in the divine. The same is beautifully expressed through the Vedic word *śraddhā* (*śrat* = truth, *dhā* = to hold),[3] i.e. faith or conviction which leads to the realization of truth: *śraddhayā satyamāpyate* (*YV* 19.30). It is not without reason then that the very sequence of Vedic Saṁhitās points to this fact in order of priority as follows:

> *Ṛk = jñāna; Yajuḥ = karma; Sāma = upāsanā; Atharva = vijñāna.*
> – Saraswati 2008: 60

In other words, the Vedic view of *bhakti* is inclusive and is well integrated with *jñāna* and *karma*. Obviously, the post-Vedic triple manifestation of human endeavour, viz. *jñāna-mārga*, *karma-mārga* and *bhakti-mārga* (Plott 1974: 1) is based on this very inherent Vedic foundation.

III

The Vedic notion of *bhakti* reflects a firm faith in the existence of a Supreme, Divine principle invoked through various names of deities which may be taken as various forms of personal gods and addressed by several seers as seekers or devotees. The divine is addressed as Agni, Indra, Varuṇa, Yama, Mātariśvan, etc. in the Vedas; it is contemplated as the Supreme Lord as also called in affectionate terms as father, mother, brother, friend, guest and so on. The seeker prays for divine grace, bliss, help, protection, mercy, benediction, benevolence and love.

The Vedic conception of God presents both the dimensions of the divine – *nirguṇa* as well as *saguṇa*:

> *sa paryagācchukram-kāyam-vraṇam-*

---

3 *Vācaspatyam*, vol. VI, p. 5149 and *Śabdakalpadrumaḥ*, vol. V, p. 154.

snāviraṁ śuddhamapāpaviddham ।
kavirmanīṣī paribhūḥ svayambhūryā-thātathyato
'rthān vyadadhācchāśvatībhyaḥ samābhyaḥ ॥ – *YV* 40.8

He [the man who knows] has attained the bright, the unbodied, the unwounded, the unsinewed, the pure, attained. That which evil has not penetrated. He, the Poet, the wise, the (all) encompassing, the self-existent, has prescribed aims, according to fundamental principles, unto the everlasting years.

The divine is enunciated as *sat* (ever existent), *cit* (all knowing) and *ānanda* (pure bliss) in the following verses:

Ever Existent and All knowing (Sat and Cit)

anuttamā te maghavannakirnu na tvāvāṁ asti devatā vidānaḥ ।
na jāyamāno naśate na jāto yāni kariṣyā kṛṇuhi pravṛddha ॥
– *ṚV* I.165.9

Oh bounteous self! nothing done by you is unavailing. No nature's force could be as effective. No one that is to be born, nor any one that has been born could surpass you in these deeds which you have achieved, Oh exceedingly mighty self!

Pure Bliss (Ānanda)

yo bhūtaṁ ca bhavyaṁ ca sarvaṁ yaścadhitiṣṭhati ।
svaryasya ca kevalaṁ tasmai jyeṣṭhāya brahmaṇe namah ॥
– *AV* 10.8.1

Let our homage be to him, the Lord Supreme, who superintends all that ever was, and all that ever will be, and all (that now exists); His only is heavenly bliss.

Only One

Moreover, the supreme is stated to be only one:

yo devānāṁ nāmadhā eka eva । – *AV* 2.13

The deities are many, but the Supreme Deity, who is the goal of devotion, is one and one only.

One in Many

Even though God is one, he is addressed by numerous names and expressed through several features.

nāmāni te śatakrato viśvābhir gīrbhir īmahe ।
indra abhi mātiṣāhye ॥ – *R̥V* III.37.3

Oh performer of hundred selfless deeds! we recite your many names in all our hymns for strength and for the triumph over evils.

* * *

ekaṁ vā idam vi babhūva sarvam ॥ – *R̥V* VIII.58.2

That which is one has become this All.

Further, there are various other aspects of the divine so beautifully expressed in several Vedic hymns such as creator, sustainer and destroyer (*R̥V* X.121.1); as saviour (*R̥V* III.62.9), as omnipresent (*R̥V* I.97.6) and as omnipotent (*YV* 10.24, 12.14).

IV

As regards the nature and eligibility of a *bhakta* (devotee), the Vedic verses enunciate numerous aspects of human nature which can be interpreted to be the attributes thereof:

Piety

śuddhā pūta bhavata yajñiyāsaḥ । – *R̥V* X.18.02

May you all be diligent in your sacrificial works; may you enrich yourself with progeny and affluence and may be pure in mind and clean in body.

Sinlessness

apa naḥ śośucadaghamagne śuśugdhyā rayim ।
apa naḥ sośucadagham ॥ – *R̥V* I.97.1

Shining brightly, Agni, drive away our sin, and shine thou wealth on us. Shining bright, drive away our sin.

→

Sacrificing Nature

stomaśca yajuśca ṛk ca sāma ca
bṛhacca rathantaraṁ ca ।
svardevā aganmāmṛtā abhūma prajā
pateḥ prajā abhūma veṭ svāhā ॥ – *YV* 18.29

Oh enlightened ones! we (the devotees) have reached the world of bliss. We have become immortal. We have become the children of the creator Lord. *Veṭ Svāhā.*

Charitableness

śatahasta samāhara sahasrahasta saṁkira । – *AV* 3.24.5

May you gather as if you are a hundred handed; may you distribute as if you are a thousand handed.

Friendship

dṛte dṛṁha mā mitrasya mā cakṣuṣā
sarvāṇi bhūtanī samīkṣantām ।
mitrsyāhaṁ cakṣuṣā sarvāṇi bhūtanī samīkṣe
mitrasya cakṣuṣā samikṣāmahe ॥ – *YV* 36.18

May all beings look on me with the eye of a friend; may I look on all beings with the eye of a friend; may we look on one another with the eye of a friend.

Compassion

pṛṇīyād innādhamānāya tavyān drāghī
yāṁsamanu paśyeta panthām ।
o hi vartante rathyeva cakrānya
manyam upa tiṣṭhanta rāyaḥ ॥ – *ṚV* X.117.5

It is expected of every rich man to satisfy the poor implorer; let the rich person have a distant vision (for, a rich of today may not remain rich tomorrow). Remember that riches revolve from one man to another, as revolve the wheels of a chariot.

Joyfulness

viśvadānīṁ sumanasaḥ syāma paśyema
nu sūryam uccarantam ।
tathā karad vasupatir vasūnāṁ devām̐
ohāno 'vasāgamiṣṭhaḥ ॥ – *Ṛ̥V* VI.52.5

May we, at all seasons be possessed of healthy minds: and may we behold the sun, when he arises. May the affluent Lord of riches, observant, conveyer of our oblations to Nature's bounties, make us worthy of these rewards.

Fearlessness

indra āśābhyas pari sarvābhyo abhayaṁ karat jetā śatrūnvicarṣaniḥ । – *Ṛ̥V* II 41.12

May the resplendent Lord, the conqueror of adversaries and all-wise, provide us security from fear from all quarters.

Good Conduct

parimā 'gne duścaritādbādhasvā mā sucarite bhaja ।
udāyuṣā svāyuṣodasthāmamṛtā anu ॥ – *YV* 4.28

Bar me, Oh Agni! against evil conduct, make me a sharer in good conduct. I have risen up with life, have risen up with good life, following the immortals.

V

It will also be rewarding to delineate upon the subjective, mental modes of a devotee (Sharma 1979: 150-55) as suggested through the following Vedic verses:

Restlessness

uduttamaṁ varuṇa pāśam asmad avādhamaṁ
vi madhyamaṁ śrathāya ।
athā vayam āditya vrate
tavānāgaso aditaye syāma ॥ – *Ṛ̥V* I.24.15

Oh venerable Lord! loosen the bonds that hold me, loosen the bonds upper, middle and lower. We shall obey your eternal laws, faithfully follow your command and thereby avoid sin.

Affliction

imaṁ me varuṇa śrudhī havam adyā ca mṛḷaya ।
tvām avasyurā cake ॥ – *ṚV* I.25.19

I invoke you, Oh venerable Lord! to make this day a happy one. I implore you for your helpful blessings.

Goodwill (Śivasaṅkalpa)

yajjāgrato dūramudaiti daivaṁ tadu
suptasya tathaivaiti ।
duraṅgamāṁ jyotiṣāṁ jyotirekaṁ tanme
manaḥ śivasaṅkalpamastu । – *YV* 34.1

May the divine essence that goes far away, from the waking, and likewise from the sleeping, and that one far-travelling Light of lights, may that my Mind resolve on what is good.

* * *

yena karmāṇyapaso manīṣiṇo yajñe
kṛṇvanti vidatheṣu dhīrāḥ ।
yadapūrvaṁ yakṣmantaḥ prajānām tanme
manaḥ śivasaṅkalpamastu ॥ – *YV* 34.2

May that by which wise men, skilful in rituals, and steady in assemblies, perform their tasks, that peerless Spirit that lies in all creatures, may that my Mind resolve on what that is good.

* * *

yatprajñāmuta ceto dhṛtiśca yajjyotir-
antaramṛtam prajāsu ।
yasmānna ṛte kiñcana karma kriyate
tanme manaḥ śivasaṅkalpamastu ॥ – *YV* 34.3

May that which is deep knowledge, intellect, memory, that which is the deathless Flame in living beings, without which nothing whatever is done, may that my Mind resolve on what that is good.

* * *

yenedaṁ bhūtaṁ bhuvanaṁ bhaviṣyat-
parigṛhītamamṛtena sarvam ।
yena yajñastāyate saptahotā tanme
manaḥ śivasaṅkalpamastu ॥ – *YV* 34.4

May that immortal Essence by which all the past and present world is comprehended, by which the ritual spreads with the seven priests, may that my Mind resolve on what is good.

* * *

yasminṛcaḥ sāma yajuṁṣi yasmin
pratiṣṭhitā rathanābhāvi-vārāḥ ।
yasmiṅśicittaṁ sarvamotaṁ prajānāṁ
tanme manah śivasaṅkalpamastu ॥ – *YV* 34.5

May that in which the *Ṛk*, the *Sāman*, the *Yajus* are held firm, like spokes in the nave of a chariot-wheel, in which all thoughts of living beings lie interwoven, may that my mind resolve on what is good.

* * *

suṣārathiraśvāniva yanmanuṣyānnenīyate
'bhīṣubhirvājina 'iva ।
hṛtpratiṣṭhaṁ yadajiraṁ javiṣṭham
tanme manaḥ śiva-saṅkalpamastu ॥ – *YV* 34.6

May that which guides men like a good charioteer who controls fleet-footed horses with the reins, that which abides in the heart, most swift and active, may that my mind resolve on what that is good.

Faith in the Divine Power

ā ghā gamadyadi śravat sahasriṇībhirūtibhiḥ ।
vājebhir upa no havam ॥ – *ṚV* I.30.8

When He listens to our invocations, He assuredly comes to us with thousands of generous bounties and benedictions.

Self-Surrender

yam agne manyase rayiṁ sahasāvannamartya ।
tam ā no vājasātaye vi vo made yajñesu citram ā bharā vivakṣase ॥
– *ṚV* X.21.4

Oh powerful and immortal fire divine! may you give us precious wealth which you deem best for our sustenance, in our various benevolent works. Verily, you are great.

Contemplation

vi me karṇā patayato vi cakṣur vīdaṁ
jyotir hṛdaya āhitaṁ yat ।
vi me manaś carati dūra ādhīḥ kiṁ
svid vakṣyāmi kim u nū maniṣye ॥ – *ṚV* VI.9.6

My ears open to hear, my eyes to see this Light within my spirit that shines beyond; My mind roams with its thoughts in the distance; What shall I speak, and what, verily, shall I think?

Identification

yad agne syām ahaṁ tvaṁ tvaṁ vā ghā syā aham ।
syuṣṭe satyā ihāśiṣaḥ ॥ – *ṚV* VIII.44.23

If, Oh God! I were Thou and Thou were I, Thy prayers should have their due fulfilment here.

Realization

tvayed indra yujā vayaṁ prati bruvīmahi spṛdhaḥ ।
tvam asmākaṁ tava smasi ॥ – *ṚV* VIII.92.32

Supported by Thee Oh God! may we answer all who defy us. Thou art ours and we are Thine.

VI

In this process, the devotee establishes several sorts of relationships with the Divine and while addressing Him, seeks love and benediction of God in various expressions such as the following ones:

As a Father to the Son

sa naḥ piteva sūnave 'gne sūpāyano bhava ।
sacasvā naḥ svastaye ॥ – *ṚV* I.1.9

Lord, be unto us easy of access, as a father is to his son, May you be ever-present with us for our sake.

* * *

trātā no bodhi dadṛśāna āpirabhi
khyātā marḍitā somyānām ।
sakhā pitā pitṛtamaḥ pitṝṇāṁ kartemu
lokam uśate vayo-dhāḥ ॥ – *ṚV* IV.17.17

May you be our preserver, watching and blessing all and bestowing felicity on those who are worthy and offer libations. May you be a friend, a sire, most fatherly of fathers, giver of food, bestowing heavenly bliss upon him who desires it.

* * *

tvaṁ hi naḥ pitā vaso tvaṁ mātā śatakrato babhūvitha ।
adhā te sumnam īmahe ॥ – *ṚV* VIII.98.11

Bounteous One! Thou art our Father; and our Mother, Oh Lord! Thou hast been. Now we pray for Thy bliss.

* * *

agniṁ manye pitaram agnim āpim
agniṁ bhrātaraṁ sadam it sakhāyam । – *ṚV* X.7.3

The Deity I deem my Father, my Kinsman, my Brother, deem Him my Friend for ever.

* * *

sakṛt su no maghavannindra mṛḷayādhā piteva no bhava ।
– *ṚV* X.33.3

Show Thy mercy on us once, Oh Gracious Lord! Be like a Father to us.

yo naḥ pitā janitā yo vidhātā … । – *ṚV* X.82.3

He is our father, our begetter, our creator.

As a Mother to the Child

yas te stanaḥ śaśayo yo mayobhūryena
viśvā puṣyasi vāryāṇi ।
yo ratnadhā vasuvidyaḥ sudatraḥ
sarasvati tamiha dhātave kaḥ ॥ – *ṚV* I.164.49

Oh Sarasvatī! That exhaustless breast of Thine which is the source of well-being, with which Thou nourishes all good things, which contains treasure, possesses wealth, confers good gifts, That Thou lay bare here for our nourishment.

* * *

prati me stomam aditir jagṛbhyāt
sūnuṁ na mātā hṛdyaṁ suśevam ।
brahma priyaṁ devahitaṁ yad astyahaṁ
mitre varuṇe yan mayobhu ॥ – *ṚV* V.42.2

May the infinite and indivisible Lord accept my affectionate and delightful praise, as a mother welcomes her son. I address this inspired, bliss-giving prayer to the virtuous and friendly Lord, which he surely would love to accept.

* * *

… *vayaṁ syāma mātur na sūnavaḥ* ॥ – *ṚV* VII.81.4

May we be like sons of Thee, the mother.

As a Friend to the Friend

tvaṁ jāmirjanānām agne mitro asi priyaḥ ।
sakhā sakhibhya īḍyaḥ ॥ – *R̥V* I.75.4

Oh foremost fire-divine! indeed you are alone your kin amongst men, you are their beloved friend, a friend whom friends may supplicate.

* * *

bhavā no agne sumanā upetau sakheva sakhye । – *R̥V* III.18.1

Be kind to us when we approach you, O Adorable Lord! May you be fulfiller of our aspirations like a friend to a friend.

* * *

bhavā naḥ sumne antamaḥ sakhā vr̥dhe ॥ – *R̥V* VIII.13.3

Be Thou most near to us for bliss, a friend to aid.

As a Lover to the Beloved

apaghnanneṣi pavamāna śatrūn
priyāṁ na jāro abhigīta induḥ ।
sīdan vaneṣu śakuno na patvā somaḥ
punānaḥ kalaśeṣu sattā ॥ – *R̥V* IX.96.23

Oh flowing elixir! eulogized, you come chasing our foes, as a lover to his darling, or as a bird flies back to her nest. You finally settle in the reservoirs, having been mixed with water.

* * *

jāraḥ kanīna iva cakṣadāna r̥jrāśvaḥ … ॥ – *R̥V* I.117.18

As a youthful gallant, has given me a hundred and one privileges for personal use.

As a Husband to the Wife

pari ṣvajante janayo yathā patiṁ maryaṁ
na śundhyuṁ maghavānam ūtaye ॥ – *R̥V* X.43.1

(May the poems) embrace just as women embrace men, their husbands free from defect, for the sake of protection.

* * *

patir iva jāyām abhi no ny etu dhartā divaḥ savitā viśvavāraḥ ||
– *R̥V* X.149.4

As a husband proceeds to his wife, so may the blessings of the supreme creator, the upholder of the cosmos, whom every one reveres, hasten to us.

As a Guest to the Host

viśveṣām aditir yajñiyānāṁ viśveṣām atithir mānuṣāṇām |
agnir devānām ava āvr̥ṇānaḥ sumr̥ḷīko bhavatu jātavedāḥ ||
– *R̥V* IV.1.20

The universal fire-divine is the mother of all those divine powers, to whom the worship is offered. May He be dear like a guest to all men. Receiving the offered homage, may He, the knower of all that is born, be gracious to us.

* * *

preṣṭhaṁ vo atithiṁ stuṣe mitram iva priyam |
agniṁ rathaṁ na vedyam || – *R̥V* VIII.84.1

I adore fire-divine dear as a guest and loving as a friend who brings us riches as if laden on a chariot.

* * *

viśo-viśo vo atithiṁ vājayantaḥ purupriyam |
agniṁ vo duryaṁ vacaḥ stuṣe śūṣasya manmabhiḥ ||
– *R̥V* VIII.74.1

Oh adorable Lord! desirous of strength and food, we glorify you with hymns for the attainment of happiness. You are dear and familiar friend and dear like the guest in every home.

As a Preceptor to the Disciple

imāṁ dhiyaṁ śikṣamāṇasya deva kratuṁ
dakṣaṁ varuṇa saṁ śiśādhi | – *R̥V* VIII.42.3

Oh All-pervading Deity! sharpen the intelligence, wisdom and insight of him who is striving for enlightenment.

* * *

ācārya upnayamāno brahmacāriṇaṁ kr̥ṇute garbhamantaḥ ।
– *AV* 11.5.3

The *ācārya* (teacher) initiating the *brahmacārī* (pupil) makes him (as it were) a (spiritual) child within him.

VII

It is also worth mentioning here that there are three layers of prayer suggested through the Vedic verses, viz. *stuti* (adulation, eulogizing), *prārthanā* (solicitation, seeking) and *upāsanā* (waiting, worshipping or approaching respectfully) (Saraswati 2001: 426). Out of these, *stuti* is simply singing the attributes of the divine, preferably in musical chants, while *prārthanā* is an earnest urge for divine benediction which is sought after exhaustion of human endeavour. Last, *upāsanā* signifies coming close to the divinity, not in a physical sense but in an intrinsic and essential manner.

Eulogizing (Stuti)

mahīr asya praṇītayaḥ pūrvīr uta praśastayaḥ ।
nāsya kṣīyanta ūtayaḥ ॥ – *R̥V* VI.45.3

Vast are His designs, manifold are His praises, and His protections are never withdrawn.

* * *

ya eka it tam u ṣṭuhi kr̥ṣṭīnāṁ vicarṣaṇiḥ ।
patir jajñe vr̥ṣakratuḥ ॥ – *R̥V* VI.45.16

May you glorify that resplendent Lord, who, alone and on His own, supervises, and is the Lord of each and everyone – the showerer of blessings.

* * *

mā cid anyad vi śaṁsata sakhāyo mā riṣaṇyata ।
indram it stotā vr̥ṣaṇaṁ sacā sute muhur ukthā ca śaṁsata ॥
– *R̥V* VIII.1.1

Oh friends, do not worship anybody but Him, the divine one. Let no grief perturb you. Praise him alone, the radiant, the showerer of benefits. During the course of self-realization, go on repeatedly uttering hymns in his honour.

Accordingly, there are ample verses in the Vedas which not only make mention of *stuti* (eulogy) in clear terms but also exhort the seeker/devotee to address and invoke the divinity in various names so as to please it and attain the desired goal.

Seeking (Prārthanā)

There are several statements in the Vedas which invoke the divine for bestowing the best upon his seekers:

ime ta indra te vayaṁ puruṣṭuta ye
tvārabhya carāmasi prabhūvaso ।
nahi tvad anyo girvaṇo giraḥ saghat kṣoṇīr
iva prati no harya tad vacaḥ ॥ – *ṚV* I.57.4

Much praised and most opulent soul, we, the sense organs belong to you; we glorify you alone accept our offerings. None other than you is entitled to receive our devotion. May you love and cherish our prayers as the mother-earth cherishes its creatures.

* * *

manye tvā yajñiyaṁ yajñiyānāṁ
manye tvā cyavanam acyutānām ।
manye tvā satvanām indra ketuṁ
manye tvā vṛṣabhaṁ carṣaṇīnām ॥ – *ṚV* VIII.96.4

I deem Thee as the Holiest of the holy, I deem Thee as the Shaker of the unshaken; I deem Thee, Oh God! as the Banner of heroes, I deem Thee as the Chief of the people.

* * *

saṁ no bhavatu bhuvanasya yaśpatiḥ । – *YV* 36.2

Whatever distressing lacuna I have in my vision, in my heart or in my thought, may the Lord Supreme remove that, may gracious to us be He, who is the lord of the whole universe.

Approaching (Upāsanā)

The Vedic word *upāsanā* is in fact the original appellation for the idea of *bhakti*. Several usages of the verb *upa*+ √*ās* and its equivalents are scattered in all the four Vedas such as:

upa tvāgne dive dive doṣāvastardhiyā vayam ।
namo bharanta emasi ॥ – *Ṛ̥V* I.1.7

Day and night, we approach you, Lord, with reverential homage through sublime thoughts and noble deeds.

* * *

tava śarman priyatame dadhānā
upa stheyāma śaraṇaṁ na vṛ̥kṣaṁ ॥ – *Ṛ̥V* VII.95.5

And placing us under Thy protection, Thou most beloved! May we approach Thee as a tree for shelter.

* * *

ambho amo mahaḥ saha iti tvopāsmahe vayam । – *AV* 13.4.50

We worship you as fruitfullness, as strength, as might, as overpowering force.

* * *

ambho aruṇaṁ rajataṁ rajaḥ saha iti tvopāsmahe vayam ।
– *AV* 13.4.51

We worship you as ruddy strength as silvery emotion and as overpowering force.

* * *

uruḥ pṛ̥thuḥ subhūrbhuva iti tvopāsmahe vayam । – *AV* 13.4.52

We worship you as excellent, huge, happy and becoming.

* * *

pratho varo vyaco loka iti tvopāsmahe vayam । – *AV* 13.4.53

We worship you as vast, the cest, pervading and the overlooker.

As mentioned above, the very notion of *upāsanā* presupposes a basic duality between the deity and the devotee. But it needs to be reiterated that the Vedic view of celestial love does not offer a structured theory of a personal god and the individual devotee; rather, it suggests a broad, impersonal idea of emotional intensity of love between the human and the divine. More significantly, the Vedas reflect a sense of divinity lying within the heart of the devotee himself which elevates and inspires him into noble thought and lofty activity so as to enable him for reaching out to the Divine.

VIII

This brings us to the goal of *bhakti*. The Vedic view proclaims that the deity being invoked is not essentially the destination, it is just a direction to the final goal of divine bliss lying within the heart of each soul. The ultimate aim of all mortal aspirations is therefore the attainment of immortality, but there are other mediate and moderate objects as well which are sought through prayers such as:

Bodily Health

ayuto 'hamayuto ma ātmāyutam me
cakṣurayutaṁ me ।
śrotramayuto me prāṇo 'yuto me
'pāno 'yuto me vyāno 'ayuto ahaṁ sarvaḥ ॥ – *AV* 19.51.1

Undivided I am my soul, undivided my sight, undivided my hearing; undivided my in-breathing, undivided my out-breathing, undivided my diffusive breath, undivided the whole of me.

* * *

vaṇma āsannasoḥ prāṇaścakṣurakṣnoḥ śrotraṁ karṇayoḥ ।
apalitāḥ keśā asoṇā dantā bahu bāhvorbalam ॥
urvorojo jaṅghāyorjavaḥ pādayoḥ ।
pratiṣṭhā ariṣṭāni me sarvātmānibhṛṣṭaḥ ॥ – *AV* 19.60.1-2

May there be voice in my mouth, breath in my nostrils, sight in my eyes, hearing in my ears; may my hair not turn grey or my teeth turn purple; may I have much strength in my arms. May I have power in my thighs, swiftness in my legs, steadiness in my feet. May all my limbs be uninjured and my soul remain unconquered.

Intellectual Strength

yāṁ medhāṁ devagaṇāḥ pitaraścopāsate tayā māmadya medhayāgne medhāvinaṁ kuru । – *YV* 32.14

Oh Adorable Lord, make me wise today by bestowing upon me that wisdom, which the learned and elders so keenly desire.

Emotional Well-being

ayaṁ mitro namasyaḥ suśevo rājā sukṣatro ajaniṣṭa vedhāḥ ।
tasya vayaṁ sumatau yajñiyasyāpi bhadre saumanase syāna ॥
– *R̥V* III.59.4

The adorable self-radiant Lord of illumination, the benign creator of the universe, has come with sovereignity over all and with vigour. May we enjoy the grace of Him, the holy and rest in His propitious loving kindness.

Release from Suffering and Sin

viśvāni deva savitar duritāni parā suva ।
yad bhadraṁ tan na ā suva ॥ – *R̥V* V.82.5

Remove from us, Oh divine creator! all the ills and evils and bestow upon us that, what is good and beneficial.

Acquisition of Wealth

indra śreṣṭhāni draviṇāni dhehi cittiṁ
dakṣasya subhagatvam asme ।
poṣaṁ rayīṇāṁ ariṣṭiṁ tanūnāṁ svād
mānaṁ vācaḥ sudinatvam ahnām ॥ – *R̥V* II.21.6

Oh resplendent Lord! bless us with the best of treasures, the spirit of ability and fortune. May we obtain from you an abundance of wealth, healthy bodies, sweetness of speech and auspiciousness of days.

* * *

vayaṁ syāma patayo rayīṇām ॥ – *Ṛ̥V* X.121.10

May we be the possessors of grand riches.

Divine Protection or Grace

indra vājeṣu no'va sahasrapradhaneṣu ca ugra ugrābhirūtibhiḥ ।
– *SV* 598, 798

O invincible resplendent Lord, May you, with insuperable defences, protect us in the struggles of hard life.

Accomplishment of Happiness/Joy

giribhrajo normayo madanto bṛ̥haspatimabhyarkā anāvan ।
– *Ṛ̥V* X.68.1

Like joyous streams bursting from the mountain, to Bṛ̥haspati, our hymns have sounded.

IX

As already stated, the ultimate aim of Vedic *bhakti* is nothing less than immortality, which is so frequently being aspired for in the Vedic prayers as follows:

yatra jyotir ajasraṁ yasmiṁl loke svarhitam ।
tasmin māṁ dhehi pavamānāmṛ̥te
loke akṣita indrāyendo pari srava ॥ – *Ṛ̥V* IX.113.7

Where eternal lusture glows, the realm in which the light divine is set, place me, Purifier, in that deathless, imperishable world. For Indra, flow thou on, Indu! Make me immortal in that realm.

The following verse from the Vedas beautifully expresses this ultimate and the highest level of *bhakti,* i.e. the experience of enjoying infinite bliss of the Supreme:

> *apāma somamamṛtā abhūma āgana jyotiravidāma devān* ।
> *kiṁ nūnamasmānkṛṇavadarātiḥ kimu dhūrtiramṛta martyasya* ॥
> – *ṚV* VIII.48.3

> As we drink the elixir of divine bliss, we become immortal; we attain the heavenly light, we have known the secrets of divine forces. Now that would the malignant do to Harm us? Oh immortal! what man's deception Now to us?

After the dawn of divine inspiration, the devotees start paying obeisance to him, not once or twice, but on all days and at all times.

In this state of ecstasy, the devotee bows down to the divine and exclaims:

> *divo nu māṁ bṛhato antarikṣādapāṁ*
> *stoko 'bhyapatadrasena* ।
> *samindriyeṇa payasāhamagne*
> *chandobhiryajñaiḥ sukṛtāṁ kṛtena* ॥ – *AV* 6.124.1

> From the vast sky, or from the mid-space, a drop of water with pleasure fall upon me. Oh adorable Lord! may I be united with Power of my sense organs, with milk, with sacrifices and with the fruit of pious deeds.

At this advance stage of *bhakti*, the devotee desires nothing but the extreme, eternal friendship with the divine:

> *dūṇāśaṁ sakhyaṁ tava gaur asi vīra gavyate* ।
> *aśvo aśvāyate bhava* ॥ – *ṚV* VI.45.26

> Your friendship, Oh brave resplendent Lord! is not easily lost. You give wisdom to him who aspires for wisdom and vitality to him who aspires for vitality.

In fact, the *bhakta* has now realized the value of divine benediction and so he does not want to lose it at any cost:

mahe ca na tvām adrivaḥ parā śulkāya deyām ।
na sahasrāya nāyutāya vajrivo na śatāya śatāmagha ॥
– *Ṛ̥V* VIII.1.5

Oh God! I would not sell Thee for the highest price; Not for a thousand, nor for ten thousand, Oh Mighty one! nor for an infinite amount, Oh Lord of Countless wealth!

It is also noteworthy here that it is not only the devotees who seek the divine, the divine himself seeks them and urges upon them to sing his own eulogies:

arcata prārcata priyamedhāso arcata ।
arcantu putrakā uta puraṁ na dhṛ̥ṣṇvarcata ॥

ava svarāti gargaro godhā pari saniṣvaṇat ।
piṅgā pari caniṣkadad indrāya brahmodyatam ॥
– *Ṛ̥V* VIII.69.8-9

Sing you all and sing; Oh *priyamedhas*! sing your songs; Let children, too, sing; Sing to him, who is a refuge like mighty fortress; Let the *gargara* (violin) sound; Let the *godhā* (lute) send its resounding voice; Let the string send its tunes around; To God is our hymn unpraised.

What follows from the above description is that the Vedic prayers are a fine expression of *bhakti* – intensive as well as extensive. To quote:

It is interesting to find that in the Veda itself there are prayers of the typically *bhakti* type, containing sentiments and ideas associated with the cult. The very *kīrtana* form of prayer with its mass appeal appears in the Veda. – Bose 1966: 233

trātāram indram avitāram indraṁ
have have suhavaṁ śūram indram ।
hvayāmi śakraṁ puruhūtam indraṁ
svasti no maghavā dhātvindraḥ ॥ – *Ṛ̥V* VI.47.11

(I invoke) God, the rescuer, God, the Saviour, Mighty God, happily invoked at each invocation. God, Powerful, invoked by many, I invoke, May God, the Bounteous, confer on us blessing.

X

On the basis of above delineation, the Vedic view of *bhakti* can be summed up in the following five aspects:

i. *Bhakti* as a prayer signifies the ritual aspect of singing eulogies to the divine.

ii. *Bhakti* as a means to the goal, both mundane as well as supreme, has been well-reflected in the Vedas.

iii. *Bhakti* as a moral principle motivates the seeker for self-upliftment and encourages him to practise self-elevation as well, while praying to the higher powers for help.

iv. *Bhakti* is a gesture of reciprocation wherein the devotee prays and seeks something from the divine while offering the best of his own.

v. *Bhakti* in the form of prayer is an expression of inner satisfaction experienced by the seeker after attainment of his desired goal.

The most remarkable feature of *bhakti* in the Vedas is that it is not just effortless seeking, rather, it is an earnest quest of the devotee for winning the battles of life and attaining happiness with a full sense of determination and self-participation. It prays for divine help but insists on maximum effort by oneself:

icchanti devāḥ sunvantaṁ na svapnāya spr̥hayanti ।
yanti pramādam atandrāḥ ॥ – *R̥V* VIII.2.18

Nature's bounties favour those who are active in work and do not indulge in sleep. They bless those who are not drowsy and who realize the ecstasy of joy.

* * *

... *na r̥te śrāntasya sakhyāya devāḥ* ॥ – *R̥V* IV.33.11

Not without toil, the divines get friendly with men.

Ordinarily, *bhakti* is associated with sentimentalism and deep sense of pain or deprivation on the part of the seeker. But the more numerous and characteristic Vedic prayers express the feelings of joy and fulfilment in the mind of the seeker when he is immersed in the thoughts of the deity. It is not without reason then that the most typical devotional prayers in the Veda are the songs which appear to be flowing forth from a heart filled with sheer ecstasy:

> *agniṁ mandraṁ purupriyaṁ śīraṁ pāvakaśociṣam* ।
> *hṛdbhirmandrebhirīmahe* ॥ – *ṚV* VIII.43.31
>
> We worship with joyous hearts, the joyous deity dear to all, effulgent, holy, purifying.

From this point of view, the Vedic idea of *bhakti* is unique in the sense that herein the devotee not only invokes divinity in its various manifestations but also enkindles the latent divinity lying in the heart of his own being:

> *vayaṁ ghā te tve idvindra viprā api ṣmasi* ।
> *nahi tvadanyaḥ puruhūta kaścana maghavannasti marḍitā* ॥
> – *ṚV* VIII.66.13
>
> Truly God! We are Thine, we worshippers depend on thee. Except Thee, Oh much-invoked! there is none, Oh Mighty one! to show us grace.

It is due to this very aspect of Vedic *bhakti* that the devotee is inspired to have noble thought and undertake good action so that he not only comes closer to the deity he worships but also feels a strong bond of love and fellowship with all beings of the universe. The genuine celestial love elevates the *bhakta* and he rises above all selfish desires, his *bhakti* results in altruistic aspirations such as the following:

> *yāṁśca paśyāmi yāṁśca na teṣu mā sumatiṁ kṛdhi* । – *AV* 17.1.7
>
> Among those, whom I see and those, whom I do not see, may you cultivate friendship for me.

The most characteristic feature of Vedic *bhakti* is its genuinely collective and universal spirit. It is therefore that most of the

Vedic prayers are in the first-person plural like the following ones:

agne naya supathā rāye asmān… । – *R̥V* I.189.1

Oh adorable God! may you lead us along the wholesome path for our prosperity.

* * *

… suvīryasya patayaḥ syāma ॥ – *R̥V* X.131.6

May we be lords of hero vigour!

* * *

… nr̥bhir nr̥vantaḥ syāma ॥ – *R̥V* VII.41.3

May we be rich herpes.

* * *

… jīvā jyotir aśīmahi ॥ – *R̥V* VII.32.26

May we live and have light.

To re-iterate in brief, a seeker in the Vedic view of *bhakti* is not only eulogizing the divine but is also engaged in his own inner quest for exploring the divinity within himself. All his prayers are an expression of the same intense sense of bonding with the divine which binds him to other manifestations of the divine as also radiates within him and the outside world:

tasminnidaṁ saṁ ca vi caiti sarvaṁ
sa otaḥ protaśca vibhūḥ prajāsu ॥ – *YV* 32.8

Therein unites and therefrom issues the whole. The Lord is the wrap and woof in all the created beings.

To sum up, it would be appropriate to quote the following words of a poet critic:

The R̥gvedic hymns constitute not only the profoundest expression of the feeling of devotion to a personal Deity, but the wealth of devotional mood and attitude here, as well as their literary expression, far outshines anything in the

> best examples of later devotional poetry. Not only did the Vedic poets approach their deities as friends, as sons and as servants, i.e. in *sakhya*, *vātsalya* and *dāsya* as the later devotional schools would say, but they gave expression also to what has been considered as later development, the *madhura bhāva*, the approach in which God is the lover and the devotee the beloved .... – Raghavan 1956: xxxi, quoted by Bose 1966: 234

Lastly, to conclude with a Vedic prayer which characterizes the essence of Vedic *bhakti*:

> *gāyanti tvā gāyantriṇo 'rcantyarkamarkiṇaḥ* ।
> *brahmāṇastvā śatakrata udvaṁśamive yemire* ॥ – *SV* 1344
>
> Oh Lord with hundred names! the chanters chant of thee, and to thee the singers sing their songs, and those who pray, raise thee Oh Lord! as they raise a beam to the house.

9

Yajña in Vedic Tradition

THE chapter proposes to present a philosophical background of *yajña* in Vedic tradition of India as available in the original sources and also to propound scientific aspect of *yajña* in contemporary scenario.

I

In Vedic view *yajña* is stated to be the navel of universe[1] and the noblest of acts[2] since it is based on fostering the feeling of sacrifice among different levels of existence. Accordingly, the principle of interdependence is the inherent idea which pervades in all the aspects of *yajña* – physical or subtle, individual or social, ritual or spiritual. The basic thought behind the Vedic practice of *yajña* is the sense of offering oneself for the other which operates within the human body as also in the society and the world at large. Therefore, the seemingly simple act of *yajña* in Vedic tradition has a lot to contribute towards individual dignity, social solidarity and environmental well-being.

Etymologically the term *yajña* signifies: propitiating the natural forces like fire, air, rain, sky, earth, etc.; partaking of

---

1 *ayaṁ yajño bhuvanasya nābhiḥ* । – *YV* 23.62

2 *yajño vai śreṣṭhatamaṁ karma* । – *ŚatBrā* 1.7.1.5

available resources in a shared manner and providing for all those who are not having enough to sustain themselves.[3]

However, it needs to be clarified at the outset that the very first derivation of the term *yajña*[4] suggests its contribution to environmental equilibrium where every aspect of cosmos is offering itself for each other. This idea has its genesis in the Vedic philosophy according to which creation of the cosmos has also been described in the form of *yajña*. All the divine forces joined together to offer their best for the same.[5] It is, therefore, in the form of reciprocal offering that *yajña* evolves as a principle of environmental well-being. This is well expressed in the *Bhagavadgītā* also.[6]

It is an established fact that the offerings made into the fire of *yajña* give rise to cloud formation which eventually results in rain.[7] Hence this mutual partaking of five basic natural elements is the key factor for maintaining the balance of Nature. From this point of view, *yajña* helps in keeping the environment at peace, not only by simple offerings made in to fire but also in a well developed scheme of preparing the altar (earth), igniting the flame (fire), pouring purified butter and offering herbs for purification of atmosphere (air and sky) and ultimately giving rise to rain (water).

---

3 *√yaj devapūjāsaṅgatikaraṇadāneṣu* । – *Pāṇinīya Dhātupāṭhaḥ* 1.729

4 There are many synonyms of the term like *homa*, *havana* and *agnihotra*, but *yajña* is the most pervasive and the most ancient out of these all. This is so because *homa* or *agnihotra* pertains to *deva-yajña* only while the epithet *yajña* includes all the five types mentioned in Vedic sources.

5 *yajñena yajñamayajanta devāstāni dharmāṇi prathamānyāsan* ।
– *R̥V* X.90.16

6 *devān bhāvayatānena te devā bhāvayantu vaḥ* ।
parasparaṁ bhāvayantaḥ śreyaḥ parama vāpsyatha ॥ – *Gītā* III.11

7 *annād bhavanti bhūtāni parjanyād anna-sambhavaḥ* ।
yajñād bhavati parjanyo yajñaḥ karma-samudbhavaḥ ॥ – *Gītā* III.14

Viewed from this angle, the principle of *yajña* helps in promoting a feeling of mutual care and concern among different levels of existence – animate as well as inanimate, micro as well as macro and human as well as the divine. So the same act of offering to fire becomes a mode of worship when it operates between the human and the divine while it assumes the form of an act of mutual coordination when it operates between two human beings. More importantly, it raises to the level of cosmic welfare when an animate being invokes the environmental forces and makes faithful offerings to them. It is, therefore, that on the one hand Vedic *yajña* ordains to invoke gross environmental elements like earth, sky, air, fire, water, rain and rivers, and on the other hand, implores subtle forces such as mind (*manas*), speech (*vāk*), time (*kāla*), knowledge (*jñāna*), etc. Not only this, there are Vedic prayers for abstract notions like mutual concord (*saṁjñāna*),[8] coordination (*saṅgaṭhana*)[9] and collaboration (*saṁvanana*)[10] among different domains of family, society and the world. Fostering of such fine feelings among all the human beings and elements of the world makes it the most secular practice for environmental dignity. Above all, it proclaims to perpetuate an emotional bond among various aspects of the universe. It is therefore that the Vedas proclaim human beings as kin of *yajña*.[11]

Coming down from the cosmic to the communitarian level,

---

8 *yena devā na viyanti no ca vidviṣate mithaḥ* ।
tat kr̥ṇmo brahma vo gr̥he saṁjñānaṁ pūruṣebhyaḥ ॥ – *AV* 3.30.4

saṁjñānaṁ naḥ svebhiḥ saṁjñānam araṇebhiḥ ।
saṁjñānam aśvinā yuvām ihāsmāsu ni yachatam ॥ – *AV* VII.52.1

9 *saṁ gacchadhvaṁ saṁ vadadhvaṁ saṁ vo manāṁsi jānatām* ।
devā bhāgaṁ yathā pūrve saṁjānānā upāsate ॥ – *R̥V* X.191.2

10 *etaṁ me stomaṁ tanā na sūrye dyutadyāmānam vāvr̥dhanta nr̥ṇām* ।
saṁvananaṁ nāśvyaṁ taṣṭevānapacyutam ॥ – *R̥V* X.93.12

11 *sa cetayanmanuṣo yajñabandhuḥ* । – *R̥V* IV.1.9

it is noteworthy that the Vedic vision of *yajña* leads to societal well-being as well. *Yajña* is the key factor for an ethical social organization according to which all members of the society are obliged to perform this reciprocal act for a smooth functioning of society.

The basic principle of organismic unity and social solidarity operates in this realm as well, where various sections of society, just like different organs of a body, function in full coordination for the welfare of one organism, i.e. the society. It is not without reason then that the term *yajña* is usually translated as oblation, offering and also sacrifice (Monier-Williams 2005: 839), but actually the inherent "feeling of sacrifice" and not "sacrifice in literal sense" is essential to the practice of *yajña* in original Vedic tradition.

According to Vedic thought, every human being is born along with three vital obligations such as: *ṛṣi-ṛṇa* (debt to the sages), *pitṛ-ṛṇa* (debt to one's ancestors) and *deva-ṛṇa* (debt towards the divine powers),[12] which he must always remember to repay to the divine powers through performance of *yajña*. That is why one is obliged to wear the sacred thread consisting of three cotton strands not only to remind him of the three debts incurred by him but also to enable him for performing the daily *yajñas*.[13] This idea of three debts (and three strands of the sacred thread associated with the performance of *yajña*) is in fact a symbolic reminder for giving back to the society whatever one has gained from it (Cromwell 1974: 210). In other words, when the *yajña* is performed by an individual with some selfish desire,

---

12 *jāyamāno vai brāhmaṇastribhirṛṇavā jāyate* ।
brahmacaryeṇa ṛṣibhyo yajñena devebhyaḥ ।
prajayā pitṛbhyaḥ ... । – *TaitSaṁ* 6.3.10.55

13 *yajñopavītaṁ paramaṁ pavitraṁ prajāpateryatsahajaṁ purastāt* ।
āyuṣyamagryaṁ pratimuñca śubhraṁ yajñopavītaṁ balamastu tejaḥ ।
yajñopavītamasi yajñasya tvā yajñopavītenopanahyāmi ।
– *Pāraskara Gṛhyasūtra* 2.2.11.1-2

it becomes a mere mechanical ritual. But the same act, when performed with a selfless motive, becomes spiritual and leads to universal welfare where each member of society is working for the benefit of others.

In fact, the Vedic paradigm of *yajña* is not rights-oriented, rather, it is duty-oriented. Therefore, the later Vedic texts prescribe five types of *yajña*s for every householder.[14] Details of these five types of *yajña*s are given hereunder:

i. *Brahma-yajña*:[15] It is enjoined for every householder to study and meditate over the teachings of scriptures so as to propitiate the ancient seers.

ii. *Deva-yajña*:[16] As enunciated in Vedic tradition, the daily rituals for a householder include the offering into fire (*agnihotra*), which is eulogized in the *Chāndogya Upaniṣad*[17] as a mother whom her hungry children approach with love because it fulfils the aspirations of all those who offer oblations into it. *Devayajña* is prescribed so as to

---

14 In the *āśrama* system of later Vedic tradition, a householder or *gṛhastha* is held to be the most important of the four *āśrama*s since it sustains all the other three, viz. student life (*brahmacarya*), ascetic life (*vānaprastha*) and the life of a recluse (*saṁnyāsa*):

catvāra āśramaḥ gārhasthyamācāryakulaṁ maunaṁ vānaprasthyamiti ।
– *Āpastamba Dharmasūtra* II.9.21.1

yathā nadīnadāḥ sarve sāgare yānti saṁsthitim ।
tathaivāśramiṇaḥ sarve gṛhasthe yānti saṁsthitim ॥ – *MS* 6.90

yathā vāyuṁ samāśritya vartante sarvajantavaḥ ।
tathā gṛhastham āśritya vartante sarva āśramāḥ ॥ – *MS* 3.77

yasmāt trayo 'py āśramiṇo jñānenānnena cānvaham ।
gṛhasthenaiva dhāryante tasmājjyeṣṭhāśramo gṛhī ॥ – *MS* 3.78

15 *atha brahmayajñaḥ svādhyāyo vai brahmayajñaḥ* । – *ŚatBrā* 11.5.6.1

16 *yadagnau juhotyapi samidhaṁ tad devayajñaḥ santiṣṭhate* । – *TĀ* 2.10

17 *yatheha kṣudhitā bālā mātaraṁ paryupāsate* । *evaṁ sarvāṇi bhūtānyagnihotramupāsata iti* । – *ChāUp* 5.24.5

gratify the gods and discharge one's duties towards the environmental forces like the sun, the rain, the wind and waters.

iii. *Pitṛ-yajña:*[18] Serving one's mother, father and ancestors with love and respect is also envisioned to be a form of daily *yajña* (duty) since in this way the continuity of the progeny is preserved and carried forward in a meaningful manner.

iv. *Balivaiśvadevayajña*[19] or *Bhūta-yajña:*[20] Offering of cooked food to all beings including gods, humans, animals and insects is also enjoined as a daily ritual. It is worth mentioning here that Vedic view regards the whole universe as a single, seamless unit in which all living beings have their appropriate places (Kumar 2005c: 63). Hence, one is not only obliged to look after other human beings but also to care for the welfare of other living beings such as the cow, the dog, the crow and the insects.

v. *Atithi-yajña* or *Nṛ-yajña:*[21] Each one of the householders is also obliged to treat and serve the guests by offering of food, clothes and shelter. "He who cooks for himself, verily eats sin alone"[22] is the famous Vedic principle according to which one should share with fellow human beings whatever he/she has for eating. This daily observance in Vedic tradition gave rise to the idea of *yajñaśeṣa* (food left after *yajña*), i.e. eating only after feeding others.[23]

---

18 *yad pitṛbhyaḥ svadhā karotyapyapastat pitṛyajñaḥ* । – *TĀ* 2.10

19 *yatra viśve devā ijyante tad vaiśvadevikam karma* ।
– *Parāśara-Mādhavīya,* quoted by *Kane* 1941, vol. II, part I: 741

20 *yadbhūtebhyo baliṁ harati tad bhūtayajñaḥ santiṣṭhate* । – *TĀ* 2.10

21 *nṛyajño 'tithipūjanam* । – *MS* 3.70

22 ... *kevalāgho bhavati kevalādī* ॥ – *ṚV* X.117.6

23 *yajña-śiṣṭāśinaḥ santo mucyante sarva-kilbiṣaiḥ* ।
bhuñjate te tv aghaṁ pāpā ye pacanty ātma-kāraṇāt ॥ – *Gītā* III.13

→

Obviously, the practice of above five types of daily *yajña*s helps in developing a cooperative model of living rather than the competitive one. Moreover, *yajña* being laid out as a daily practice, coupled with the chanting of Vedic *mantra*s (sacred verses), in correct pronunciation (Bhargava 2006) gives it an obligatory status and also generates positive vibrations to purify the environment.

As already stated, *yajña* is held to be a metaphor of coordination in Vedic tradition right from the beginning of creation and the maintaining of societal balance, going up to the harmonious living of an individual in a familial set-up. In its ritual form, it involves a perfect blending of five physical elements – earth, water, air, sky and fire – while in its nature of obligatory acts, it provides a fine formula for societal well-being.

Not only this, the Vedic paradigm of *yajña* goes beyond humans and envisages dignity for all forms of existence – be it animals, birds or insects. The same can be substantiated from the Vedic ideal of *yajña* as elaborated above. In the contemporary consumeristic society, the idea and practice of *yajña* can contribute a lot not only in improving relationships among human beings but also in maintaining a balance between external and internal environment for a fair and peaceful living on the planet earth.

This brings us to the point of *mantra*s ordained for chanting in the Vedic *yajña*. Accordingly, the *mantra*s included in *svastivācana* chapter of Vedic *yajña* are culled from the four Vedas and are mostly in the form of prayers to the divine forces/ natural powers for bestowing their benign blessings not only on the devotee but on all the human beings. This can be confirmed from the frequent use of word *naḥ* (upon us all). Similarly, the *mantra*s of *śāntikaraṇa* chapter are chanted for bringing peace

---

← *yajña-śiṣṭāmṛta-bhujo yānti brahma sanātanam* ।
nāyaṁ loko 'sty ayajñasya kuto 'nyaḥ kuru-sattama ॥ – *Gītā* IV.31

upon the whole of universe including sun, rain, air, water, herbs, plants and human beings. Once the sacred fire is ignited and offerings of purified butter and dried herbs are put into it along with the chanting of *mantras*, then at the end of each offering these words are uttered:

- *agnaye/vāyave/viṣṇave/indrāya-**svāhā**.*
- ***idanna mama.***

Which mean to say that this offering is for the specific divine/natural force and not for me. It is meant to inculcate a sense of selflessness, which is central to the practice of *yajña*.[24]

More importantly, the two words *svāhā* and *idanna mama* are such an integral part of all the offerings put into sacred fire that it is aptly said:

- *svāhā vāṭ vai yajñasyātmā* । (*svāhā* is the soul of *yajña*).
- *idanna mama vai yajñasya prāṇaḥ* । (*idanna mama* is the vital force of *yajña*).
- *surabhirvai yajñasya sāraḥ* । (fragrance emanating from *yajña* is the essence of *yajña*).[25]

It needs to be highlighted that in Vedic *yajña*, there is a special sense of sanctity in the chanting of *mantras*[26] and coordinating

---

24 *gata-saṅgasya muktasya jñānāvasthita-cetasaḥ* ।
yajñāyācarataḥ karma samagraṁ pravilīyate ॥ – *Gītā* IV.23

The commentator of the *Śrīmad Bhagavadgītā*, Rāmacandrācārya while interpreting the above verse, has explained the word *yajña* as *lokasaṁgraha* which clearly signifies social welfare.

– Vide *Padayojanā* commentary on the above

25 Vide "Yajnā-saṁskṛti" in *Videha-Vāṇī* (Hindi) II, Ajmer: Vidyananda Videha, 1983, pp. 174-77.

26 (i) "The *mantra* is neither a mere sound nor sheer magic. Words have not only a sound but also a meaning, which is not apparent to all those who simply hear the sound. Living words have, furthermore a power that transcends the purely mental plane. →

all the physical elements mentioned above. Otherwise, simply putting woods or purified butter in fire will not result in such a magical effect as the Vedic *yajña* emanates.

As regards the idea of gender in the context of *yajña* in Vedic tradition, it may be said with certainty that women had equal rights to perform the household ritual. In fact, the Sanskrit term *patnī* for a wife is derived from her obligatory equal status in the fire ritual.[27] It is therefore that in Vedic tradition no married man can perform the ritual without his wife by his side.[28] That is also the secret of the epithet *dharmapatnī*,[29] to be used for a duly wed wife as per Hindu law.

There are several Vedic references of husband and wife performing the fire ritual together.[30] Even the wedding ceremony

---

← To acquire this energy of the word one has to grasp not only its meaning but also its message, or its vibrations, as they are sometimes called in order to stress the link with the sound itself." – Panikkar 2001: 39

(ii) "Every *mantra* in the Vedas has been linked with a *devatā* that symbolizes an eternal energy field of specific flow of cosmic consciousness. Whenever a *mantra* is enunciated or chanted in a specific rhythmic manner. Its associated sonic waves expand in a specific pattern and after traversing across the layers of energy-particles in the surrounding space reach and penetrate the corresponding cosmic nuclei of divine powers." – Acharya 2003: 49

27 *patyurno yajñasaṁyoge* । – *Aṣṭādhyāyī* 4.11.3

28 *ayajñiyo vā eṣa ya 'patnīkaḥ* । – *ŚatBrā* 3.3.3.1

ayajño vā eṣa yo 'patnīkaḥ । – *TaitBrā* 2.2.2.6

29 *patnītvamasi dharmaṇā 'ham gṛhapatistava* । – *AV* 14.1.51

30 *tān yajatrāṁ ṛtāvṛdho 'gne patnīvatas kṛdhi* ।
madhvaḥ sujihva pāyaya ॥ – *ṚV* I.14.7

yā daṁpatī samanasā sunuta ā ca dhāvataḥ ।
devāso nityayāśirā ॥ – *ṚV* VIII.31.5

in Vedic tradition is performed as a ritual and both the husband and wife together make offerings into fire while chanting the *mantras*.[31] Not only this, women alone could also perform *yajña* as reflected in many Vedic verses.[32]

In fact, keeping the fire of *yajña* alive is held to be the foremost duty of a wife in Vedic tradition and hence a man, who does not have a wife, is held to be unfit for the sacred acts.[33] In other words, anybody who performs a *yajña* without his wife does only half of the ritual.[34] Even king Rāma had to place a golden statue of Sītā, when he decided to perform the Vedic ritual of Aśvamedha according to *Rāmāyaṇa*.

However, the ennobling ethos of *yajña* in the original Vedic tradition got a bit diminished later when it was restricted to the ritual being performed in a mere mechanical manner. This was burdened with the rigid priestly involvement and caste-driven restrictions of the later Vedic period. The same is reflected very well in the golden goose episode of the *Mahābhārata*,[35] where it is suggested that the real sense of selfless offering means much more than the pomp and show pertaining to *yajña*. However, it needs to be mentioned that up to the *Rāmāyaṇa* period, *yajña*s of different kinds were being performed with full faith and are said to be yielding desired results too as can be seen in Putrakāmeṣṭi Yajña[36] performed by King Daśaratha for availing progeny.

---

31 *punaḥ patnīmagniradādāyuṣā saha varcasā* ।
dīrghāyurasyā yaḥ patirjīvāti śaradaḥ śatam ॥ – *ṚV* X.85.39

32 *purukutsānī hi vām adāśad dhavyebhir indrāvaruṇā namobhiḥ* ।
athā rājānaṁ trasadasyum asyā vṛtrahaṇaṁ dadathur ardhadevam ॥
– *ṚV* IV.42.9

33 *ayajño vā eṣa yo 'patnīkaḥ* । – *TaitBrā* 2.2.2.6

34 *jaghanārdho vā eṣa yajñasya yatpatnī* । – *ŚatBrā* 1.3.1.12

35 Aśvamedhika Parva, chapter 30, verses 1-120.

36 *sa cāpyaputro nṛpatistasmin kāle mahādyutiḥ* ।
ayajatputriyāmiṣṭiṁ putrepsurarisūdanaḥ ॥
– *Vālmīki Rāmāyaṇa*, Bāla-Kāṇḍa 1.16.9

This brings us to the point of different forms of *yajñas* in later Vedic tradition which were being performed for fulfilling of various desires – individual, familial or social, e.g. *iṣṭa* (individual and familial) and *āpūrta* (social).[37] The *Bhagavadgītā* describes five types of *yajña* on the basis of various offerings such as *dravya-yajña, tapo-yajña, yoga-yajña, svādhyāya-yajña* and *jñāna-yajña*[38] in ascending order and another three levels of *yajña* – *sāttvika, rājasika* and *tāmasika* – depending upon the intention of the agent in descending order.[39]

What follows from the above brief delineation is that *yajña*, which arose as a mode of worship and a symbolic practice of cosmic welfare in the early Vedic tradition, came to be a means for mutual coordination in the later Vedic tradition (up to the period of Upaniṣads) where kings like Janaka (*BṛUp* 4.1.1) and householder sages like Vājaśravas (*KaṭhUp* 1.1.1) organized huge *yajñas* in the form of congregations where all the intellectuals were invited and were paid large amount in lieu of delivering discourses. Gradually, although the original idea of *yajña* as a symbol of cosmic welfare eloped, yet it is still being practised as a mode of worship on specific occasions. But it has come to

---

37 *udbudhyasvāgne pratijāgṛhi tvamiṣṭāpūrte saṁsṛjethāmayam ca* ।
– *Vājasaneyī Saṁhitā* 15.54

ekāgnikarma havanaṁ tretāyāṁ yacca hūyate । *antarvedyāṁ ca yadvānamiṣṭamityabhidhīyate* । *vāpīkūpataḍāgāni devatāyatanāni ca* । *annapradānamārāmaḥ pūrtamityabhidhīyate* । – *Mahābhārata* (quoted by Aparārka in his commentary on the *Yajñavalkya Smṛti*, p. 290)

38 *dravya-yajñās tapo-yajñā yoga-yajñās tathāpare* ।
svādhyāya-jñāna-yajñāś ca yatayaḥ saṁśita-vratāḥ ॥ – *Gītā* IV.28

39 *aphalākāṅkṣibhir yajño vidhi-dṛṣṭo ya ijyate* ।
yaṣṭavyam eveti manaḥ samādhāya sa sāttvikaḥ ॥ – *Gītā* XVII.11

abhisandhāya tu phalaṁ dambhārtham api caiva yat ।
ijyate bharata-śreṣṭha taṁ yajñaṁ viddhi rājasam ॥ – *Gītā* XVII.12

vidhihīnam asṛṣṭānnaṁ mantra-hīnam adakṣiṇam ।
śraddhā-virahitaṁ yajñaṁ tāmasaṁ paricakṣate ॥ – *Gītā* XVII.13

be only a short-cut ritual act of igniting the fire in a small lamp which continues till date in diverse forms of Vedic tradition.

In brief, it may be said that Vedic *yajña* sanctifies the earth, propitiates the fire, purifies the air, creates positive sound vibrations in the sky and paves the path for rainwater. It is not without reason then, that *yajña* is held to be the key for environmental balance. Even though the times have changed and it will be futile to think of bringing back the ideal form of *yajña* in Vedic tradition, yet not only the basic idea of offering oneself for the other at all levels is worth emulating at the familial and social level but also the therapeutic aspect of *yajña* needs to be taken into account for the microcosmic as well as macrocosmic well-being.

These days, many experiments are being carried out in several places to check the efficacy of *yajña*. This is a pointer beyond doubt that several scientific facts[40] and certain therapeautical benefits[41] of *yajña* are being proven in such experiments, which is a pointer to the practice of *yajña* being helpful for individual, social and universal welfare.

To conclude, let us invoke the divine forces to enable us all for protecting and propagating the inherent feeling of *yajña*.

---

40 "There are two basic energy systems in the physical world: Heat and sound. In performing *yajña*, these two energies, viz. the heat from *yajña*'s fire and the sound of the Gāyatrī and other *mantra*s, are combined to achieve the desired physical, psychological and spiritual benefits.

The fumigation of specific substances in the *yajña*-fire is a scientific method of subtilization of matter into energy and expanding its potential and positive effects in the surrounding atmosphere. The electromagnetic waves generated therapy help in transmitting, at cosmic level, the desired sonic signals 'stored' in the *mantra*s, which are chanted during the process of sacrificing the special materials in the fire." – www.awgp.org

41 Vide: www.homatherapie.de; yagyopathy.com; www.homatherapyindia.com; www.homahealth.com

10

Vedic View of Language as Power

THE chapter proposes to propound the Vedic vision of "language as power" available in early Vedic sources.

The Veda is held to be the original source of knowledge in Indian tradition. It also signifies Śruti, the vibrating spoken word or an utterance of the preceptor which is directly heard by the disciple. This orality of knowledge in Vedic view is the cornerstone for Indian philosophy of language,[1] which accords supreme authority to verbal testimony among all modes of knowing. It is, therefore, that the Vedic view of language is basically focused on ideational rather than the physical or written form of language.[2]

1 "Where in the Indian tradition language is thought to be truly and most fully experienced in its oral form, the modern view tends to restrict language to the printed word and then analyse it for a one-to-one correspondence with objective reality. As Klaus Klostermier has observed, contemporary linguistic philosophy sees the word only as a carrier of information and basically studies those aspects of language that a computer can store and retrieve." – Coward 1992: 114

2 From this point of view, Saussure's *langue* (language) seems to be nearer to the Vedic idea of language rather than the *parole* (speech). – Vide F. de Saussure, "Cours de Linguistic Generale", quoted by Raja 1963: 104

Language as Divine Power

Supremacy of the word is based on the Vedic notion of language which holds that speech or the idea of speech, i.e. *vāk* is a creative force, a power extraordinary; so much so that the same is stated to be a divine word (*daivī vāk*) which has manifested itself in various forms. Accordingly, *vāk* has two aspects – transcendent and the immanent: the former exists in the spiritual plane while the later manifests itself at the material level:

> *devīṁ vācamajanayanta devāstāṁ*
> *viśvarūpāḥ paśavo vadanti* ।
> *sā no mandreṣamūrjaṁ duhānā*
> *dhenurvāgasmānupa suṣṭutaitu* ॥ – *Ṛ̥V* VIII.100.11

> The divine powers produce the Goddess of speech; even animals of every kind utter some words; may She, the speech, the all-gladdening cow, yielding food and drink, come to us, worthily lauded.

There are two levels of speech in Vedic view: higher and lower, i.e. *parā* and *aparā*, *amṛtā* and *martyā*, *daivī* and *mānuṣī*. Out of these, *parā* (transcendent) *vāk* is unmanifest and impersonal, while *aparā* is the *vāk* in which the distinction of syllables is manifest. It is in this background that the four parts and the seven forms of speech are suggested in the following Vedic verse:

> *catvāri śṛṅgā trayo asya pādā dve śīrṣe sapta hastāso asya* ।
> *tridhā baddho vṛṣabho roravīti maho devo martyām̐ ā viveśa* ॥
> – *Ṛ̥V* IV.58.3

> Four are the horns, three are his feet, his heads are two, his hands are seven; this triple-bound showerer of benefits roars aloud. That mighty divine is enshrined in the hearts of all mortals.

The Vedic view of language equates it with the divine power *Brahman*; the *Ṛgveda* clearly states that there are as many words as there are manifestations of the supreme *Brahman*:

sahasradhā pañcadaśānyukthā yāvad
dyāvāpṛthivī tāvadittat ।
sahasradhā mahimānaḥ sahasraṁ yāvad
brahma viṣṭhitaṁ tāvatī vāk ॥ – *ṚV* X.114.8

The fifteen chief forms are found in thousands of places; this is as vast as heaven and earth in measure; the thousand great cosmic powers are in a thousand cosmic places; the divine speech (*vāk*) spreads forth as much as the creator (*Brahman*).

The above verse signifies that *vāk* is not only described as the highest reality, *Brahman*; it is also said to be coextensive with *Brahman* in the *Ṛgveda*; "the *Brahman* which is both transcendent Reality and the supreme word" (Padoux 1992: 1-2).

Even in the exegetical texts of Vedas, *vāk* is repeatedly said to be *Brahman*:

a. *vāgbrahma* । – *GoBrā* 1.2.10
b. *vāgvai brahma* । – *AitaBrā* 6.3
c. *prajāpatirvai vāk* । – *TaiBrā* 1.3.4.5
d. *vāgvai prajapatiḥ* । – *ŚatBrā* 5.1.5.6
e. *yā sā vā brahmaiva tat* । – *JaiUpBrā* 2.13.2

This clearly indicates that language is held to be the supreme power in Vedic view.

Significantly the term *śakti* appears in several verses of the *Ṛgveda* (III.57.3; VII.68.8; X.88.10), though it is not exactly in the sense of power as was suggested in the later texts of Indian tradition. It may be mentioned here that the notion of power generally points to the idea of authority commanded through the use of language and the same is suggested more appropriately by compound phrases like *vāk-śakti* or *vāg-vibhava* (power of description, command of language) (Monier-Williams 2003: 612). But the real significance of Vedic view lies in the fact that herein *vāk* is not only held to be a medium or tool for power, rather, it is stated to be power itself.

Vāk as a Feminine Force

Numerous synonyms of "speech" have been given in Vedic lexicon, out of which *vāk* (speech) is enumerated as the fiftieth and happens to be the foremost.[3] Interestingly, out of these fifty-seven synonyms, forty-four are feminine in nature which again is an indication of speech as the creative female power (Abhayadeva 2006: 172).

More notably, there is a whole hymn in the *Ṛgveda* exclusively devoted to *vāk,* the feminine force. In this remarkable hymn, *vāk* is personified and glorified as supreme power:

> *ahameva svayam idaṁ vadāmi juṣṭaṁ*
> *devebhiruta mānuṣebhiḥ* ।
> *yaṁ kāmaye tantamugraṁ kṛṇomi taṁ*
> *brahmāṇaṁ tamṛṣiṁ taṁ sumedhām* ॥ – *ṚV* X.125.5

I verily of myself announce the truth that is approved of by both, the divine ones and humans; I make one formidable, a sage, a seer, and a wise whomsoever I choose.

Daughter of Sage Ambhṛṇa, Vāk is said to be capable of creating both – the eloquent as well as the silent. Vāk is depicted here as an all-pervasive power which encompasses all that is there in the universe. All the creatures of living world draw their food from this divine power called *vāk*; those who do not know of it, become bereft of this world:

> *maya so annamatti yo vipaśyati yaḥ prāṇiti ya īṁ śṛṇotyuktam* ।
> *amantavo māṁ ta upa kṣiyanti śrudhi śruta śraddhivaṁ te vadāmi* ॥ – *ṚV* X.125.4

---

[3] *ślokaḥ, dhārā, ilā, gau, gāndharvī, gaurī, gabhīrā, gambhīrā, mandrā, mandrājanī, vāśī, vāṇī, vāṇīcī, vāṇaḥ, pavīḥ, bhāratī, dhamaniḥ, nālīḥ, meliḥ, menā, sūryā, sarasvatī, nivit, svāhā, vāgniḥ, upabdiḥ, māyuḥ, kākut, jihvā, ghoṣaḥ, svaraḥ, śabdaḥ, svapnaḥ, ṛk, hotrā, gīḥ, gāthā, gaṇaḥ, dhenāḥ, gnāḥ, vipāḥ, nagā, kaśā, dhiṣaṇā, nauḥ, akṣaram, mahī, aditi, śaci, vāk, anuṣṭup, dhenu, valguḥ, galdā, saraḥ, suparṇī, bekurā.* – *Nighaṇṭu* 1.11

> Through me alone, whosoever eats, eats food. It is through me that one sees, breathes, hears and speaks; those who are ignorant of me are sure to perish; may you hear, I tell you the truth, and you have to accept it.

Akṣara: The Eternal Syllable

Besides *Brahman*, language is also expressed as *akṣara* in Vedic depiction. *Akṣara*, another epithet for word, which signifies the eternal, imperishable aspect of speech, is, in fact, a syllable:

> An irreducible ultimate or impartible unit of speech, which is the symbol of motion or pulsation, since all speech is a visible activity against the spectrum of silence. – Agrawala 1963: 153

Akṣara is the primal, imperishable principle of word-power and is associated with the verses of the *Ṛgveda* (*ṛca*s). It is proclaimed in the *Ṛgveda* itself:

> *ṛco akṣare parame vyomanyasmindevā adhi viśve niṣeduḥ* ।
> *yastanna veda kimṛcā kariṣyati ya ittadvidusta ime samāsate* ॥
> – *ṚV* I.164.39

> The Supreme Reality (*Brahman*) is omnipresent like space and eternal like his word and all nature's bounties have their repose in him. What will he, who knows not this (divine principle), do with Veda? But they who know it, they come close to him.

Evidently the above verse highlights the Vedic idea of speech as impersonal power. It means that *parā* or *parameṣṭhinī vāk* is just in the form of sound, i.e. *dhvanyātmikā* since the distinct syllabic sounds of vowels are not manifested in it. This form of *vāk* is actually silence which is present in the hearts of all creatures: *vāgghṛdaye* (*TaiBrā* 3.10.8.4).

Brāhmaṇa texts have extended this imagery to convey that the speech of human beings is *nirukta* (syllabic), while of the animals, birds and reptiles is *anirukta* (non-syllabic):

> *vadiṣyatīti tadetatturīyaṁ vāco niruktaṁ yanmanuṣyā vadantyathaitatturīyaṁ vāco'niruktaṁ yatpaśavo vadantya-*

> *thaitatturīyaṁ vāco 'niruktaṁ yadvayāṁsi vadantya-thaitatturīyaṁ vāco 'niruktaṁ yadidaṁ kṣudraṁ sarīsṛpaṁ vadati* ।
> – *ŚatBrā* 4.1.3.16
>
> He said: if they have assigned to me a fourth part each time for my share, then speech shall speak intelligibly only one fourth part. Hence only that fourth part of speech is intelligible which men speak, but that fourth part of speech leasts speak is unintelligible; and that fourth part of speech which birds speak is unintelligible and that fourth part of speech which the small vermin here speaks is unintelligible.

Here, a mention must also be made of infinite and finite forms of speech. The same is expressed as the "thousand-syllabled speech" and "one-syllabled *akṣara*" according to an interpretation:

> The doctrine of *parame vyoman* is mentioned several times in the *Ṛgveda* as typical of the highest transcendent *Brahman* who is the source of the thousand-syllabled speech (*sahasrākṣarā parame vyoman*, I.164.41), or of the one-syllabled *akṣara* that is *oṁkāra*.
> – Agrawala 1963: 153

Obviously in Vedic view, "thousand" signifies the infinite world of the *deva*s while the "hundred" symbolizes the finite world of human beings.

Oṁ: The Subtlest Speech Form

This brings us to the significance of *oṁ* in Vedic view. It is held to be the best name of Divine Supreme, who is addressed by several appellations (Saraswati 2003: 6-19); while all other names refer to any particular aspect or attribute of the divine, *oṁ* embraces all that is there. Only God is signified by the term *oṁ*, whereas all other names like Agni, Viṣṇu, Śiva may mean other objects as well. *Oṁ* is indeclinable (*avyaya*) having no change in number, gender, person or case. In *oṁ* (*a+u+m*): *a* (अ) is the first letter of the phonetic alphabet; *u* (उ) is the last phonetic pure vowel, *m* (म्) is the last letter and all the three together are the integral limits of sounds which we use in our language.

- *a* = Supreme Self
- *u* = Lower Self
- *m* = Primordial Nature (Das 2012: 1)

All these are indicated by the single syllable *oṁ*. The sound of the monosyllable *oṁ* and its exalted status in Vedic tradition points to the infinite power of finite word. *Oṁ* is said to be the essence of Vedas:

> *athai 'kasyaivā 'kṣarasya rasaṁ nā 'śaknodātum* । *omityetasyai 'va* । *se 'yaṁ vāgabhavat omeva nā maiṣā* । – *JaiUp* 1.1

> Now of one syllable, he was not able to take the sap: of *oṁ*, just of that.

As leaves are held together by a spike, so all the worlds merge into the sound *oṁ*. The sound *oṁ* is the whole universe.

> *tānyabhyatapattebhyo 'bhitaptebhya oṁkāraḥ saṁprāsravattadyathā śaṅkunā sarvāṇi parṇāni saṁtṛṇṇānyevam-oṁkāreṇa sarvā vāk saṁtṛṇṇoṁkāra evedaṁ sarvamoṁkāra evedaṁ sarvam* । – *ChāUp* 2.23.3

> On them (those syllables), he brooded; from them thus brooded upon the syllable *oṁ* (the symbol of *Brahman*) issued forth: just as by the ribs of the leaf all parts of the leaf are permeated, so by the syllable *oṁ* all the words are permeated. The syllable *oṁ* verily – all is this.

Oṁ is held to be the basic symbol, the subtlest speech form and the most primary sound of Vedic language.[4] Dwelling upon the potential depth of *oṁ*, Thomas Coburn (1984: 542) rightly says:

---

4 "It may be worth noting that this extolling of *oṁ*, as containing the very essence of the Vedas, shows how in Indian thought, as early as Vedic times, the condensed, the concentrated has always been given primacy over the extended, the diluted. There is nothing more powerful than *oṁ*, for within this one syllable (which should be uttered at the beginning of any Vedic text) is encapsulated the whole of the Veda." – Padoux 1992: 18-19

Auṁ does not mean any one thing; rather, it symbolizes everything.

Three Vyāhṛtis

Along with *oṁ*, there is also this Vedic idea of three utterances (*vyāhṛtis*) – *bhū, bhuvaḥ, svaḥ*. Three *vyāhṛtis* signify three levels of the cosmos respectively, i.e. earth, mid-space and sky. It is enjoined in Vedic sources that these three syllables must be uttered before the well-known Gāyatrī verse.

In Vedic view, three regions of physical universe are explained as earth (*bhū*), mid-space (*bhuvaḥ*) and the highest abode above (*svaḥ*) – these three utterances are therefore indicative of three planes of existence:

> *bhūrbhuvaḥ suvariti vā etāstisro vyāhṛtayaḥ* । *tāsāmuha smāitāṁ caturthiṁ māhācamasyaḥ pravedayate* । *maha iti* । *tadhrahma* । *sa ātmā* । *aṅgānyanyā devatāḥ* । *bhūriti vā ayaṁ lokaḥ* । *bhuva ityantarikṣam* । *suvarityasau lokaḥ* । – *TaiUp* 1.5.1

> *Bhūḥ, bhuva* and *suva* are three sacred utterances. Besides these the fourth, the *mahā* has been tought by the son of *māhācanas*. That is *Brahman*. That is *ātman*. All other gods are the other limbs. *Bhū* is this world; *bhuva* is the sky and *suva* is the other world.

Accordingly, all the Vedic verses are interpreted in three ways, i.e. physical (*ādhibhautika*), atmospheric (*ādhidaivika*) and spiritual (*ādhyātmika*).

> *prajāpatirvā idaṁ ... trayasya vedasya rasamādadā iti* । *sa bhūriryevargvedasya rasamādatta* । *se 'yampṛthivyabhavat* । *tasya yo rasaḥ prāṇodat so 'gnirabhavadrasasya rasaḥ* । *bhuva ityeva yajurvedasya rasamādatta* । *tadidamantarikṣamabhavat* । *tasya yo rasaḥ prāṇedat sa vāyurabhavadrasasya rasaḥ* । *svarityeva sāmavedasya rasamadatta* । *so 'sav dyaurabhavat* । *tasya yo rasaḥ prāṇedat ādityo 'bhavadrasasya rasaḥ* ।
>
> – *JaiUpBrā* 1.1.1

> Prajāpati verily ... let me take the sap of the threefold knowledge (*veda*). Saying *Bhūs* he took the sap of the *Ṛgveda*. That became this earth. The sap of it which streamed forth became Agni (fire), the sap of the sap. Saying *bhuvas*, he took the sap of the *Yajurveda* that became this atmosphere. Saying *svara*, he took the sap of the *Sāmaveda* that became yonder sky. The sap of it which steamed forth became Āditya (sun), the sap of the sap.

These three great utterances are said to be the sap of three Vedas: *bhū* is the sap of the *Ṛgveda*. The sap of this sap became fire from which this earth has originated; *bhuvaḥ* is the sap of the *Yajurveda* and it is the source of mid-space, the sap of this sap became air (*vāyu*); *svaḥ* is the sap of the *Sāmaveda* – that became the sky and the sap of this sap is sun (Āditya).

Mantra as Word-power

The Vedic term *mantra* is another example of word-power; it is derived from root √*man* and signifies a special sort of word which is the result of serious contemplation and carries a certain inherent weightage. These *mantra*s are not the words of ordinary speech, rather they are held to be of divine origin and directly received by the *ṛṣis*, the extraordinarily gifted beings. It is noteworthy here that the Vedic *mantra* is unique in this sense also that it cannot be covered under any other linguistic category as such. Hence, the following statement of Gonda (1964: 245, 268) is well founded:

> Holy or sacred word has been enumerated in twelve different types by a modern scholar, Friedrich Heiler, but the well-known Indian *mantra* is, in these pages conspicuous by its absence. Vedic *mantra* may therefore be described as a power (*śakti*) in the form of formulated and expressed thought.

Needless to say that the Vedic *mantra* itself denotes the power of language. In the words of Sir John Woodroffe (1950: 83):

> *Mantra* is a power (*mantra-śakti*) which lends itself impartially to any use.

Another contemporary scholar Frits Staal (1979: 9) holds that the *mantra*s are not for naming anything but for ritualistic actions. He has suggested that

> *mantra*s began as sentences attached to ritual actions, and that these *mantra*s, ritual action units were the raw data from which language arose.

It is, therefore, that the Vedic *mantra*s are said to have a capacity for putting one in direct touch with the divine power; this is the reason that correct accent (*svara*) plays an important part in pronouncing Vedic verses so that positive vibrations are produced and negative ones are thwarted.[5]

Two Aspects of Speech

What follows from the above is that there are two aspects of the Vedic diction: benign as well as fierce. The former is manifested in most of the epithets ascribed to eulogize Goddess Sarasvatī, where adjectives like *vājinīvatī, dhiyāvasu* and *pāvakā,* are used (*ṚV* I.3.10-12).

Significantly, Sarasvatī is also described as one of the synonyms of speech in Vedic lexicon and continues to be held as the Goddess of language and learning. So, there is no denying the fact that *vāk* as Sarasvatī is the purifying power in Vedic view. But the fierce aspect of speech is also delineated in Ṛgvedic

---

5 In this connection, there is a legend which describes that the faulty recitation of Vedic verses results just in contrast to the desired ones:

duṣṭo padaḥ svarato varṇato vā mithyā prayukto na tamartham āha ।
sa vāgvajro yajamānaṁ hinasti yathendraśatruḥ svarato 'parādhāt ॥
– Quoted in *Mahābhāṣya* of Patañjali 1.1.1

verses through epithets like *ghorā* and *vṛtraghnī*.[6] The *Aitareya Brāhmaṇa* also describes *vāk* as thunderbolt:

a. *vajra eva vāk* । – 2.21
b. *vāgghi śastram* । – 3.44

Speech and Mind; Speech and Breath

Vedic view holds that Vāk is herself the creator and is no less than his majesty, Prajāpati: *vāgvai prajāpatiḥ* । (*ŚatBrā* 5.1.5.6; 13.4.1.15).

It is, therefore, that when Prajāpati desired to procreate, he thought of none else but Vāk as his consort and planted his seed in her as the mother of universe:

> *prajāpatirvā idameka āsīttasya vāgeva svamāsīodvāg dvitīyā sa aikṣatemāmeva vācaṁ visṛjā iyaṁ vā idam sarvaṁ vibhavantyeṣyatīti sa vācaṁ vyasṛjata* । – *TāṇḍyaBrā* 20.14.2

> Prajāpati was alone, Vāk was his own form and Vāk was his other part; he decided to procreate and looked at Vāk, thought of Vāk as everything, and created Vāk.

Interestingly, Prajāpati is also identified with the principle of mind in Vedic cosmogony because no creation can take place without the involvement of mind and no speech can be fruitful if it is bereft of mental activity. So, an imagery of *vāk* and *manas* (matter and mind) as a pair is also available in Vedic literature:

prajāpatirvai manaḥ । - *ŚatBrā* 4.1.1.22
vāk ca vai manaśca devānāṁ mithunam । – *AitBrā* 5.23

Besides, a couple of *vāk* and *prāṇa* is also suggested therein because the association of spoken word with vital breath is no secret:

---

[6] *uta syā naḥ sarasvatī ghorā hiraṇyavartaniḥ* ।
vṛtraghnī vaṣṭi suṣṭutim ॥
yasyā ananto ahrutas tveṣaścariṣṇurarṇavaḥ ।
amaścarati roruvat ॥ – *ṚV* VI.61.7-8

vāk ca vai prāṇaśca mithunam । – *ŚatBrā* 1.4.1.2

The above statements signify that mind (*manas*) and life (*prāṇa*) are the two unmanifested principles while *vāk* (matter) is the manifest – these are three constituents of Prajāpati and also of material *prakṛti* symbolized as *vāk*:

tredhā vihitā hi vāk । – *ŚatBrā* 6.5.3.4; 10.4.5.2

As already mentioned above, this personification of *vāk* as a feminine force is quite common in Vedic view. The same is expressed in several statements available in Vedic texts such as follows:

i. *yoṣā hi vāk* । – *ŚatBrā* 1.4.4.4
ii. *vāgiti strī* । – *JaiUpBrā* 4.22.11
iii. *vāg yoniḥ* । – *AitBrā* 2.38

The idea is originally suggested in a *Ṛgveda* hymn where Gaurī is stated to be the symbol of *vāk*:

gaurirmimāya salilāni takṣatyekapadī dvīpadī sā catuṣpadī ।
aṣṭāpadī navapadī babhūvuṣī sahasrākṣarā parame vyoman ॥
– *ṚV* I.164.41

The divine speech has been uttered enabling the thoughts to flow, and is one-footed, two-footed, four-footed, eight-footed, nine-footed or infinite in the innermost region of heart.

Various adjectives of speech used in the above verse can be explained in many ways but the most convincing interpretation is given by V.S. Agrawala (1963: 154-55) who says:

Pada is equivalent to "motion", and *ekapadī* (one-footed) is that which is capable of undivided motion, i.e. absence of all motion in different directions. *Ekapadī* therefore refers to the principle of rest or stasis (*sthiti*), the locking of directional motions in the centre (*hṛdaya*). ... *Dvipadī* refers to that phase of *vāk* in which the original transcendental Reality becomes relative for the sake of manifestation. *Catuṣpadī* as the symbol of *vāk* is mentioned in *Ṛgveda* I.164.45. Here, the three feet

> are said to be hidden in the cave, i.e. unmanifest and only the fourth feet becomes manifest as human speech. It exactly corresponds to the conception of four-footed *Puruṣa*, of whom *tripāda* is "above" and one *pāda* is this manifest cosmos. … *Aṣṭapadī* (eight-footed) cow involves the symbolism of the number 8, e.g. in *Ṛgveda* I.164.27. … Here *vāk* is the cow and Agni (*prāṇa*) is her calf. … When we refer to the *vāk* as *aṣṭapadī*, there is verily a reference to it as identical with Agni, with Vasus, with *Ṛgveda*, etc. an established symbolism at several levels of reference, of which the basic conception is that of *aṣṭākṣarā* Gāyatrī. *Navapadī:* The conception of nine-footed cow exhausts all the possibilities of numerical manifestation since nine is the highest numerical in the series 1, 2, 3. … The maximum number of consonants that can be tagged to the utterance of one vowel is nine. That indicates the maximum limit of manifestation *navo navo bhavati jāyamāna* (*ṚV* X.85.19).

The metaphor of a cow for *vāk* is also used in *Ṛgveda* I.164.9:

> *yuktā mātāsīddhuri dakṣiṇāyā atiṣṭhadgarbho vṛjanīṣvantaḥ* ।
> *amīmedvatso anu gāmapaśyadviśvarūpyaṁ triṣu yojaneṣu* ॥
>
> The mother (i.e. space) comes in contact with the southern yoke (southern hemisphere). Her embryo (water vapour) stood in the clouds. The calf (i.e. year) lowed (or desired to follow) the rays and saw the sun in all the three zones of the heavens.

Significantly, it is evident from the above depiction that Gaurī as well as Gau are both enumerated as appellations of speech in Vedic lexicon; *vāk* is described in the imagery of these cosmic creatures, viz. she-buffalo and the cow, because both of them are derived as symbols of movement and signify the strength of the spoken word and of its vibrating effect.

Conclusion

To sum up, it may be stated that the idea of *vāk* as the creative female force and mother of the universe is inherent in Vedic cosmology. The *mantra* below clearly reflects the same:

catvāri vākparimitā padāni tāni vidurbrāhmaṇā ye manīṣiṇaḥ ।
guhā trīṇi nithitā neṅgayanti turīyaṁ vāco manuṣyā vadanti ॥
– *ṚV* I.164.45

> Four are the definite grades of speech; those learned ones, who are wise, know them; three deposited in secret, indicate no meaning; humans speak the fourth grade of speech.

Four grades of speech are: *oṁ, bhuḥ, bhuvaḥ* and *svaḥ* which are also known as *parā, paśyantī, madhyamā* and *vaikharī. Parā* is the innermost at the origin; *paśyantī* pertains to heart, *madhyamā* to intellect and *vaikharī* is phonetically expressed through the organs of speech.

The *Śatapatha Brāhmaṇa* echoes the same when it states that it is speech which pervades all the divine spheres:

vāgeva devāḥ । – *ŚatBrā* 14.4.3.13

Finally, the Vedic idea of speech as power gets expressed in the important doctrine of *veda-apauruṣeyatva* (see Kumar 2006b: 235-51), i.e. word is not only authorless and impersonal, but also eternal and imperishable.

The *ṛṣi*s are not accepted to be the authors of Vedas but only the seers or the mere channels through which the transcendent word passes to make itself available to humans at the start of each creation cycle (Coward 1992: 106). In the words of Sri Aurobindo, the language of the Veda is:

> a rhythm not composed by the intellect but heard, a Divine word that came vibrating out of the Infinite to the inner audience of the man who had previously made himself fit for the impersonal knowledge. – 1998: 10

It is in the above background that the Vedic idea of Vācaspati (Lord of the word) can also be comprehended since Prajāpati or the creator manifests his creative powers by means of *vāk* (word):

prajāpatirvai vācaspatiḥ । – *ŚatBrā* 5.1.1.16

In fine, *vāk* is the most exalted universal principle in Vedic view:

ādityādhi madādityā adhi sarve tapanti । *devīṁ vācamajanayanta yadvāgvadantī* । *anantāmantādadhi nirmitāṁ mahīm* । *yasyā devā adadhurbhojanāni* । *ekākṣarāṁ dvipadāṁ ṣaṭpadāṁ ca* । *vāca devā upajīvanti viśve* । *vāca devā upajīvanti viśve* । *vāca gandharvāḥ paśavo manuṣyāḥ* । *vācīmā viśvā bhuvanānyarpitā* ।। *sā no hava juṣatāmindrapatnī* । *vāgakṣara prathamajā ṛtasya* । *vedānaṁ mātā 'mṛtasya nābhiḥ* ।

– *TaiBrā* 2.8.8.4-5

There is no end to Vāk, it is beyond the entire creation, immeasurable. All the gods, the *gandharvas*, human beings and animals live within it and are fed within it. Within the Vāk do all the regions reside. Vāk is the first born syllable of the order, the mother of the Veda, the navel of immortality.

Let us, therefore, conclude by praying to Vāk as follows:

iyaṁ yā parameṣṭhinī vāgdevī brahmasaṁśitā ।
yayaiva sasṛje ghoraṁ tayaiva śāntirastu naḥ ॥ – *AV* 19.9.3

May this divine speech, which is sanctified by Supreme *Brahman*, and with which the fierce forms are also created; May this supreme Goddess, bestow peace upon us!

11

Fundamentals of Vedic Education

THE word *veda* is derived from the root √*vid* (to know) and is aptly looked upon as the stock of knowledge.[1] Vedic knowledge is basically progressive and ascent-oriented in the sense that life according to Vedic view is nothing but moving ahead and marching forward in all its aspects.[2] The Veda impels man to become human and procreate the divine[3] by rising above petty cravings and following the pure, divine path of progress.

The Veda is not only the fountainhead of Indian philosophy and culture, language and literature, but also of Indian education. The Veda proclaims that even though the human being is not born perfect, he can and should strive for the higher goals in life through self-motivated aspirations as well as noble inspirations from the learned and the realized ones. This is the core of Vedic education which aims at arousing an internal quest for awakening the human consciousness.

II

According to Vedic philosophy, the basic nature of a human being is integral, therefore, true education should aim at revealing his

1 *sarvajñānamayo hi saḥ* । – *MS* 2.7

2 *ārohaṇamākramaṇaṁ jīvato jīvato 'yanam* । – *AV* 5.30.7

3 … *manurbhava janayā daivyaṁ janam* ॥ – *ṚV* X.53.6

overall potential. In other words, the principal objective of Vedic education has been to inspire man and inculcate in him both the curiosity and the capacity to comprehend each and everything around him in its true sense. From Vedic point of view, education is not merely a collection of information, but realization of the divinity already inherent in man. The Vedic philosophy of education cultivates a holistic view beyond the multiplicities of human experience; it strives not only for intellectual quest but also for spiritual accomplishment which is the main feature of Indian philosophy. The Veda declares that *vidyā* (true knowledge) is the knowledge of the self and it is the means for attaining immortality. The main subject of teaching, according to Vedic view is this philosophy of self (*ātma-vidyā* or *brahma-vidyā*) which is the science of sciences, he who does not know it, cannot achieve anything even after knowing everything else; but he who has known it, has known all that is worth knowing.

It needs to be emphasized that the Vedic philosophy of education is not only a view of life, but also a way of life; although it lays greater stress on the knowledge of the self, it does not negate the world. The Veda draws a clear distinction between *vidyā* and *avidyā*,[4] the knowledge of the essence and the knowledge of phenomena; between the knowledge of the self and the knowledge of the things: *parā-vidyā* and *aparā-vidyā* (*MuUp* 1.4) to use the Upaniṣadic terminology. In fact, the Vedic philosophy of education admits both, but there is never any doubt as to which one is higher and more desirable. It is not merely a "question of survival" that the Vedic education focuses upon, but also the "question of significance", which is its prime concern. Knowledge of things and processes as also of many more mundane subjects is very much there (as is evident from the exhaustive list of various professions enumerated in the 30th

4 *vidyāñcāvidyāñca yastadvedobhayaṁ saha* |
avidyayā mṛtyuṁ tīrtvā vidyāyamṛtamaśnute || – *YV* 40.14

chapter of the *Śukla Yajurveda* (30.5-7)), but it is only secondary; the nature of reality or truth is the most important subject worthy of teaching and learning.

III

As mentioned above, human life, according to Vedic philosophy, is a path to perfection initiated by one's own "aspiration" but there is no denying the fact that in this constant journey towards progress, one does need "inspiration" and derives guidance from his ancestors and seniors. It is not without reason then that the Vedic seers themselves refer to their forefathers as great pathfinders[5] from whom they have heard the Vedic word of wisdom and carried forward the stream of knowledge for future generations. It is in this background that the Veda is held to be *śruti*, i.e. directly heard by the disciple from the mouth of his preceptor, so it also incorporates the idea of *guru–śiṣya* relationship in the Vedic philosophy of education and signifies an integral approach towards the alround development of an individual seeker under the able and immediate guidance of an enlightened seer. In fact, the "seeker with a quest" and the "seer with a vision" are the two parameters of Vedic education.

From this point of view, the most important idea is that God, the Supreme Divine Being, is the first and foremost teacher of humankind,[6] it is he who manifests this divine knowledge called the Veda in the beginning of creation for the benefit of humanity.[7] The same divine knowledge is at first realized by the seven sages who are stated to be the sons of heaven and fathers of humanity.[8]

---

5 *idaṁ nama ṛṣibhyaḥ pūrvajebhyaḥ pūrvebhyaḥ pathikṛdbhyaḥ* ।
– *ṚV* X.14.15

6 *Ṛgvedādibhāṣyabhūmikā*, Vedotpattiviṣaya, pp. 07-19.

7 *evaṁ vā are 'sya mahato bhūtasya niḥsvaśitametadyadṛgvedo yajurvedaḥ sāmavedo 'tharvāṅgirasaḥ* । – *ŚatBrā* 14.5.4.10

8 *adhā māturuṣasaḥ sapta viprā jāyemahi prathamā vedhaso nṝn* ।
– *ṚV* IV.2.15

The symbolic sense of such cryptic references is that man begets human and divine in his own being through self-consecration and exaltation by the realized souls. In other words, there is an intimate relationship between life and education, because life in Vedic view, as already stated, is a continued course of preparation for higher goals and education is the process which prescribes and paves the path for such goals.

Accordingly, the main aim of Vedic education is to enable an individual and inspire him to transcend the limitations of sense-bound experience and reason-bound intellect and to awaken a higher level of consciousness by which he can comprehend the underlying essence of everything around him. Once this genuine awareness is generated within the seeker, he travels from the known to the unknown in order to gain access to the deeper, wider and higher realms of experience. It is in this basic exploration of truth that the seeker knocks into the domain of an illumined seer who has already realized the truth and is empowered to direct his disciple towards the infinite source of knowledge.

It is also worth mentioning in this regard that the Vedic view of education implies an active and participatory pattern wherein both the teacher and the taught are in direct contact with each other and are equally involved in the search for truth. Hence, it is the science and art of interrelationship between the two who have embarked upon a pursuit for perfection through personal aspiration and mutual inspiration. The whole lot of Vedic education is moulded in this intimate relationship between the teacher and the taught. This is based on a double track of training in the sense that it is a course of self-direction on part of the disciple and a motivating model of instruction on part of the preceptor (Kumar 2005b: 90-92).

IV

It is in the above background that the Vedic preceptors are called *ṛṣis*,[9] the enlightened seers who have realized the truth. The Vedic ideal of teacher is exemplified in the Vedic concept of *ṛṣi*, the most ancient Indian icon of *guru*. The *ṛṣi* (illumined seer) epitomizes an immediate perception of reality, coupled with basic intuition, unruffled concentration and compassionate wisdom:

> It was the *ṛṣi* who came to be acknowledged as the teacher and revered as *guru* or *ācārya*. It is to the *ṛṣi* that the pupils went in search of training and knowledge and the Vedic teacher–pupil relationship came to be determined by the profound and even inscrutable ways by which the teachers and pupils (*guru*s and *śiṣya*s, developed their modes and methods of exploring knowledge, discovering the aim and meaning of life and practising disciplines for arriving at psychological perfection.
>
> – Joshi 1988: 33

The *ṛṣi* (Vedic teacher), endowed with noble qualities as enunciated above, is usually described to live in his hermitage in the forest along with his wife and children, and the disciple is also admitted into his family (*gurukula*). The entry into the resident centre of learning is not through any formal test, but it is held to be an important event in the life of the pupil, and is celebrated in the shape of a significant ritual named *upanayana saṁskāra*. The disciple is brought to the *ācārya* by his parents, hence it is termed as *upanayana*, i.e. bringing closer. This initiation ceremony is, in fact, a beginning of a long-term relationship between the *guru* and the *śiṣya*.

The *gurukula* system of education not only provides a strong foundation for over all individual grooming but also leads to social solidarity. The *gurukula* is a place where students from all walks of life not only stay and study together, as enjoined by the

---

9 *sākṣātkṛtadharmāṇa ṛṣayo babhūvuḥ* । – *Nirukta* 1.20

Veda, but also work collectively for the betterment of society. It has been described in the Vedic verses that the teacher admits the student into his fold just like a mother conceives her child and protects the womb with care. The *ācārya* keeps him within his fold for three nights (*AV* 11.5.3) (because night is a symbol of darkness or ignorance) before he initiates him to Vedic learning. This is equated to a new birth, for the pupil emerges as a *dvija* (twice-born) after the ceremony. The parents had given him a physical birth only, while the *ācārya* gives him a second, spiritual birth. In the words of the noted Vedic interpreter, Sāyaṇa, "the teacher recreates the pupil in a new body of learning".[10]

The *ācārya* is like a pregnant spiritual mother to the pupil. Through the *upanayana* ceremony, he regenerates the life of his pupil, both physically and spiritually, and teaches him the discipline of life to develop in himself the purity of body, heart and mind. The *ācārya*, who has himself led his life fully performing his duties as a householder, is keen on serving the society through educating and training the youth of the country. Therefore, he does not live for himself alone; he becomes a *bhūtakṛt* (man-maker) (*AV* 6.133.5). That is why the parents bring their child to the teacher and request him to make a human being out of him (*YV* 2.33).

In this way, the *ṛṣi* (ideal teacher) as conceived in the Vedic system of education interweaves his own life with the life of his disciples and sets upon shaping their personality through triple methods of instruction, example and influence. So, professional competence and power of communication are not the only instruments of a good teacher; he has to be discerning as well as simple, stern as well as accessible, learned as well as kind. It is only to such a worthy and wise teacher that the student approaches and addresses for guidance to the righteous path and teaching of the immortal truth (*ṚV* III.43.5). Such a teacher is verily fit to be an *ācārya*, another Vedic word for the *guru*,

---

[10] Sāyaṇa on *Śatapatha Brāhmaṇa* 11.5.4.

who teaches more through his conduct than words (*Nirukta* 1.2), he not only teaches various topics of the textbook but also sharpens the grasping power of the student and imparts guided training to him for acquiring fluency of words as well as potency of intentions.

It is not without reason, then, that the teacher is eulogized through various epithets (Kumar 2005b: 93-94) in Vedic verses such as:

i. *Śākta* (*R̥V* VII.103.5), i.e. a capable person who is fit to instruct through words as well as deeds.

ii. *Purohita* (*YV* 11.81), since he is the intellectual leader of the society at large.

iii. *Mr̥tyu* (*AV* 11.5.14), since he dispels and destroys the darkness of ignorance from the hearts of his disciples.

iv. *Varuṇa* (*AV* 11.5.14), since he is worth choosing and fit for controlling the forces of evil.

v. *Soma* (*AV* 11.5.14), since he is soft-spoken and pleasant so that the students come to him without fear.

vi. *Oṣadhi* (*AV* 11.5.14), just as the medicines cure ailments, similarly, the teacher removes the physical as well as mental diseases of the pupils.

vii. *Payaḥ* (*AV* 11.5.14), the teacher, like milk, is a source of nourishment, intellectual as well as spiritual for his students.

viii. *Br̥haspati* (*YV* 36.2), since he has to be the master of his subject and with his knowledge, can remove the shortcomings of his disciples.

ix. *Vācaspati* (*AV* 1.1.2), since the teacher has to be adept at communicating through words.

x. *Vāstoṣpati* (*AV* 1.1.2), since he is the owner of wealth, mental and spiritual.

xi. *Vipra* (*R̥V* IV.2.15), since he is intelligent and sharp.

xii. *Vedhasa* (*R̥V* IV.2.15), since he is the architect of his disciples' personalities.

xiii. *Muni* (*R̥V* X.136.4), since he has the capacity to contemplate and ponder over various subjects.

xiv. *Kavi* (*R̥V* III.8.4), since he is imaginative and has a creative bent of mind.

xv. *Kuvid* (*R̥V* 3.43.5), since he knows the drawbacks and weakness of his disciples.

V

This brings us to the eligibility of the pupil in Vedic view. Numerous epithets used as adjectives of the pupil denote various aspects of studentship but the most important of them is his intent for learning, so much so that he has to take a vow to that effect and has to prepare himself as a *vratacārī* (*YV* 1.5) and follow strict discipline laid out by the teacher. The intense desire of the student is also expressed by the term *śikṣamāṇa* (*R̥V* VIII.42.3) used in Vedic verses for him, while his newly achieved existence as an initiated learner is described by the word *dvija*. The disciple has to be *medhāvī* (intelligent), *tapasvī* (hardworking), *śuci* (pure in body and mind) and *apramatta* (relentless) (*Nirukta* 2.1) in observing his resolve to know the truth.

On the other hand, there are certain negative aspects of personality which should be avoided by the student, if he intends to learn the Supreme Truth. He should not be an *asūyaka* (calumnious), *anidaṁvid* (one who is not initiated) and *anupasanna* (who has not approached the *ācārya* himself) (*Nirukta* 2.1).

In accordance with its concern for final ends, the Vedic philosophy of education accepts *brahmacarya*, a system of self-discipline as a prerequisite for anyone aspiring to attain higher knowledge (*Brahman*). The conception of *brahmacarya* lays greater emphasis on discipline (*caryā*) rather than mere learning or knowledge (*Brahman*) (Vedamitra 1964: 14). Actually, *Brahman* signifies the Supreme Reality, the highest truth. In order to attain this highest knowledge, only the *brahmacārī* (a man of spiritual training) is eligible. Stern simplicity, selflessness and sublimation of the sensual instinct assisted by the quiet natural surroundings of forest life are an essential part of this education that aimed at an integral development of physical and moral stamina as well as spiritual power (Bose 1951: 55).

In Vedic view, *brahmacarya* does not merely mean physical continence, but encompasses in its fold much more than that because the word *Brahman* connotes various senses such as:

a. the pious effusion or utterance,
b. the sacred word, the Veda,
c. the Brāhmaṇa portion of the Veda,
d. the sacred syllable *oṁ*,
e. the one universal soul,
f. the final emancipation, and
g. the one who prays, a devout religious man, etc. (Monier Williams 1966: 738).

In fact, the idea of *brahmacarya* as enunciated in the Vedas is so wide that it covers the whole gamut of existence in it, it is the profound principle which creates and sustains the universe. The Supreme Being Himself is described as the first *brahmacārī*. The fire, the sun, the moon, the water, the clouds, the rain, the earth, the sky, the heaven and the mid-region are all manifesting the principle of *brahmacarya*. All creatures of the world, the wild and tame animals, winged birds and the wingless ones are observing *brahmacarya*; the king protects his kingdom through it and the gods have conquered death by following it (*AV* 11.5.17, 19). Even females are enjoined to follow *brahmacarya* (*AV* 11.5.18). The *R̥gveda*, *Yajurveda* and *Atharvaveda* – all of them refer to young maidens completing their education as *brahmacāriṇīs* and then marrying equally learned and young bridegrooms (*ṚV* VII.1.6, III.55.16; *YV* 8.1; *AV* 11.5.18).

The subtle technique of purifying the individual through *saṁskāra* is also a very important feature of Vedic education well reflected in the practices and austerities prescribed for the *brahmacārī*. The *brahmacārī* is required to put the sticks (*samidhā*) in fire as if to inspire him to kindle the fire of intellect within him. This is meant to be an initiation into an eventful and enrapping life of self-reliance, self-confidence and controlled thought as well as action. The disciple is invigorated with a spirit of confidence that he will succeed with self-determination and tireless perseverance (Apte n.d.: 252). The rituals create in him a faith that the supernatural powers are at his back to bless his endeavour with success; they instill in him an ambition to become as powerful as Indra, as lustrous as the sun, whom he offers his prayers morning and evening, and as shining as the fire, whom he worships; there is nothing impossible to achieve for such a disciple, who imbibes a conviction and the confidence that he is powerful enough to face even death and death dare not touch him.

VI

According to the Vedic philosophy of education, the student, disciplined through *brahmacarya*, should not live a cloistered life, cut-off from society. On the other hand, after being consecrated, he takes hold of the work and constantly brings them near him (*AV* 11.5.6). It is ordained as the usual practice for him to go about begging for the upkeep of the *āśrama* of his *ācārya* (*ŚatBrā* 11.3.3.5), this rule is, in fact, prescribed for the student to develop in him a sense of humility. Hence, whatever his social status, the student is required to beg alms in the neighbourhood, as if he is poor and so become devoid of shame (Das 1986: 81). This practice also helps him in establishing a contact between worldly life and the hermitage.

> It is like a ritual for the cultivation of impersonal relations in life. This contact of the recluse with the world is a valuable collective to the exaggerated subjectivity of isolated meditative life in the hermitage. Isolation and intercourse thus lead to a higher synthesis of the inner and the outer, *puruṣa* and *prakṛti*, self and the world. – Mookerji 1974: xxx

Briefly put, the *brahmacārī*, after his initiation into a new life, whereby he is recreated by his *guru*, has to undergo a dual course of discipline, physical as well as spiritual. This is in other words, the Vedic way of education in which the studentship is evolved into a science or art of life. It is evidently and essentially a method of self-direction for the student, guided by an enlightened teacher, of course.

Further, it needs to be mentioned that the Vedic system of education is free and flexible in the sense that the teacher is not bound with the rigidities prevalent in the examination-oriented modern system of education. Therefore, he is free to use separate methods of teaching for different students. Since all the students are not of the same calibre, the teacher employs different degrees of discipline for each one of them and does not demand from the student more than the highest effort of which he is capable.

> *akṣaṇvantaḥ karṇavantaḥ sakhāyo manojaveṣvasamā babhūvuḥ* ।
> *ādadhnāsa upakakṣāsa u tve hṛdā iva snātvā u tve dadṛśre* ॥
> – *ṚV* X.71.7

> There are pupils who are well endowed with sight and hearing but are unequal in the quickness of their mind. Some look like pools that reach to the mouth or armpit and some are like lakes in which a man can bathe.

It is the poetic description of different levels of receptivity of the student.

What follows from the above is that the Vedic view of education has a proper perspective, i.e. the overall development of an individual to grow into the highest possibilities which are already latent in him: physical, mental, intellectual, ethical and spiritual. It is actually a demand for self-determination by the individual who is consistently and systematically resolved in the integral and character-building principles of Vedic education. The fundamental aim of Vedic education is therefore a pursuit for perfection and involves a search for truth and a will to realize the higher and holistic development of personality. The Vedic seers are sure that no education is successful if it does not bring a radical change in human consciousness and character; true education transforms the knower in the process of knowing, since it is a harmonious method of understanding rather than piecemeal collection of some subjects and topics prescribed in the syllabus. Hence, while laying great emphasis on the role of the teacher as a guide and an example himself for inspiring and enkindling the quest within the students, Vedic philosophy of education also envisages that the basic, inherent tendency of the learner is the most important factor in the process of learning.

VII

To sum up, it may be said that the Vedic ideal of education is to make one transcend from high to higher and then lead him to the highest, it teaches the path of perfection and leads one towards immortality. In other words, the purpose of Vedic education is not only humanization, but divinization of humanity against the tendency of sheer mechanization and massive industrialization in today's world. Until that goal is achieved, real education is not complete, it must continue uninterruptedly. The essence of education is ever the same. The forms may change and the details may differ but the central insights always remain the universal. Therefore, we must look back to our past heritage not for clinging to it but for reanalysing it and drawing such eternal inputs that can sustain our present and strengthen our future.

The crisis of contemporary education is that today "our knowledge is provisional, empirical, specialized, knowing more and more about less and less, a scheme of limited orderliness but quite unrelated to any first principles or purposes". Rightly did T.S.Eliot lament that "Where is the wisdom in all this profusion of knowledge; where is knowledge, in the crowd of information". True education does not cease with the getting of a degree from some recognized university, rather, it starts from the point where one has been stimulated towards life and the totality of his being. It is here that the Vedic philosophy of education comes to our rescue, since it is basically a training in totality, an attempt to lead man towards his own evolution, a quest of the spirit behind this universe. That is what makes it perennial, a philosophy of life for ever and so it is relevant up to the period of humanity and the point of universality. The man-making nature and the character-building aspect of this education are the eternal needs of mankind (Kumar 1999c: 20-21).

Today, like all other systems of human society, education has also become utilitarian in character, where there is no intrinsic relationship between the teacher and the taught or the learner and his life. So, there is a renewed necessity of looking at these issues because the predicament in which we are living today is getting deeper day by day. We need to draw our attention to these fundamental principles of Vedic vision with a view to invigorate our ways of thinking so that the bliss of benign education is universally enjoyed by one and all and the whole humanity is motivated for enkindling the divine light of true knowledge:

> *ā no bhadrāḥ kratavo yantu viśvato 'dabdhāso aparītāsa udbhidaḥ* ।
> *devā no yathā sadam id vṛdhe asannaprāyuvo rakṣitāro dive dive* ॥ – *ṚV* I.89.1

May noble wisdom come to us from all sides, undeceived, unhindered, overflowing. So that the *deva*s may always help us onward, unceasing in their care, our guardians day by day.

12

Vedic View of Cosmic Harmony

Parity between Microcosm (Piṇḍa) and Macrocosm (Brahmāṇḍa)

In this chapter I intend to explore and expound the Vedic idea of inherent synergy between the gross (embodied) and the subtle (disembodied) levels of existence. The scope of this exposition is mainly restricted to the Vedic sources in original, i.e. the four Vedic Saṁhitās, Brāhmaṇas, Āraṇyakas and the Upaniṣads.

Humanity today is passing through a critical phase when all aspects of the universe seem to be in a conflicting mode and the quest for harmony is far greater than ever. It is in this background that the profound Vedic vision can offer fresh insights for future possibilities.

II

Veda is the most ancient available literary document (Radhakrishnan 2007: 63) of the world and it proclaims that life is a divine opportunity. It exhorts all human beings as the sons of immortality[1] and enunciates that there is complete coordination among all aspects of existence in the universe. The Vedic principle of *ṛta* (see Kane 1973: 2) represents the

---

1 *ṚV* X.13.1

sublime inviolable moral regularity of cosmos as also the inner harmony and order of a man's conduct (vide Kumar 2005a: 28). Accordingly, it signifies that there is a parallelism between the embodied human being and the disembodied cosmic existence. The same is suggested by an oft-quoted (but anonymous) dictum of Vedic interpretation, that the human body is a micro model of the macrocosm: *yathā piṇḍe tathā brahmāṇḍe*:

> In Sanskrit religio-philosophical literature, *piṇḍa* and *brahmāṇḍa* are used as a pair to speak of everything from an individual to all the creation around him. – Aklujkar 2001: 42

It means that just as the human body is an abode of the individual self, the entire cosmos is the abode of the Supreme Self.

> The earth is whose base (foot or *pramā*), the midspace whose belly, and who has made the sky his head, to him, the Eldest Lord Supreme, let our homage be.[2]

From this point of view, anyone, who aims to resolve all sorts of conflicts[3] and attain harmony, has to begin with the immediate rather than the mediate, proximate rather than the remote and visible rather than the invisible. It goes without saying that the most immediate reality for everyone is one's own personal experience and the real conflict is also not with others, but with oneself. It is so because the seeds of conflict or amity are actually rooted in the mind of an individual and if the mind is attuned in such a manner that there is no intrapersonal disturbance, then interpersonal disputes will automatically

---

2 *yasya bhūmiḥ pramānatarikṣamutodaram* ।
divaṁ yaścakre mūrdhānaṁ tasmai jyeṣṭhāya brahmaṇe namaḥ ॥
– *AV* 10.7.32

3 "All our lives are in contradiction, and therefore in conflict, either the conflict born of trying to conform, conflict through fulfilment, or the conflict engendered by social influence. Conflict does produce a certain result by the use of the will, but conflict never is creative." – Krishnamurti 2013: 14

be dissolved. Consequently, a harmonious complementarity between bipolar opposites such as untruth and truth, darkness and light, mortality and immortality will also be accomplished. In other words, if we aspire to achieve global peace, then first we have to be at peace within ourselves.

III

It is in this background that the Vedic view propounds a complete, cohesive philosophy of life in which body, mind and the sense organs of a person are all working in complete cooperation for a healthy and happy living. Vedic Saṁhitās abound in such prayers where not only the physical health is aspired for, but the mental strength and spiritual power are also sought:

yanme chidraṁ cakṣuṣo hṛdayasya manaso
vātitṛṇṇaṁ bṛhaspatirme taddadhātu ।
śaṁ no bhavatu bhuvanasya yaspatiḥ ॥ – *YV* 36.2

Whatever distressing lacuna I have in my vision, in my heart or in my thought, may the Lord Supreme remove that. May gracious to us be He, who is the Lord of the whole universe.

It must be reiterated that to accomplish this goal of perfect harmony, one has to begin with one's own self, i.e. to control and contain negative emotions such as anger, greed, hate and jealousy, as is manifested in the following Vedic prayers:

… *mo ahaṁ dviṣate radham* ॥ – *Ṛ̥V* I.50.13

May I never be swayed by (my weak impulses like) aversion.

* * *

mā no dvikṣata kaścana । – *AV* 12.1.24

Let no one so ever hate us.

On the other hand, positive feelings such as universal empathy, global concord and cosmic goodwill need to be strengthened as is expressed in the following Vedic verses:

saṁjñānaṁ naḥ svebhiḥ saṁjñānam araṇebhiḥ ।
saṁjñānam aśvinā yuvam ihāsmāsu ni yachatam ॥ – *AV* 7.52.1

May there be proper understanding with our own people, proper understanding with strangers; Oh twins divine (Aśvinau)! may both of you develop proper understanding among us here.

It is also noteworthy here that the Vedic view is not prescriptive, it does not enjoin one to act in a certain way, rather, it directs one for self-motivation and exhorts to first elevate oneself through auto-suggestions like the following and then seek divine help for the same:

paro 'pehi manaspāpa kimaśastāni śaṁsasi । – *AV* 6.45.1

Oh evil thought! go far away, why do you suggest abominable things. Get away.

* * *

yo naḥ svo 'raṇo yaśca niṣṭhyo jighāṅsati ।
devāstaṁ sarve dhūrvantu ॥ – *SV* 1872

Whoever, our hostile kin or an outsider, wants to destroy us; May all the *deva*s discomfit him!

IV

There is no denying the fact that universal conflict between evil and good, ignoble and noble is eternal. There are several depictions of this constant struggle in the Vedic literature which narrates it in the form of a battle between divine and demonic forces (*devāsura-saṅgrāma*).[4] But actually this struggle is only metaphorical in the sense that there is an inner essence to the literal depiction; it emphasizes upon the supremacy of right over wrong, light over darkness and immortal spirit over mortal physicality.[5]

---

[4] vide *ŚatBrā* 11.1.6.10

[5] *asato mā sad gamaya*
tamaso mā jyotir gamaya
mṛtyor mā amṛtaṁ gamaya । – *BṛUp* 1.3.28

More importantly, this tussel is not only in the outer physical world, but also in the inner mental space of every human being, so the Vedas propose an optimistic outlook according to which truth always prevails over falsity and light over darkness; that is why an alert human being crosses over from untruth towards truth[6] and there is always a transition from darkness to light:

jyotiṣā bādhate tamaḥ । – *R̥V* X.127.2

Darkness is replaced with the lustre of light.

It is this positive message of Vedic sources which can guide humanity in its search for a holistic development and also provide an everlasting link between both the realms: individual as well as universal. Therefore, the well-known Vedic prayer for cosmic peace actually culminates in an explorative journey for self-enrichment:

dyauḥ śāntirantarikṣaṁ śāntiḥ pr̥thivī śāntirāpaḥ śāntiroṣadhyaḥ śāntiḥ vanaspatayaḥ śāntirviśve devāḥ śāntirbrahma śāntiḥ sarvaṁ śāntiḥ śāntireva śāntiḥ sā mā śāntiredhi । – *YV* 36.17

May the sky be peaceful; may the mid-space be peaceful; may the earth be peaceful; may the waters be peaceful; may the annual plants be peaceful; may the forests be peaceful; may all the bounties of Nature be peaceful; may the knowledge be peaceful; may all the things be peaceful; may there be peace and peace only; may such a peace come to me!

The ultimate phrase of this prayer "may that peace come to me which is pervading the whole cosmos" is actually the clue for resolution of all inner conflicts. It means that there is peace throughout the external world, provided there is peace within one's own heart since no idea of harmony can be actualized if one is mentally disturbed oneself.

---

6 *idamahamanr̥tatsātyamupaimi* । – *YV* 1.5

According to Vedic view, a human being is the most fortunate one, who, in spite of possessing several animal instincts, can overcome all of these and transform oneself totally, so much so that his ascent and upliftment can take him to the level of divinity.[7] In a Ṛgvedic verse, six such embodied animal instincts are desired to be thwarted:

ulūkayātuṁ śuśulūkayātuṁ jahi śvayātumuta kokayātum ।
suparṇayātumuta gṛdhrayātuṁ dṛṣadeva pra mṛṇa rakṣa indra ॥ – *ṚV* VII.104.22

Oh Lord of resplendence! destroy the evil feelings, whether these come in the fiendish garb of an owl, or of an owlet, or of a dog, or of a wolf, or of a falcon or of a vulture.

The following six negative attitudes respectively symbolize six creatures other than human beings such as:

- darkness | owl
- anger | owlet
- jealousy | dog
- lust | wolf
- pride | falcon
- greed | vulture

Significantly, it is implied herein that such degrading inner instincts are more harmful than the external enemies, because these endanger the saner aspect of humanity. At the same time, it is only given to the human beings that they can first distinguish between good and evil, and then overcome the later by strengthening the former.

Accordingly, it is envisaged in Vedic sources that the finest formula for resolving a conflict between vice and virtue begins from within each one of us; those who know their immortal inner being, they are truly the knowledgeable ones, because only they are capable of realizing the essence of Supreme universal power:

---

7 *pṛthivyā ahamudantarikṣamāruham antarikṣāddivamāruham* ।
divo nākasya pṛṣṭhāt svarjyotiragāmaham ॥ – *YV* 17.67

ye puruṣe brahma viduste viduḥ parameṣṭhinam ।
yo veda parameṣṭhinaṁ yaś ca veda prajāpatim ।
jyeṣṭhaṁ ye brāhmaṇaṁ vidus te skambhamanusaṁviduḥ ।
– *AV* 10.7.17

They who recognize the Lord Supreme in *puruṣa* (the embodied human), they know the Parameṣṭhi (the Lord of the highest abode). He, who knows the Parameṣṭhi and he who knows the creator (Prajāpati); Those who know the eldest Lord Supreme (*Jyeṣṭha Brahman*), they come to know the Skambha (the support of the universe).

V

As already mentioned, human body is held to be the microcosm and is stated to be the sacred substratum of immortal spirit in Vedic view. It is said to be the most coveted creation of the divine:

sarvaṁ saṁsicya martyaṁ devāḥ puruṣam āviśan । – *AV* 11.8.13

Having fused the mortal man complete, the divine forces entered the human form.

* * *

sarvā hyasmin devatā gāvo goṣṭha ivāsate । – *AV* 11.8.32

For all deities are dwelling within (the human body), as cows stay in a cow-stall.

The human body is ordained as the first and foremost means for fulfilling one's obligations[8] to oneself, to the family and society at large; it is held to be the most superior model of complementarity and coordination among its different parts. It is therefore held to be a sacred dwelling for different divine faculties.

In another Vedic verse, it is stated that thirty-three gods have entered the human body, just as these divine forces have formed the cosmic abode of the Supreme Self.[9] Therefore,

---

8 *iyaṁ te yajñiyā tanūḥ* । – *YV* 4.13

9 *yasya trayastriṁśad devā aṅge gātrā vibhejire* ।
tān vai trayastriṁśad devān eke brahamvido viduḥ । – *AV* 10.7.27

he who knows this body (*piṇḍa*), verily knows the cosmos (*brahmāṇḍa*).

It is, therefore, that the human body represents the whole cosmos; it needs to be respected and cared for, but only as a means to the ultimate goal of self-realization and not only as an end in itself. The value of mortal human body lies in the fact that it is an abode of the immortal self.

The Veda proclaims that human life is a rare gift wherein all the three regions of the cosmos are represented; the highest or uppermost part of human body is, in fact, the parallel of the celestial sphere, the middle portion symbolizes midspace while the lower part indicates the terrestrial earth. Anyone, who realizes the spiritual secret of this splendour bestowed upon him in the form of human body, will not only be enabled to live a life of harmony amongst all parts of it but will also experience amity amidst the variety of existence within oneself; this sentiment is echoed in the following proclamation of *Yajurveda* 7.5:

> *antaste dyāvāpr̥thivī dadhāmyantardadhāmyurvantarikṣam* ।
> *sajūrdevebhiravaraiḥ paraiścāntaryāme maghavan mādayasva* ॥
>
> Oh human being! I lay heaven and earth within you, I lay midspace in you. Live the life of amity and harmony amidst the bounties of Nature. Help the needy, show cordiality even to those who envy you.

VI

In accordance with the above, the Vedic view propounds that once the individual is at peace with himself, he can proceed on the path of happiness for others around him. The first significant outcome of this positive attitude is genuine gender-equality; the seemingly eternal conflict between male and female is not real in Vedic view, because both male and female are held to be twin aspects of the same reality. As per Vedic cosmogony, the

Supreme Being divided himself into two equal halves in the beginning of creation.[10]

Needless to say that one of the most disturbing problems of human existence today is the widely prevalent gender conflict. So, the Vedic idea of perfect parity between male and female is an important source in the direction of cosmic harmony (for details, see Kumar 1998a). According to Vedic delineation, there is complete equality between both the sexes; none is better or worse half – there are just two equal halves of the same substance.[11] This is more eloquently expressed in the Vedic marriage ceremony wherein a perfect companionship between the husband and wife is solicited; so much so that they are said to act like a single unit, that is why both of them are designated as *dampatī*[12] (two owners of the house) after marriage. In fact, marriage in Vedic view is said to be an inseparable bond which is undertaken to accomplish all the religious duties together for the welfare of family and society, and ultimately for the fulfilment of a higher goal in life, i.e. *dharma* (obligation). It is not without reason then that the wife is stated to be *dharmapatnī* (lawful partner in sacred rituals, since she occupies a more exalted status in the familial role), while the husband is held to be merely a *gṛhapati* (householder).[13]

VII

This brings us to the point of pleasure and good, desired and the desirable, i.e. *preyas* and *śreyas* to use the Vedic terms. The Vedic view does not deplore enjoying the physical pleasures of life but exhorts humanity to practise restraint in every field of life; this

---

10 *sa vai naiva reme, tasmādekākī na ramate sa dvitīyamaicchat sa haitāvānāsa yathā strīpumāṁsau saṁpariṣvaktau sa imamevātmānaṁ dvedhāpātayat tataḥ patiśca patnī cābhavatāṁ* ... । – *BṛUp* 1.4.3

11 *tasmādidamardhavṛgalamiva svaḥ* । – *BṛUp* 1.4.3

12 *ihemāvindra saṁ nuda cakravākeva daṁpatī* । – *AV* 14.2.64

13 *patnī tvamasi dharmaṇāha 'ṁ gṛhapatistava* । – *AV* 14.1.51

restrained and regulated conduct at micro and macro levels is expressed through the terms *ṛta* and *satya* in Vedic philosophy. Accordingly, *ṛta* represents cosmic order at the global level while *satya* suggests moral strength at the individual level; both of these principles are stated to be originated from the blazing *tapas*[14] (spiritual fire, purifying and refining human nature (Bose 1951: 7)) of the Supreme. It is reaffirmed in the *Atharvaveda* that *ṛta*, *satya*, *tapas*, and many more such values are lodged in the different limbs of the Supreme Being (Skambha):

kasminnaṅge tapo asyādhi tiṣṭhati
kasminnaṅga ṛtamasyādhy āhitam ।
kva vrataṁ kva śraddhāsya tiṣṭhati
kasminnaṅge satyamasya pratiṣṭhitam । – *AV* 10.7.1

In which part of him the austerities (*tapas*) abide; in which part of him the eternal law (*ṛta*) is laid; where the vow (*vrata*); in which part of him resides the faith (*śraddhā*), in which part of him is the truth (*satya*) well established.

There is no doubt about the fact that the contemporary consumeristic attitude has taken us to an alarming level of ecological imbalance while the Vedic view propounds a balance between indulgence (*bhoga*) and abstinence (*tyāga*) so that there is a harmony between the external Nature as well as internal nature:

Enjoy it, knowing full well that it will have to be renounced. Do not be greedy. To whom do the riches belong?[15]

This fine formula for enjoying the bounties of Nature without harming or exploiting the ecosphere is another aspect of Vedic view of complementary for cosmic harmony which is expressed in such Vedic prayers as the following one addressed to mother earth:

---

14 *ṛtaṁ ca satyaṁ cābhiddhāt tapaso 'dhyajāyata* । – *ṚV* X.190.1

15 *tena tyaktena bhuñjīthāḥ mā gṛdhaḥ kasya sviddhanam* । – *YV* 40.1

pṛthivi mātarmā hiṁsīrmo'haṁ tvām । – *YV* 10.23

Oh Mother Earth! may you not injure me, nor do I hurt you.

Here, earth is depicted as a personified form of all the natural resources which actually symbolize cosmic existence. But the emotional bond depicted between a human being and the earth is worth emulating. Vedic view propounds a complete communion between man and Nature; the external as well as internal space have to work in unison because all forms of existence are intertwined in an integral relation.

It means that the human beings across cultures should not only strive for conservation of natural resources but also have a genuine concern and practise a sense of respect towards them. In fact, the totality of an inclusive view is much more relevant for cosmic harmony than the fragmented approach being adopted today. The traditional Vedic view in this regard is that the management of natural resources has to be based on inter-generational equity which is inherent in the Indian notion of three debts, i.e. *ṛṇatraya* (for details, see Kumar 2005b: 155-57). The same is very beautifully described by a contemporary thinker in following words:

> We have not inherited the land from our ancestors, we have borrowed it from our children. – Kumar 1999b: 63

It is noteworthy that empathy for fellow-beings is the cornerstone of cosmic harmony, so the Vedic view aspires that:

… *pumān pumāṁsaṁ pari pātu viśvataḥ* । – *ṚV* VI.75.14

May one person protect the other.

According to Vedic philosophy, this type of feeling has to be inculcated by one and all, since the whole universe is just a single dwelling for all its inhabitants:

yatra viśvaṁ bhavateyakanīḍam । – *YV* 32.8

All this world is in fact the common nest.

Therefore, Vedic prayers like the followings ones for a disease-free and healthy existence of all the residents of this universe are but natural:

> ... *viśvaṁ puṣṭaṁ grāme 'smin anāturam* । – *R̥V* I.114.1
>
> All beings around us are nourished and become exempt from disease.
>
> * * *
>
> *sarvamijjagadayakṣmaṁ sumanā asat* । – *YV* 16.4
>
> May all the living beings of this world be free from diseases and be hail and hearty.

The Veda, in fact, even goes beyond empathy among human beings and envisages sympathy and friendship for each and every being of the cosmos:

> *mitrasyāhaṁ cakṣuṣā sarvaṇī bhūtāni samīkṣantām* ।
> *mitrasya cakṣuṣā samīkṣāmahe* ॥ – *YV* 36.18
>
> May all the beings look at me with friendly eye. Thus, may we all be looked at with a friendly eye.

It is in this background that welfare of bipeds as well as quadrupeds is desired for at several places in the Vedas:

> *śaṁ naḥ kuru prajābhyaḥ abhayaṁ naḥ paśubhyaḥ* ।
> – *YV* 36.22
>
> May you grant happiness to our progeny and safety to our cattle.

VIII

What follows from the above is that the Vedic view emphasizes upon an underlying unity of the entire cosmos; all the living and non-living beings are, in fact, various reflections of the same Supreme Reality which has manifested itself in many forms:

> ... *ekaṁ vā idaṁ vi babhūva sarvam* ॥ – *R̥V* VIII.58.2
>
> One is that which manifests in all.

Therefore, he who sees divinity in all the manifested forms of cosmos, has to respect each and every entity thereof.

Another aspect of mutual care and concern in Vedic view is expressed through the principle of sacrifice (*yajña*) which is a key concept for cosmic harmony. The principle of *yajña* is also operating at both the levels: individual as well as global. The individual *yajña* is an internal process wherein the human body itself is the altar; speed, sight, vitality and mind are the various priests.[16] At the cosmic level, *yajña* is being performed by several forces of Nature like the sun, fire, air, water, earth and sky. A sense of genuine gratitude towards all these natural forces impels one to offer his best for them, so that they too shower their choicest blessings on humans in return. This reciprocal gesture, known as *yajña* in Vedic tradition, is the secret of ecological balance and spiritual satisfaction. The universe is created, sustained and destroyed through the cosmic principle of *yajña*. That is why the Vedas proclaim *yajña* to be the best of actions[17] which is said to be the fulfiller of all desires. Accordingly, each householder is supposed to observe five types of daily *yajña*s through which the supreme knowledge (*brahma-yajña*), divine forces (*deva-yajña*), ancestors including one's parents (*pitṛ-yajña*), fellow human beings and the guests (*nṛ-yajña* or *atithi-yajña*) as well as all other living beings (*bhūta-yajña*) are propitiated.[18]

IX

Another significant concept of the Vedic philosophy is the triple interpretation of all its verses, viz. spiritual (*ādhyātmika*),

---

16 ... *vāgvai yajñasya hotā* ... ।
... *cakṣurvai yajñasyādhvaryuḥ* ... ।
... *prāṇo vai yajñasyodgātā* ... ।
... *mano vai yajñasya brahmā* ... । – *BṛUp* 3.1.3-6

17 *yajño vai śreṣṭhatamaṁ karma* । – *ŚatBrā* 1.7.3.5

18 *adhyāpanaṁ brahmayajñaḥ pitṛyajñastu tarpaṇaṁ* ।
homo daivo balirbhūto nṛyajño 'tithi pūjanaṁ ॥ – *MS* 3.70

atmospheric (*ādhidaivika*) and material (*ādhibhautika*). It implies that there is an inherent amity amongst the grossly physical, the supraphysical or the middle and the subtle spiritual level. Accordingly, whatever takes place within oneself, is known as *adhyātma*,[19] i.e. the self, mind, sense organs, vital air, etc. which are dwelling within the body are included in this category. But the same divine forces, which have been interpreted as *adhyātma* earlier, can also be explained as *adhidaivata* when they are pervading the external physical world. So the sun, moon, air, planets, sky, etc. – these are all *ādhidaivika* in nature.[20] The third term *adhibhūta* denotes all other living beings, who represent these divine forces at gross material level.[21] For example, fire can be interpreted in these three ways:

i. from *adhyātma* point of view, it is speech within the body.
ii. at the *adhidaivata* level, it is the subtle, deified fire as also the physical and visible fire which burns.
iii. from *adhibhūta* aspect, it represents the embodied speaker (vide S.D. Satavalekar n.d.: 1-5).

This provides for an integral insight into the comprehensive vision of Vedas and also paves a path for a broader understanding of the text within its proper context.

X

To sum up, it may be said that the Vedic philosophy presents a holistic vision of the universe in which the individual as well as universal realms are held to be two ends of the same single thread. In other words, there is an essential unity between the two levels of existence since an embodied individual being is

---

19 *tadetat catuṣpād brahmaś* । *vāk pādaḥ prāṇaḥ pādacakṣuḥ pādaḥ śrotraṁ pāda ityadhyātmam …* । – *ChāUp* 3.18.2

20 … *athādhidaivatam agniḥ pādo vāyuḥ pāda ādityaḥ pādo diśaḥ pāda itya … dhidaivataṁ…* ॥ – *ChāUp* 3.18.2

21 … *yasya sarvāṇi bhūtāni śarīraṁ … ityadhibhūtam* ॥ – *BṛUp* 3.7.15

held to be the micro model of the disembodied macro-cosmic universe. Accordingly, whatever takes place at the personal level does definitely affect the universal existence. Therefore, each one of us is potentially capable as well as morally responsible for our own individual state of being and also of the world around us. Let us then conclude by the following Vedic verse wherein universal well-being is sought:

> *śṛṇotu naḥ pṛthivī dyaurutāpaḥ sūryo nakṣatrairurvantarikṣam śṛṇvantu no vṛṣaṇaḥ parvatāso dhruvakṣemāsa iḍayā madantaḥ ādityairno aditiḥ śṛṇotu yacchantu no marutaḥ śarma bhadram* ॥ – *ṚV* III.54.19

> May the fire divine, the messenger of nature's bounties manifested in various forms, guide us everywhere along sinless paths! May the lord of earth and heaven, the cosmic watery space, the sun and the vast firmament with constellations, listen to our prayers!

13

Persona of Women in the Vedas

THE present chapter proposes to expound and examine the rendering of women in the Vedas. The study is limited in its scope as it pertains to the four Vedic Saṁhitās only, with some occasional references to the subsequent Vedic literature.

I

The Vedas are a rich matrix of knowledge and have a distinguished place in the world literature for various reasons: historical, philosophical, linguistic and otherwise. But they are singularly unparalleled in that they accord the highest esteem to a woman as an individual and an equally respectable status as a member of the family and society. The Vedic depiction of women not only portrays their role in family and society, but also their affinity with the cosmic creative process and their identity as symbols of power and glory.[1] Needless to say that the Vedic view of women is a holistic one in which males and females are described as integrally complementary, none is better or worse half, they are just two equal halves of the same substance, two aspects of the same reality (*BṛUp* 1.4.3).

1 *yasyāṁ bhūtaṁ samabhavat*
yasyāṁ viśvamidaṁ jagat ।
tāmadya gāthāṁ gāsyāmi
yā strīṇāmuttamaṁ yaśaḥ ।। – *Pāraskara Gṛhyasūtra* 1.7.2

The women are depicted in the Vedas from several perspectives and a framework of the persona of women may be defined through different delineations. But the dignified pictures of woman-power that emerge from these enunciations are uniformly impressive and eternally enviable. However, it must be clarified and emphasized at the outset that a study of this type should be descriptive as well as evaluative and research and reflection, both are called for herein; we should neither decry our past without deciphering it, nor should we eulogize it, without telescoping our views therein. It is with this idea that we can now analyse the portrayal of women in the Vedas from two angles:

I. the outer form, i.e. the narrative angle, and

II. the inner content, i.e. the semantic angle.

II

From the point of view of narration, any serious reader of Vedic verses might notice, without delving deep into their semantic aspect, that there are three types of expressions available in the Vedas, viz. *First Person, Second Person* and *Third Person*. To illustrate this point, we may refer to a statement of Yāska, the famous Vedic etymologist, as follows:

> *tāstrividhā r̥caḥ* । *parokṣakr̥tāḥ pratyakṣakr̥tāḥ ādhyātmikyaśca* । *tatra parokṣakr̥tāḥ sarvābhirnāmavibhaktibhirvyajyante prathamapuru-ṣaiścākhyātasya* । *atha pratyakṣakr̥tā madhyamapuruṣayogāḥ* । *tvamiti ca sarvanāmnā* । *athādhyātmikya uttamapuruṣayogāḥ* । *ahamiti caitena sarvanāmnā* । – *Nirukta* 7.1

> There are three kinds of verses – indirect, direct and spiritual. Out of these three, the indirect ones are those which are used with all the declensions of the noun but in the third person of the verb. The direct type verses are those which have the second person verb and the pronoun "you" being used therein. The third type, i.e. the spiritual ones are those, where the first person verb is used and pronoun "I" is employed.

In view of the above, if we now closely look at the form of Vedic expressions, indicating all the three forms which have been suggested by Yāska in his magnum opus, *Nirukta*, but in a reverse order, the following points are worth mentioning.

First Person Expressions

This type of utterances in the Veda are marked by the pronoun "I" and have been termed as of an "autobiographical style" by a modern Vedic scholar (Vedalankara 1976: 116-19). Accordingly, we may refer to a hymn (125.1-8) of the tenth *maṇḍala* of the *Ṛgveda*, popularly known as Vāgambhṛṇī hymn. The narrative style of this hymn is autobiographical and it has been stated by Kātyāyana in his Vedic index that the daughter of Sage Ambhrṇa, Vāk Āmbhṛṇī, is eulogizing herself in this particular hymn.[2] But there is no doubt that the verses of this, as well as other Vedic hymns of this sort can be and have been interpreted to signify the self-eulogistic statements of a bold, confident and straightforward woman (Vedalankara 2042 (Saṁ): 23, 72) of the Vedic age. Two examples can be quoted here:

> *ahaṁ janāya samadaṁ kṛṇomiyahaṁ dyāvāpṛthivī ā viveśa* ।
> – *ṚV* X.125.6
>
> I rouse, and order battle for the people and pervade heaven and earth.
>
> * * *
>
> *yaṁ kāmaye taṅtamugraṁ kṛṇomi*
> *taṁ brahmāṇaṁ tamṛṣiṁ taṁ sumedhām* ॥ – *ṚV* X.125.5
>
> I make anyone I wish, an aggressive person, or a scholar; a seer or an intelligent one!

Of course, such statements have also been interpreted as indicating the omnipresent, supreme, divine power, by none

---

2 *vāgāmbhṛṇī tuṣṭavātmānam* । – *Sarvānukramaṇī*, quoted by Sāyaṇa in his commentary on the hymn

else than Sāyaṇa[3] himself, but still there is no denying the fact that the same is expressed in feminine gender and first person.

There is another such hymn in the *Ṛgveda* (X.159.1-6), where Indrāṇī, the wife of Indra, is eulogizing herself; she not only commands her household but is also the all-powerful source of strength for her husband Indra. She is the daughter of Puloma and is therefore called Paulomī while her own name is Śacī, which itself signifies action according to *Nighaṇṭu* 2.1. So Indrāṇī, Śacī or Paulomī is a symbol of bravery and courageous action. Just as Indra is knwon for his valour in the Vedas, similarly his wife commands respect for her strength and status. To quote her own statements from the Veda:

> *mama putrāḥ śatruhaṇo 'tho me duhitā virāṭ* । – *ṚV* X.159.3
>
> My sons are destroyers of enemies and my daughter is great!
>
> * * *
>
> *ahaṁ keturahaṁ mūrdhā* ... । – *ṚV* X.159.2
>
> I am the flag of my family and forehead of society!

Second Person Expressions

There are a whole lot of Vedic verses which seem to be directly addressed to a woman, irrespective of the deity invoked or the seer mentioned therein; these are the statements of the middle type, i.e. the second person verb is used in such sentences. It is worth quoting a few examples of this type as follows:

> *viśvaṁ jīvaṁ carase bodhayantī viśvasya vācamavidan-manāyoḥ* । – *ṚV* I.92.10
>
> You are generating motion in every living being and understand the voice of each adorer!
>
> * * *

[3] Sāyaṇa in interpretation of the above.

... devānāmasi svasā । – *ṚV* II.32.6

You are the sister of gods!

* * *

ambitame nadītame devitame sarasvati ।
apraśastā iva smasi praśastimamba naskṛdhi ॥ – *ṚV* II.41.16

Oh the best of mothers! the best of rivers and the best of goddesses, we have become like unadorables, please make us all adorable!

* * *

arvācī subhage bhava sīte vandāmahe tvā ।
yathā naḥ subhagā sasi yathā naḥ suphalā sasi ॥ – *ṚV* IV.57.6

Oh fortunate one! Oh named as Sītā! you please approach us, we adore you so that you may be both propitious and fruitful for us.

* * *

utthāya bṛhatī bhavodutiṣṭha dhruvā tvam । – *YV* 11.64

Oh steady woman! arise and awaken your greatness!

As is clear from the above, these and many more such statements of the Vedas are enough to show and establish that a woman symbolizes wisdom, power and radiance. It is in this background that she is addressed as a *samrājñī*[4] (illuminant, empress) of the house. The Veda goes even a step further and blesses her as follows:

prabhudhyasva subudhā budhyamānā ।
dīrghāyutvāya śatasāradāya ॥ – *AV* 14.2.75

Oh wise woman! awake and keep awakened: live as long as hundred years!

---

4 *samrājñī śvaśure bhava samrājñī śvaśrvāṁ bhava* ।
nanāndari samrājñī bhava samrājñī adhi devṛṣu ॥ – *ṚV* X.85.46

yathā sindhurnadīnāṁ sāmrājyaṁ suṣuve vṛṣā ।
evā tvam samrājñyedhi patyurastaṁ paretya ॥ – *AV* 14.1.43

Third Person Expressions

The Vedic Saṁhitās also abound in such statements where the woman is described as an individual and the style of expression employed there is mostly in third person. Some select expressions in this narrative form may be quoted here which throw sufficient light on the persona of women:

vṛṣā jajāna vṛṣaṇaṁ raṇāya tamu cinnārī naryaṁ susūva ।
– *ṚV* VII.20.5

The Supreme Lord, the mighty Vṛṣā as a father, begets a heroic son for the battle while the lady as a mother brings him forth.

* * *

uta tvā strī śaśīyasī puṁso bhavati vasyasī ।
adevatrādarādhasaḥ ॥ – *ṚV* V.61.6

A woman, who is an accomplisher of praiseworthy deeds is more noble than a man who reverences not God and does not offer wealth in charity.

* * *

vi yā jānāti jasurim vi tṛṣyantaṁ vi kāminam ।
devatrā kṛṇute manaḥ ॥ – *ṚV* 5.61.7

For she discerns one who is wear and worn, one who thirsts and is in want and she sets her mind towards God.

* * *

uta ghā nemo astutaḥ pumām̐ iti bruve paṇiḥ ।
sa vairdeya itsamaḥ ॥ – *ṚV* V.61-8

And I proclaim that the man, her other half, the greedy, is not worth of commendation until he also becomes equally liberal in munificient donations.

* * *

vi śrayantāmṛtāvṛdhaḥ pra yai devebhyo mahīḥ ।
pāvakāsaḥ puruspṛho dvāro devīrasaścataḥ ॥ – *ṚV* I.142.6

Let the bright upkeepers of divine knowledge, adorable, pious and gracious, women of substance, be respected by noble men.

* * *

... striyā aśāsyaṁ manaḥ । – *R̥V* VIII.33.17

The mind of a woman (being sensitive and delicate), resists control.

* * *

imā nārīravidhavāḥ supatnīrāñjanena sarpiṣā saṁ viśantu ।
anaśravo 'namīvāḥ suratnā ā rohantu janayo yonimagre ॥
– *R̥V* X.18.7

Let these women who are not widows and have noble husbands, adorn themselves with fragrant cosmetics, cremes and perfumes. Let women adorned with jewels be without tears and free from sorrow, let them ride the carts first!

III

Another significant feature worth noting from the point of view of expression in the Vedas is that numerous adjectival epithets have been employed therein which denote various aspects of women's persona. It is quite interesting to derive the exact meaning of such expressions because it may help in getting a better idea of different roles of women in home and in society. For intance, a woman as wife is denoted by three words: *jāyā*, *jani* and *patnī*. Of these, *jāyā* is the woman who gives birth to one's progeny, *jani* is the mother of children and *patnī* is the co-partner in the religions duties (Rao Shastri 1969: 30). What is more important to mention here is that we neither find the word *bhāryā* as a synonym of wife nor *bhartā* as an apellation for husband which mean the dependent one and the provider, respectively. Hence, we might observe that woman was not held to be a liability in the Vedic age; lack of this single expression in Vedic Saṁhitās is enough evidence for such an observation. On the other hand, we have many more such terms which go on to prove that the woman was accorded the highest respect in Vedic society. To quote a few such terms as follows:

1. *Aditi*, because she is not dependent. – *YV* IV.19, *Nirukta* 4.22
2. *Aghnyā*, for she is not to be hurt. – *YV* 8.43
3. *Bṛhatī*, for she is liberal (at heart). – *YV* 11.64
4. *Brahmā*, for she is the creator. *ṚV* 8.33.19
5. *Candrā*, because she is happy. – *YV* 8.43
6. *Devakāmā*, since she is pious. – *AV* 14.2.17
7. *Devī*, since she is divine. – *AV* 14.1.45; *YV* 4.23
8. *Dhruvā*, for she is firm. – *YV* 11.64
9. *Havyā*, because she is worthy of invocation. – *YV* 8.43
10. *Iḍā* for she is worshippable. – *YV* 8.43
11. *Jyotā*, because she is illuminating, bright. – *YV* 8.43
12. *Kāmyā*, because she is lovable. – *YV* 8.43
13. *Kṣamā*, for she is tolerant/indulgent/patient. – *AV* 12.1.29
14. *Mahī*, since she is great. – *YV* 8.43
15. *Menā*, because she deserves respect. – *Nirukta* 3.21.2
16. *Nārī*, for she is not enimical to anyone. – *AV* 14.1.59
17. *Purandhīḥ*, for she is munificent. – *YV* 22.22
18. *Rantā*, because she is lovely. – *YV* 8.43
19. *Ṛtāvarī*, *Ṛtacit* (*ṚV* IV.16.10), for she is the preserver/ fosterer of truth. – *ṚV* 2.41.18
20. *Sañjayā*, since she is victorious. – *ṚV* 10.159.3
21. *Sarasvatī*, since she is scholarly. – *YV* 20.84
22. *Siṁhī*, since she is courageous. – *YV* 5.12
23. *Śivā*, for she is benevolent. – *AV* 14.1.64
24. *Śivatamā*, since she is the noblest. – *ṚV* X.85.37
25. *Strī*, since she is modest. – *ṚV* V.14.6; *Nirukta* 3.21.2

26. *Subhagā*, because she is fortunate. – *YV* 8.43
27. *Subudhā*, for she is knowledgeable. – *AV* 14.2.75
28. *Sumaṅgalī*, since she is auspicious. – *AV* 14.2.26
29. *Suśevā*, for she is pleasant. – *AV* 14.2.26
30. *Suvarcā*, since she is splendid. – *AV* 14.2.47
31. *Suyamā*, since she is self-disciplined. – *AV* 14.2.18
32. *Syonā*, for she is noble. – *AV* 14.2.27
33. *Vīriṇī*, since she is mother of brave sons. – *R̥V* X.86.9-10
34. *Viśrutā*, since she is learned. – *YV* 8.43
35. *Yaśasvatī*, for she is glorious. – *R̥V* 1.79.1
36. *Yoṣā*, beause she is intermingled with man, she is not separate. – *R̥V* I.92.11, *AV* XIV.1.56, *Nirukta* 3.5.1

Of course, these words have separate connotations and various shades of their meaning can be exactly grasped only by referring to the context. Still, they are quoted here with a view to suggest the respectable status of women in the Vedic society (Kumar 1999a: 32-33).

IV

As regards the content of the Vedas connoting the identity and status of women, we find that there are three levels (Upadhyaya 1974: 1-41) of their persona suggested therein such as follows:

i. The transcendent women in the form of deities invoked in Vedic hymns.
ii. The extraordinarily gifted women described as female seers of Vedic hymns.
iii. The ordinary women depicted as daughter, wife, mother, sister, etc.

There are more than twenty female deities and as many as twenty-seven female seers in the *R̥gveda* alone (*Br̥Up*) I.128-29, II.82-84: 18). These deities are described as personified female charm, grace and freedom, e.g. Goddess Aditi is etymologically explained as unbinding freedom of boundlessness, she is the mother of gods (*Nirukta* 4.22). In fact, she denotes the endless expanse of the infinite cosmic power. Similarly, Vāc, who is the seer as well as a deity signifies the feminine counterpart of the creating and annihilating God. Her hymn is interpreted as in honour of the primal energy of life and is made the basis of Śāktism. She is the energy drawing forth from *Paramātman*, the whole universe from *ākāśa* downwards (Radhakrishnan 1956: 487). Indrāṇī, the wife of Indra, who is also the seer as well as deity of a Ṛgvedic hymn, personifies a brave, bold and glorious woman who proclaims:

> *avīrāimiva māmayaṁ śarārurabhi manyate* ।
> *utāhamasmi vīriṇīndrapatnī maruttsakhā* ... । – *ṚV* X.86.9
>
> I am the mighty wife of Indra and the friend of Maruts, while this noxious being thinks that I am a weak and timid person.

Obviously, the female deities and the lady seers of the Veda are endowed with all the tender or terrific traits of a woman and that is why the pictures of Sarasvatī, Uṣā or Pṛthvī and all other Vedic goddesses are so lively that they are able to imprint the readers' minds with their impressive images.

V

But it is with regard to the third category of women stated above that the persona of women as an individual is actually concerned. Viewed from this aspect, many more rich, refined and chiselled feminine images emerge from the Vedas in several shades, prominent among them being the following:

A. Physical charm
B. Intellectual calibre
C. Familial roles
D. Social status
E. Spiritual strength.

In fact, the conception of womanhood in the Vedas is so comprehensive and impressive that right from the beautiful exterior and up to the innermost spiritual strength, both feminine grace and power are portrayed perfectly, of course, through the pictures of goddesses only. To illustrate the first point, a reference to the delineation of dawn, i.e. the Goddess Uṣā, in the Vedas will be the best. Vedic Uṣā is the personification of utter feminine charm and beauty. As many as twenty hymns of the *Ṛgveda* alone are exclusively addressed to her, which constitute the finest Vedic poetry as well as the most beautiful portrayal of feminine charm. She is described as bright and resplendent in her form, the lady of the light and the radiant mover of the sweet sounds with wealth of horses and cows (*ṚV* I.92.4, I.48.10). This brilliant daughter of the heavens is a charming, graceful lady,[5] a maiden decked by her mother, showing her form.[6]

Uṣā is even linked to a professional dancer who arrays herself in gay, embroidered garments and lays bare her breasts just as a cow yields her udder.[7] The unfailing charm of Uṣā is delicately woven as of an ancient Goddess, ever young, born again and again, decking her beauty with the self-same raiment,[8] clothed in light, the maiden appears in the eastern horizon and unveils her maddening charm[9] to her beholders.

---

5 *divo duhitā* । – *ṚV* I.113.7, I.124.3

6 *susaṅkāśā mātṛmṛṣṭeva yoṣāvistanvaṁ kṛṇuṣe dṛśe kam* । – *ṚV* I.123.11

7 *adhi peśāṁsi vapate nṛtūrivāporṇute vakṣa usreva barjaham* ।
– *ṚV* I.92.4

8 *punaḥ punarjāyamānā purāṇī samānaṁ varṇamabhi śumbhamānā* ।
śvaghnīva kṛtnurvija āmimānā martasya devī jarayantyāyuḥ ॥
– *ṚV* I.92.10

9 *eṣā divo duhitā pratyadarśi jyotirvasānā samanā purastāt* ।
– *ṚV* I.124.3
upo adarśi śundhyuvo na vakṣo nodhā ivāvirakṛta priyāṇi ।
– *ṚV* I.124.4

Uṣā, the immortal Goddess, has shone in earlier days, she shines today and she will shine hereafter, never ageing.[10] Like a shining silver wheel, she revolves ever anew[11] and truly following the eternal cosmic law, this dawn gradually diminishes the days of life for humans; she shines forth brightly, the last of the dawns, that have always gone, the first of those to come.[12] Effulgent in peerless beauty, she does not give her light with discrimination but she floods the entire world, all small and great, with her brilliant torch (*ṚV* I.124.6). Rising resplendent as from a bath, showing her charms, she approaches with light, dispelling darkness (*ṚV* V.80.5-6).

To quote Macdonell (2002: 46):

> Uṣas is the most graceful creation of Vedic poetry and there is no more charming figure in the descriptive religious lyrics of any other literature. The brightness of her form has not been obscured by priestly speculation nor has the imagery as a rule been marred by referenes to the sacrifice.

The physical charm and feminine grace of a woman is so intricately woven in the Vedic diction and depiction of female goddesses that the poetic appeal of Vedas is also enhanced substantially. Besides the beautiful Goddess of dawn, Uṣā, we can indulge in the beautifully adorned bride, Sūryā, who is wearing a lovely garment, embellished with the *gāthā* song. She had decorated herself in a beautiful way:

> *cittirā upabarhaṇaṁ cakṣurā abhyañjanam dyaurbhūmiḥ kośa*
> *āsidyadayāt sūryā patim* । – *ṚV* X.85.7

---

10 *śaśvatpuroṣā vyuvāsa devyatho adyedaṁ vyāvo maghoni* ।
atho vyucchāduttarām̐ anu dyūnajarāmṛtā carati svadhābhiḥ ॥
– *ṚV* I.113.13

11 *samānamaryaṁ caraṇīyamāsā cakramiva navyasyā vavṛtsva* ।
– *ṚV* III.61.3

12 *aminatī daivyāni vratāni praminatī manuṣyā yugāni* ।
iyuṣīṇāmupamā śaśvatīnāmāyatināṁ prathamoṣā vyadyaut ॥
– *ṚV* I.124.2

thought was the pillow of her couch, and sight the unguent of her eyes, heaven and earth were her treasure-box, when Sūryā went to her husband.

The sage, who is Sūryā herself, invites everyone to behold the comely forms of Sūryā, her border cloth and her headwear, and her garment triply parted, which have been sanctified by the priest (*R̥V* X.85.35).

VI

Vedic goddess Sarasvatī is the perfect feminine personification of mental capabilities: wisdom, imagination and creativity. She is depicted as the purifying power, the fountain-source of flowing knowledge, the mighty ocean of intellect.[13] She is the inspirer of sweet words, impeller of noble thoughts and the bearer of oblations.[14]

In this regard, it is worth stating here that Vedic Sarasvatī has usually been interpreted as a River or as the Goddess of speech; but there have also been Vedic interpreters, who have, on the basis of Vedic evidence itself,[15] presented her as a living, learned woman.[16] No doubt such interpretations should be given more priority and publicity, since they are prone to appeal to the modern, rational mindset and can also be linked to the women's education in Vedic times. Several epithets used for Sarasvatī in Vedic verses are worth quoting (Kumar 1998b: 140-42) here from this point of view:

---

13 *maho arṇaḥ sarasvatī pra cetayati ketunā* ।
dhiyo viśvā vi rājati ॥ – *R̥V* I.3.12

14 *codayitrī sūnr̥tānāṁ cetantī sumatīnām* ।
yajñaṁ dadhe sarasvatī ॥ – *R̥V* I.3.11

15 Dayananda Saraswati, in his *Bhāṣya* on *R̥V* VI.49.7, II.41.16; *YV* 9.27, 19.18, 19.82; 20.64.

16 *yoṣā vai sarasvatī* । – *ŚatBrā* 2.5.1.11

1. *Akavārī*, i.e. the faultless female. – *R̥V* VII.96.3
2. *Anumati*, i.e. the assent-giving. – *AV* VII.20.2
3. *Ambā*, i.e. the mother. – *R̥V* II.41.16
4. *Ambitame*, i.e. the best of mothers. – *R̥V* II.41.16
5. *Avitrī*, i.e. the protectress. – *R̥V* VII.96.2
6. *Asuryā*, i.e. the most powerful. – *R̥V* VII.96.1
7. *Āpapruṣi*, i.e. the radiant one. – *R̥V* VI.61.11
8. *Upastutyā*, i.e. the glorifiable. – *AV* 6.61.13
9. *Uśatī*, i.e. the eager. – *R̥V* V.43.11
10. *R̥tāvarī*, i.e. the truthful. – *R̥V* II.41.18
11. *Kanyā*, i.e. the lovely lass. – *R̥V* VI.49.7
12. *Gr̥ṇānā*, i.e. the adorable. – *R̥V* VII.96.3
13. *Gaurī*, i.e. the divine female. – *R̥V* I.164.11
14. *Ghr̥tācī*, i.e. the one who offers. – *R̥V* V.43.11
15. *Ghorā*, i.e. the strict disciplinarian. – *R̥V* VI.61.17
16. *Cikituṣā*, i.e. the inquisitive. – *R̥V* 6.61.13
17. *Citrāyuḥ*, i.e. the graceful. – *R̥V* VI.49.7
18. *Cetantī sumatīnām*, i.e. the encourager of truthful ones. – *YV* 20.85
19. *Codayitrī sūnr̥tānāṁ*, i.e. the inspirer of sweet speech. – *R̥V* 1.3.11
20. *Jāgr̥vi*, i.e. always awakened, alert. – *R̥V* VI.49.7
21. *Jujuṣāṇā*, i.e. the caring one. – *R̥V* V.43.11
22. *Tanūpā*, i.e. the protector of body. – *YV* 21.130
23. *Tanyatu*, i.e. the knowledgeable. – *R̥V* X.65.13
24. *Triṣadhasthā*, i.e. abiding in all the three levels. – *R̥V* VI.61.12
25. *Devitame*, i.e. the best of goddesses. – *R̥V* II.41.16
26. *Dhiyāvasuḥ*, i.e. the source of inspiration. – *R̥V* I.3.10
27. *Dhīnāmavitrī*, i.e. protectress of knowledge. – *R̥V* I.61.4
28. *Dhr̥ṣatī*, i.e. the strong one. – *R̥V* II.30.8

29. *Pāvakā,* i.e. the purifier. – *ṚV* I.3.10
30. *Pāvamānī,* i.e. the propitiating. – *YV* 34.55
31. *Pāvīravī,* i.e. the auspicious. – *ṚV* VI.49.7
32. *Pārāvataghnī,* i.e. the underminer of both her rivals. – *ṚV* VI.61.2
33. *Priyā,* i.e. the beloved. – *ṚV* VI.61.10
34. *Priyatame,* i.e. the most beloved. – *ṚV* VII.95.5
35. *Bṛhatī,* i.e. the vast in capacity. – *ṚV* VI.61.13
36. *Bhadrā,* i.e. the noble one. – *ṚV* VII.96.3
37. *Madhumatī,* i.e. the sweet-worded. – *AV* 5.7.4
38. *Marutvatī,* i.e. the resplendent. – *ṚV* II.30.8
39. *Marutsakhā,* i.e. the friend of vitality. – *ṚV* VII.96.2
40. *Yajatā,* i.e. the noble one. – *ṚV* V.43.11
41. *Yaśobhaginī,* i.e. the sister of fame. – *YV* 2.20
42. *Vardhayantī,* i.e. the cherisher. – *ṚV* VI.61.12
43. *Vāvṛdhānā,* i.e. the sweeping in majesty. – *ṚV* VII.59.1
44. *Vājinīvatī,* i.e. full of wisdom. – *ṚV* VI.61.4
45. *Viśvatūrtiḥ,* i.e. one who rears the world. – *ṚV* II.3.8
46. *Vīrapatnī,* i.e. damsel of the brave. – *ṚV* VI.49.7
47. *Vṛtraghnī,* i.e. destroyer of obstructions. – *ṚV* VI.61.7
48. *Vṛtrahā,* i.e. killer of evil forces. – *ṚV* IX.3.10
49. *Śagmā,* i.e. the melodious one. – *ṚV* V.43.11
50. *Śatrujayā,* i.e. suppressing her foes. – *ṚV* II.30.8
51. *Śantamā,* i.e. bestower of happiness. – *AV* VII.68.3
52. *Śivā,* i.e. the propitious. – *AV* VII.68.3
53. *Śuci,* i.e. the pious. – *ṚV* VII.95.2
54. *Śubhre,* i.e. the bright. – *ṚV* VII.95.6
55. *Sakhyā,* i.e. the friendly female. – *ṚV* VI.61.14
56. *Sajoṣā,* i.e. accompanied with her dear associates. – *ṚV* VI.49.7

57. *Saptadhātu*, i.e. comprising seven aspects. – *R̥V* VI.61.12
58. *Saptathī*, i.e. the seventh stream. – *R̥V* VII.36.6
59. *Saptasvasā*, i.e. having seven sisters. – *R̥V* VI.61.10
60. *Sādhayantī dhiyam*, i.e. perfecting our intelligence. – *R̥V* II.3.8
61. *Sindhumātā*, i.e. mother of the ocean of milk. – *R̥V* VII.36.6
62. *Sujuṣṭā*, i.e. well propitiated. – *R̥V* VI.61.10
63. *Sudughā*, i.e. liberal in proriding. – *YV* 20.75
64. *Subhagā*, i.e. the blessed one. – *R̥V* VII.95.4
65. *Sumr̥ḍikā*, i.e. the gracious one. – *AV* 7.68.3
66. *Suyamā*, i.e. the tractable. – *R̥V* IX.81.4
67. *Stuvānā*, i.e. the glorified. – *R̥V* VII.96.3
68. *Haviṣmatī*, i.e. supplying abundantly. – *YV* 20.74
69. *Hiraṇyavartani*, i.e. traversing on a golden path. – *R̥V* VI.61.7

As is clear, the above terms in Vedic verses also substantiate the view expressed by Dayananda Saraswati, who interprets Vedic verses on two levels: the transcendental as well as the empirical. Evidently, the empirical interpretation of Vedic verses will be more acceptable and relevant today than the mere ritualistic or highly spiritualistic one. The present exposition is clearly concerned with an issue which is of social significance and hence empirically relevant; therefore, this depicition of Vedic Sarasvatī as an enlightened woman is highly called for.

VII

The Vedic woman is depicted in several familial roles also, such as the daughter, the bride, the wife, the mother and the sister. The Vedic society was definitely family-oriented and a woman was the undisputed centre of household in the words of the Veda itself: *jāyedastam* (*R̥V* III.53.4). She is the equal partner in all the familial matters and an equal owner of the house; the Vedic term *dampatī* (*R̥V* VIII.31.5) is in dual number and it suggests an equal status for both, the husband and the wife.

However, it must also be mentioned here that we do find a frequent desire for the male child in the Vedic Saṁhitās but there is nowhere an explicit expression for the desire of a daughter's birth in the Vedas. Nevertheless, there are several references in the Saṁhitās which clearly convey that the daughters were lovingly caressed and affectionately brought up by the parents. There is no evidence to show that a girl child was regarded as an unwanted baby, rather, we have one statement expressing pride of a mother who has an illustrious daughter (*R̥V* X.159.3) and also a prayer for the birth of a scholarly daughter (*Br̥Up* 4.4.18). Hence, it may be deduced that the birth of a daughter was not a source of consternation to the family in the Vedic age (Altekar 1956: 3). This may also be corrobarated from an internal evidence where mention is made of twin sisters and their fond relation with the parents (*R̥V* I.185.5). We can also trace several terms to denote the young girl or the daughter such as *kanyā*, *kanā*, *kanīnakā*, *duhitā*, *putrī* and *kumārī* (*R̥V* IX.67.10, IV.32.23, X.159.3, VIII.31.8; *AV* X.3.20).

The young girl, when she reaches her marriageable age and chooses a husband for herself, adorns herself as a bride. The depiction of a lovely bride, her adornment and the marriage ceremony itself is a rare poetical treasure in the Sūryā-hymn of the *R̥gveda* (X.85.6-7, 35). The verses and the rituals based on this hymn are still prevalent in the Vedic Hindu marriage. The blessings bestowed on the lovely bride in the Veda speak volumes about the women and their auspicious place in the family. The young bride enters the home of her husband and acquires the status of wife, which is the most important aspect of a woman's personality in Vedic view. The wife is designated as *patnī* (*R̥V* I.72.5, V.44.5; *YV* 15.50; *ŚatBrā* 5.2.1.10; *TaiBrā* 2.2.2.6), since the husband cannot perform any religious rite without her[17]

[17] *ayajñiyo vā eṣa yo 'patnīkaḥ* । – *ŚatBrā* 3.3.3.1

by his side. That is why she is termed as *dharmapatnī* while the husband is merely a *gṛhapati.*[18] The respectable religious status given to a wife in the Vedic family is also suggestive of the significance of marriage in Vedic view, it is not just a contract or a compromise but a sacrament, a synthesis of spirits and harmony in thoughts,[19] which lies at the heart of Vedic marriage. Both husband and wife are essentially complementary to each other, they work for the same goal – the bearing and rearing of children and carrying forward the chain of continuity. They have equal rights as well as duties for the welfare of society at large, there is no difference at all between them.[20]

This fact is very well reflected in the Vedic marriage ceremony itself where friendship is solicited between the husband and wife (*ṚV* IV.16.10; *AitaBrā* 7.18; *ĀśvaGṛ* 1.7.19). During *Saptapadī*, an important ceremony in the marriage rituals, the bridegroom says to the bride: *sakhā saptapadī bhava* (*ĀśvaGṛ* 1.7.19) (take the seventh step along with me for friendship between both of us). It clearly shows that in the household as well as in the society, the wife had a complementary role of a friend to her husband. In fact, marriage in Vedic view is not just an external relation undertaken for physical pleasures or material comforts, but an inseparable bond which is designated as an *āśrama* (*ṚV* X.85.47; *AV* VII.36.1; *SāmaBrā* 1.3.9) meaning total functional dedication to the cause of social and religious duties wherein the wife had a prime position and shared an equal status with her husband, she was really a *sahacarī* and not an *anucarī*.

The respectable wife attains a much more elevated status

---

18 *patnī tvamasi dharmaṇāhaṁ gṛhapatistava* । – *AV* 14.1.51

19 *samañjantu viśve devāḥ samāpo hṛdayāni nau* ।
saṁ mātariśvā saṁ dhātā samu deṣṭrī dadhātu nau ॥ – *ṚV* X.85.47

20 *jāyāpatyorna vibhāgo vidyate* । *pāṇigrahaṇādadhi sahatvaṁ karmasu* । *tathā puṇyaphaleṣu ca* । *dravyaparigraheṣu ca* । – *Āpastamba Dharmasūtra* 2.6.14.16-19

in Vedic depiction, once she bears progeny and becomes the mother. Motherhood is the most coveted position of women's persona in the Vedas as well as later Hindu literature. Several Vedic goddesses have been personified as mother and given an adorable reverence, the most popular of them being that of the mother earth and her son: *mātā bhūmiḥ putro 'ham pṛthvyāḥ* (*AV* 12.1.12). The pictures of daughter and sister are also available in the Vedas and the relations of brother–sister, father–daughter, mother–son, etc. (*Ṛ̥V* I.124.7, VI.55.5) are all enunciated here. They throw sufficient light on the various familial roles played by women in Vedic society.

VIII

This brings us to the point of society, larger than the family. Women in the Vedic society enjoyed a lot of freedom and were not secluded by *purdah* (prohibited by any such custom); the fact can be corroborated from several Vedic statements such as: *yoṣā sabhāvatī* (*ṚV* I.167.3), i.e. the woman does go to the assembly or the *sabhā*; she also addresses the learned gathering: *vaśinī tvaṁ vidathamā vadāsi* (*ṚV* X.85.26).

As stated earlier, the women were given priority in riding the vehicles and enjoyed certain privileges such as *pūrvahūtī*,[21] i.e. women also went to participate in the social festivities like *samana*,[22] a general popular festivity to which women went to enjoy themselves (Macdonell and Keith 1962: 473). Moreover, the mention of a special type of marriage, in which the young maiden could herself choose a husband (*ṚV* X.27.12, X.85.4), could not have been possible in a society where women were denied liberty. We also find mention of a woman, named Viśpalā, who accompanied her husband in the battlefield (*ṚV* I.116.15) and many more Vedic verses where woman is described as *siṁhī* (*YV* V.10-12), i.e. the tigress or the fearless, courageous person.

---

21 *patnīva pūrvahūtiṁ vāvṛdhadhyā* ... । – *ṚV* I.122.2

22 *saṁhotraṁ sma purā nārī samanaṁ vāva gacchati* । – *ṚV* X.86.10

All these references go on to prove that the persona of women in Vedic delineation is both of a delicate female and a strong woman, an upholder of familial and social norms.

IX

The most significant aspect of the persona of women in Vedic society is that she is held to be morally pious, spiritually powerful and creatively potent,[23] so much so that she is elevated to the level of creator himself.[24] From this point of view, a woman is not simply a physical form or merely part of a biological species but a spirit so strong that the whole cosmos pulsates around her and she permeates the whole universe. In many of the hymns addressed to Vedic goddesses such as Vāc, Aditi, Bhūmi, Ilā, Sarasvatī or Bhāratī, one can easily discern that the feminine force is being conceived as an emphatic expression of the unity of the cosmos. The conception of these female deities is identified with the Supreme Spirit, the universal soul and the guiding principle in the scheme of creation. For example, Vāc, the Goddess of speech, herself boasts that she is mighty in her grandeur and appears from beyond the heavens and from behind the earth.[25] There are many more Vedic goddesses who are in fact personified abstractions, like Śraddhā (*R̥V* X.151.1), Anumati (*R̥V* X.167.3, *AV* VIII.20.2), Aramati (Macdonell 2002: 120), Araṇyānī (*R̥V* X.146.1), Nadyaḥ (*R̥V* X.64.9, X.75.1-9) and *apsaras*es (*R̥V* X.123.5). Their depiction in the Vedas is quite convincingly that of an equally respectable, adorable feminine and capable persona, not only on the physical plane but also in the spiritual sphere.

X

What emanates from the above short delineation is that the

23 *śuddhā pūtā yoṣito yajñiyā imāḥ* । – *AV* 11.1.17.18

24 *strī hi brahmā babhūvitha* । – *R̥V* VIII.33.19

25 *paro divā para enā pr̥thivyāḥ …* । – *R̥V* X.125.8

persona of women in the Vedas is representative of a totally cohesive identity and perfect parity with the male. It is, in fact, a model of complete complimentarity and cooperation rather than competitiveness or confrontation. In other words, the Vedic view is an elaborate and extensive, but subtle and profound paradigm of woman-power without disempowering the other half of humanity. In brief, it may be said that the comprehensiveness of Vedic vision of women is of great value in helping us to get out of the conflict models that envelope all contemporary discussions on the place of women in human society.

To conclude, I would like to quote a contemporary woman writer, Clarisse Bader:

> Has not the time arrived, we repeat, to refresh outselves. from more life-giving and generous sources. And only India has the honour of affording such sources. There is a sense of duty dominating all affections, a feeling of respect for the family life, a love for one's neighbour, a charity, including even animals in its tender effusion, a spirit of sacrifice – such are the forms of a literature, which aims not only at imagination but in strengthening the heart. – 1965: Preface

14

The Concept of Veda-Apauruṣeyatva

THE present chapter aims to expound and examine the Mīmāṁsā doctrine of *veda-apauruṣeyatva* and its counter-perspective available in source- books of other schools of Indian philosophy.

Veda is the source as well as the sustaining force of the vast and varied Indian philosophical thought. It is the storehouse of all forms of knowledge and has proved to be the pivot around which the whole lot of subsequent thought-process has been revolving since ancient times. Vedic testimony has been held to be the highest authority for all the *āstika* schools of Indian philosophy. Even the so-called *nāstika* schools of thought have developed in opposition to the Vedic view. Hence, they also owe their allegiance to the Veda in some way or the other.

The supremacy, strength and significance of Veda are derived from the fact that traditionally it is taken to be a synonym of "word" or "knowledge" which is true, complete and infallible. The unique and unparalleled distinction of Veda is its potency to denote even that which is not to be known by any other means of knowledge. Authority of Veda is actually rooted in the theory of veda-*apauruṣeyatva*, variously interpreted by several schools of Indian philosophical thought, although all of them unanimously accept its unquestionable authenticity.

II

Of all the schools of Indian philosophy, Mīmāṁsā is the most powerful champion of Vedic authority. In fact, the basic orientation of Mīmāṁsā is derived from and dependent upon Vedic sources themselves. This significant stream of Indian philosophy is deeply rooted in the interpretation of Vedic texts and seeks an inquiry into the problems relating to Vedic rituals. Etymologically, the term *mīmāṁsā* means investigating a doubtful point and arriving at a conclusion thereon.[1] Traditionally, the word has been held to express "revered thought",[2] since it deals with the interpretation of Vedic statements in accordance with the rituals based upon the sacred sanction of Vedic authority.

III

The primary aim of Mīmāṁsā school is to delineate on the true nature of *dharma* which is injunctive in nature.[3] Accordingly, the central theme of Mīmāṁsā discourse has been the analysis of *vidhi* (moral injunction). In course of discussion on *codanā* or *vidhi*, the issue of *artha* (purpose as well as meaning) also assumes significance in Mīmāṁsā because there is an underlying relationship between each word and meaning, and also between the action and its purpose. From this point of view, word, purpose and action are the three main undercurrents of Mīmāṁsā philosophy since *dharma* is accessible through words which are expressive of purpose and are grouped together and ordered according to particular component actions of the sacrifice. The blending of *śabda* and *artha*, *kratu* and *phala* has much deeper and wider implications from hermeneutic as well as moral angles.

---

1 *vicārapūrvakatattvanirṇayaḥ* । – *Nyāyakośa*, p. 654

2 *pūjitavicāravacano hi mīmāṁsāśabdaḥ* ।
– *Nyāyavārtikatātparyaṭīkā*, p. 52

3 *athāto dharmajijñāsā* । *codanālakṣano 'rtho dharmaḥ* । – *MīSū* 1.1.1-2

In other words, the following three are the basic presuppositions of Mīmāṁsā philosophy:

a. All such actions which are enjoined in the Veda, comprise of *dharma*. Interestingly, Kumārila, in his *Ślokavārttika*, has posited various other notions of *dharma* and, after rejecting all those, he has concluded that they cannot be known through Veda as *puruṣārtha*. It is only *śreya* (happiness) attainable by *dravya*, *guṇa* and *karma* which is meant by *dharma*.[4]

b. The one and only source of knowing *dharma* is the Veda as word (*śāstra*). The very definition of *śāstra* implies those activities or refraining from them which are enjoined by the *śāstra* through eternal or non-eternal statements.[5]

c. The Veda is self-validated and requires no extraneous source for its authenticity. Here a question naturally arises as to what is the basis for accepting self-validity of the Veda and how to ensure the efficacy of Vedic statements. To this, the reply of Jaimini is stated in the famous *sūtra* as follows:

> *autpattikastu śabdasyārthena sambandhastasya jñānamupadeśo 'vyatirekaścārthe 'nupalabdhe tatpramāṇaṁ bādarāyaṇa-syānapekṣatvāt* ।
> –*MīSū* 1.1.5

It means that the word and its meaning are innately related and their relation cannot be vitiated by any extraneous factor like time, space, situation or person.[6]

---

4 *śreyo hi puruṣaprītiḥ sā dravyaguṇakarmabhiḥ* ।
codanālakṣaṇaḥ sādhyāstasmāt teṣveva dharmatā ॥
– *Ślokavārttika*, Codanāsūtra 191

5 *pravṛttirvā nivṛttirvā nityena kṛtakena vā* ।
puṁsāṁ yenopadiśyeta tacchāstramabhidhīyate ॥ – Ibid., Śabdapariccheda 4

6 *na ca mithyaitaditi kālāntare deśāntare 'vasthāntare puruṣāntare vā* ।
– Śabara in his *Bhāṣya* on *Mīmāṁsāsūtra* 1.1.5

> The Mīmāṁsaka's main thesis is that *dharma* can be known only from the Vedic injunction and in order to establish the infallibility and utter reliability of the Vedic injunction, he has had to prove that: (1) Words are eternal, (2) The Denotations of Words are eternal, (3) The Relationship between Words and their Denotations is eternal, (4) the meaning of the Sentence is comprehended only on the comprehension of the meanings of the component words, and the Sentence has no meaning apart by itself. As regards the Eternality of the *Sentence*, however, that Eternality cannot belong to the Sentence composed by human beings and as such it cannot be Eternal: and for the same reason it cannot have an inherent validity, as it is open to the suspicion of having been vitiated at its source by the defects of the man pronouncing the Sentence. But this does not perturb the Mīmāṁsaka; as the only Sentence upon whose *eternality* and *validity* he is keen is the Vedic injunction, which alone is the valid source of our knowledge of *dharma*. And as all human or personal associations are open to the suspicion of being vitiated at its source, it becomes necessary for the Mīmāṁsaka to show that the Vedic Sentence is not the work of any person, that the Veda is not the work of any author and that it is Eternal and self-sufficient. – Jha 1964: 111

IV

It is against the above background that we can understand the ordering and meaning of Jaimini's *sūtra*s in the Tarkapāda, the very first section of his compendium. After introducing the basic approach of Mīmāṁsā as *dharma* and defining it as injunctive in nature, he puts forth the topic of validity of *dharma*. He goes on to elaborate that none of the accepted *pramāṇa*s can validate *dharma* as such because *pratyakṣa* is capable of denoting present objects only and the rest of the *pramāṇa*s are in one way or the other dependent upon *pratyakṣa* itself. *Dharma* is neither a physical object nor does it deal with present time alone, rather it encompasses the whole lot of past, present and future human activity and its consequences. Hence, it cannot be held that there is no means available for knowing the true nature of *dharma*.

As stated earlier, Veda (*śāstra*) is the only valid means for comprehending *dharma* according to Mīmāṁsā. Therefore, the focus and emphasis on proving the eternity and self-validity of Veda in the system is quite justified. In the fifth *sūtra* of Tarkapāda, Jaimini has dealt with this problem and asserted that, the relation of the word with its denotation is inborn, injunction is the means of knowing *dharma* and it is infallible in regard to all that is imperceptible; it is a valid means of knowledge, as it is independent (Jha 1964: 97). It is to be noted that the term *śabda* here stands for the Vedic or scriptural word, and *artha* for *dharma–adharma*, which forms the subject matter of scripture.[7] Hence, neither Jaimini nor Śabara has given a definition of "word" or "verbal cognition" in general; they have defined only the particular form of word, i.e. injunction, which is what bears upon the subject matter of Mīmāṁsā, viz. *dharma–adharma*.

But quite naturally, in the course of discussion of above themes, the basic question relating to verbal cognition in general as well as its validity and realibility has also been discussed in detail in the Mīmāṁsā sourcebooks. To grasp the real import and significance of the concept of *veda-apauruṣeyatva*, a brief outline of the more general ideas regarding this is called for as follows.

V

The idea of eternity of Veda is so significant in Mīmāṁsā system of philosophy that Jaimini himself has devoted almost eighteen *sūtra*s of his first chapter (twelve in the form of *pūrva-pakṣa* and six in the form of *siddhānta*) to establish this theory in a firm manner. It will not be out of place to discuss the opponents' arguments and Jaimini's own response to them before we deliberate upon the concept of Veda-*apauruṣeyatva* in detail. The objections raised by Jaimini in the form of *pūrva-pakṣa* to the eternity of the word are:

---

7 *Ślokavārttika*, Śabdanitytādhikaraṇam 8-13.

i. *karmaike tatra darśanāt* (*MīSū* 1.1.6): It is observed that *śabda* is produced only when some individual makes some effort in the form of action. Hence, it is to be inferred that there is a causal relation between human action and the word. Consequently, the word cannot be eternal.

ii. *asthānāt* (*MīSū* 1.1.7): The word, when uttered, does not last even for a moment. We, therefore, understand that it is destroyed. It is not seen that an object is not available even if it is present. Hence, we cannot buy the argument that the word is not available even though it is present. Nor can we say that the word has not reached its object, hence it is not being heard because word is the object of *ākāśa* which is present everywhere. But the *śabda*, once uttered, does not last in the place of hearing even for a moment.

iii. *"karoti" śabdāt* (*MīSū* 1.1.8): Since the terms like *karoti* are used with reference to the word, it is presumed that the word is produced and not eternal.

iv. *sattvāntare ca yaugapadyāt* (*MīSū* 1.1.9): It is a matter of everybody's experience that the same word is simultaneously heard but not in a uniform way at various places. This also proves that the word is not eternal because eternal objects are mostly single and uniform.

v. *prakr̥tivikr̥tyośca* (*MīSū* 1.1.10): Mutations and permutations are quite obvious in case of the words. This would not have been possible if the word was eternal. Hence, it has to be accepted that the word is not eternal.

vi. *vr̥ddhiśca kartr̥bhūmnāsya* (*MīSū* 1.1.11): The next and the last argument in favour of non-eternity of words is that the sound gets increased when there are more than one speakers.[8] It means that each speaker contributes some part of the whole word, which being cumulated, gets

[8] Śabara in his *Bhāṣya* on *MīSū* 1.1.11.

increased. This should not have been the case if the word would have been eternal. For example, a pot exists as it is, whether there is only one lamp to lighten it up or there are a thousand.[9]

In response to the above objections, Jaimini gives the following arguments and proves that the word is eternal.

a. *samaṁ tu tatra darśanam* (*MīSū* 1.1.12): As far as the first objection regarding human effort is concerned, it must be stated that even eternal word needs to be manifested and human effort has to be made for that too.

b. *sataḥ paramadarśanam viṣayānāgamāt* (*MīSū* 1.1.13): The second objection can be met with the argument that the word is only manifested by the conjunction and disjunction of air and is not actually produced. It is, therefore, that the word, being eternal, is already present but is not heard due to absence of manifesting activity.

c. *prayogasya param* (*MīSū* 1.1.14): Even the expressions like *karoti* are indicative of the usage of word and not its production.

d. *ādityavad yaugapadyam* (*MīSū* 1.1.15): Simultaneous occurrence of one word at several places can also not prove its non-eternity because the same word can be heard at different places like the same sun appearing to be present at different places.

e. *varṇāntaramavikāraḥ* (*MīSū* 1.1.16): As far as the mutations and permutations of the word are concerned, they are not real but are actually usages of one letter in place of another and that too is based on resemblance.

f. *nādavr̥ddhiparā* (*MīSū* 1.1.17): The next objection regarding

---

9 *na hi dīpasahasre 'pi vyañjake vardhate ghaṭaḥ* । – *Prabhā* on the above (Quoted by Umashankar Sharma Rishi in Hindi translation of *Mīmaṁsādarśanam*, Tarkapāda, 1.11)

increase of sound after cumulative utterance can be met with the argument that word as such is partless. Hence, the increase in word does not actually mean anything but the increase of sound (*nāda*).

VI

In this way, after meeting all the objections one by one put in by the opponent, Jaimini posits some more arguments to prove his point of view regarding eternity of word as follows:

i. *nityastu syād darśanasya parārthatvāt* (*MīSū* 1.1.18): It is a matter of common experience that the word is uttered for others' use and comprehension. If the word would have been non-eternal, nobody would have been able to communicate with others since it would have got perished just after it was uttered. Moreover, each time one hears a word, it has to be accepted as a new word, if it was to be non-eternal. Obviously, it is against the common experience. Therefore, it is logical to hold that the word is eternal.

ii. *sarvatra yaugapadyāt* (*MīSū* 1.1.19): A word once uttered denotes a whole class and not merely an individual. Hence, if it is held to be non-eternal, it will be impossible to express the relation between a word and its class. On the contrary, if it is held to be eternal, it can indicate the whole class.

iii. *saṁkhyābhāvāt* (*MīSū* 1.1.20): A word is uttered eight times but every listener can recognize that it is the same word. Nobody says that eight words have been spoken. He rather knows that the same word, which was uttered earlier, is spoken again and is comprehended as such.

iv. *anapekṣatvāt* (*MīSū* 1.1.21): No sufficient cause is available for the destruction of word. As such, it is not cogent to hold that it is non-eternal.

v. *prakhyābhāvācca yogasya* (*MīSū* 1.1.22): Some scholars believe that air is the cause of word and hence the word is non-eternal. But neither parts of air are available in the word, nor the word can be touched like air. Hence, it is not produced from air and is not non-eternal.

vi. *liṅgadarśanācca* (*MīSū* 1.1.23): Internal evidence from the Veda also suggests that the word is eternal.

VII

In this way, Jaimini in his Mīmāṁsā system has tried to establish the eternity of word after refuting all the arguments put up by the opponent. But the opponent may again raise an objection as to "the word may be eternal, but how the eternity of a sentence can be proved, since sentence is a whole consisting of several words and compounds". In other words, sentences, Vedic or otherwise, cannot be eternal, since they are composed of words and so they are produced.

Jaimini's answer to this objection is that the crux of a sentence is its verb which implies three words: *sādhya*, *sādhana* and *itikartavyatā*. Hence, a sentence is not an independent and separate entity other than the meaning of its words. It is only an understanding of a total sense of the words used in a particular sentence.

Moreover, the ordinary sentences uttered by a human being may be taken to consist of several words and so produced in that form (*MīSū* 1.1.26 and Śabara's *Bhāṣya* thereupon). But as far as the Vedic sentences are concerned, such objections are of no standing since they are not produced by anybody, and are self-validated. Sentences, ordinary or otherwise, are, according to the Mīmāṁsā, not over and above the meaning of the words which have already been proved eternal.

VIII

This brings us to the question of the relation between word and its meaning. Jaimini has propounded that the relation between word and its meaning is eternal. It is noteworthy that the Indian grammatical tradition also holds the same view.[10] According to Mīmāṁsā, word and its meaning are innately related and are not produced by anybody, not even by God. If some "person" would have caused this relation, he must be remembered like Pāṇini is remembered while using the terms *vṛddhi*, etc. Although it is also true that sometimes the memory fails and we are not able to remember certain facts due to some reason but this cannot be held true in case of words and their meanings being used in daily behaviour. Hence, it is appropriate to hold that the word and its meaning are innate, eternal and impersonal, since there is nobody available to create or to relate them.

IX

Several objections have been raised against the Mīmāṁsaka position of innateness of the relation between word and its meaning: These are as follows:

a. When the word is heard for the first time, its meaning is not known. It is known only after it is heard so many times. Hence, this relation is produced and so is non-eternal.

b. The word and its meaning are not located in the same place. Word is situated in the mouth while the meaning, i.e. the object is available somewhere on the ground.

c. The word and its meaning are understood as separate when we say:

> This is word and not the meaning. This is the meaning and not the word.

So, it is proved that they are not innately related.

---

10 *siddhe śabdārthasambandhe* । – Kātyāyana's *Vārttika, Mahābhāṣya* 1.1

d. The form of both the word and its meaning is also different. The word "cow" is *uttered* while the meaning of this word is *apprehended*. Hence, the relation between these two is born and not innate.

To the above and other such objections raised by the opponent, the Mīmāṁsā reply is that neither perception nor any other means of knowledge can prove that there is some person who created the word and its meaning.[11] Actually, it is through a continuous tradition that the relation between the word and its meaning is transmitted from one generation to another and carried forward. Never was there a time or a place where this relation was not available, because if it be accepted that it was not available somewhere at a certain point of time, then naturally the question of its beginning would arise and it would lead to an infinite regress. To avoid this fallacy of infinite regress, it has to be admitted that certain words were used for the first time and were self-related to their meanings. As such, it amounts to accept innateness of relation between word and its meaning.[12]

As stated above, the Mīmāṁsakas have postulated two theories to uphold the authority of the Vedas: (a) the eternity of the word, and (b) its non-personal origination. Obviously, the latter is dependent upon the former.[13]

In other words, the Veda is not created by any individual, be it human or divine, because, being eternal in nature, it does not need to be created at all.

The second postulate of Mīmāṁsā is slightly but significantly different from the common assumptions of other revealed faiths in as much as they state:

---

11 *puruṣasya sambandhābhāvāt । kathaṁ sambandho nāsti? pratyakṣasya pramāṇasyābhāvāt । tatpūrvakatvācchetareṣām ।*
– *Śābarabhāṣya* on *MīSū* 1.1.5

12 *tasmād avaśyam anena sambandhaṁ kurvatā kṛtasambandhāḥ । kecana śabdāḥ vṛddhavyavahāra-siddhā abhyupagantavyāḥ ।* – Ibid.

13 *vedasya nityatvenāpauruṣeyatvam ।* – *Nyāyakośa*, p. 802

> The Veda is not the word of God, but the Word itself. These two postulates of faith, based on some mystic experiences lying at the root of the whole of the *mantra* cult, have not directly helped the Vedicist to give a rational interpretation of the *mantras*, but indirectly they are suggestive of the standpoint from which an approach to such an interpretation is to be made. – Anirvan 2001: 322

X

Since we have already dealt with the issue of the eternity of the Veda or word according to the Mīmāṁsā school, it will be quite appropriate now to deal with the concept of *veda-apauruṣeyatva* in detail. It is necessary to note at the outset that the arguments of the opponent are given for refutation of the Mīmāṁsā view of the impersonality of the Veda and counter arguments are given by the Mīmāṁsaka in defence of his theory. Jaimini himself has raised two objections from the viewpoint of the *pūrva-pakṣa* in the last portion of his Tarkapāda which have accordingly been interpreted by Śabara and quoted by Sāyaṇa in his *Ṛgbhāṣyabhūmikā*.

Pūrvapakṣa

The opponents have raised two main objections against the eternality and impersonality of the Veda as follows:

A. *vedāṅścaike sannikarṣaṁ puruṣākhyāḥ* (*MīSū* 1.1.27): The Vedas must have been composed by some author just like other worldly compositions because they are named after certain persons; just as Kālidāsa has authored the *Raghuvaṁśa*, some author has composed the Vedas also because the branches of the Vedas are known as Kāṭhaka, Kauthuma, Taittirīya, etc. only on the basis of their propounders in the same way as the *Rāmāyaṇa* is known as Vālmīkīya and the *Mahābhārata* as the Vaiyāsika. The argument can be rendered as an inferential statement as follows:

vimataṁ vedavākyaṁ pauruṣeyam
vākyatvāt
kālidāsādivākyavat ।

In other words, it means that certain persons have actually authored the Vedas and hence they carry their specific names in the form of Kāṭhaka, Paippalāda, etc.

B. *Anityadarśanācca* (*MīSū* 1.1.28): Moreover, the Vedas cannot be held to be impersonal because we find many ephemeral things mentioned in them such as Babara, Prāvāhaṇi and Kusurvinda Auddālakī. On the basis of such occurrences, it can be inferred that the Vedas were not written when these persons were alive. That is why we find that many of such statements have a verb form declined in the past tense, e.g. *akāmayata*. It is, therefore, quite logical to hold that the Vedas are a work of some author.

The opponent clarifies that the names attached to a particular branch of the Veda definitely denote a relation between the creation and its creator, i.e. the Veda is the *kṛti* and some person is the *kartā*.

Moreover, the names attached to various branches of Vedas cannot simply be held to be the names of instructors or teachers of those branches, since the instructors of one branch of learning may be many but the author is usually one. Hence, if the particular branch of the Veda is carrying a particular name, it goes to prove that it is written by the author of that name.

It is quite possible that sometimes the names of the authors are not remembered after a long duration of time, but it does not mean that the work was not created at all and hence it is eternal for that matter.

Siddhāntapakṣa

To the above two main objections put up by the opponent, Jaimini has responded in the following four *sūtra*s in the form of four arguments:

i. *uktaṁ tu śabdapūrvatvam* (*MīSū* 1.1.29): It has already been stated (in the fifth *sūtra* of Tarkapāda quoted above) that we propound and subscribe to the theory of eternality of the Veda which means that there is a continued tradition of Vedic studies. Accordingly, from one teacher we go to the earlier one and then the earliest, but we cannot prove that there was a creator, since this chain is eternal.

ii. *ākhyā pravacanāt* (*MīSū* 1.1.30): Regarding the names of branches of the Veda such as Kāṭhaka, Kauthuma and Taittirīya, it is not proper to assume them as authors of the Veda. They are only interpreters or teachers of that particular Veda.

   To the above argument of Jaimini, Śabara adds the following in his *Bhāṣya*:

   > *prakarṣena vacanam ananyasādhāraṇaṁ kathādibhir anuṣṭhitaṁ syāt tathāpi hi samākhyātāro bhavanti* ।
   > *smaryate ca vaiśampāyanaḥ sarvaśākhādhyetā* । *kaṭaḥ punar imāṁ kevalāṁ śākhām adhyāpayām babhūveti* ।
   > *sa bahuśākhādhyāyināṁ sannidhānād ekaśākhādhyāyi, anyāṁ śākhāmanadhīyānaḥ, tasyāṁ prakṛṣṭatvād asādhāraṇam upapadyate viśesaṇam* ।
   >
   > – *Śābarabhāṣya* on *MīSū* 1.1.30

   Sometimes the names are given to some creation even when it is not created by some particular person but instructed or interpreted by him in an exceptionally effective manner. Seers like Kaṭha have explained the Veda in an extraordinary way, hence the names Kāṭhaka, etc. are given to the particular branch of the Veda. Similarly, the Smṛtis mention the name of

> Vaiśampāyana who has taught all the branches of the *Yajurveda* while Kaṭha had interpreted only one particular branch of it which came to be known as Kāṭhaka because he excelled and specialized in that particular branch.

Obviously, this argument of the Mīmāṁsaka carries some weight, since even in modern times, we do associate certain scholars' names with the branch of knowledge they are specializing in. This viewpoint also provides an important clue to the recognition of interpreters. Since Indian philosophy is basically a tradition-oriented philosophy, one cannot dismiss this argument simply on the face of it, for there have been great commentators like Śabara, Śaṅkara, Praśastapāda and Vātsyāyana who are no less respected than the original propounders. In this way, Mīmāṁsā does give a respectful position to the teacher and asserts that the names of great teachers, or of students for that matter, of a particular Veda are well known, but the names of their authors are not known, since the Vedas are not authored by anyone; they are eternal, impersonal and universal.

iii. *paraṁ tu śrutisāmānyamātram* (*MīSū* 1.1.31): As far as the words like Babara and Prāvāhaṇi are concerned, they denote the general and derivative sense instead of referring to any individuals bearing those names; the apparent similarity in it is based on the sound being heard.

Elaborating on this point of Jaimini, Śabara says that in history, there is no well-known person by the name of Pravāhaṇa. Hence, it is totally unfounded to hold that Prāvāhaṇi is a proper name of a person who is the son of Pravāhaṇa. Regarding the suffix "i", he says that it signifies the progeny of a person as well as the agent of a verb. To put it in simpler terms, Prāvāhaṇi means any object or individual which or who carries things forward:

> *tasmād yaḥ pravāhayati sa prāvāhaṇiḥ* ।
> – *Śābarabhāṣya* on *MīSū* 1.1.31

Evidently, the above explanation of the word "Prāvāhaṇi" is based on the principle of etymology which is highly appropriate in the case of the Vedic language.

The other part of the Vedic statement concerning "Babara" shows only the resemblance of the sound that can be heard when air blows:

> *babara iti śabdānukṛtiḥ* ।
> – *Śābarabhāṣya* on *MīSū* 1.1.31

Hence, the word *babara* is only a common noun and not proper as it is mistaken by the opponent. The air which blows and creates the sound *ba-ba-ra* is, in fact, the meaning of the word "babara" which is onomatopoeic in nature:

> *na tu manuṣyo babaranāmako 'tra vivakṣitaḥ* । *babaradhvaniyuktasya pravahaṇasvabhāvasya vāyoratra vaktuṁ śakyatvāt* ।
> – *Ṛgbhābhū*, p. 64

This argument of the Mīmāṁsakas definitely carries some weight, since in literature, the figure of speech called "Onomatopoeia" is explained as based on resonance of sounds and there are many words in all languages which testify to this trait.

iv. *kṛte vā viniyogaḥ syāt karmaṇaḥ sambandhāt* (*MīSū* 1.1.32): The opponents may argue again that there are many Vedic statements which apparently do not convey any sense and seem to be like the utterances of insane persons or children.

For example:

a. *vanaspatayaḥ satramāsata* ।
sarpāḥ satramāsata ।।

The creepers performed some rituals. The snakes performed some rituals.

b. *jaradgavo kambalapādukāyāṁ dvāri sthito gāyati madrakaṇi* ।
taṁ brāhmaṇī pr̥cchati putrakāmā rājan rumāyāṁ laśunasya ko 'rthaḥ ॥

The old ox wearing chappals and draped in a blanket, is sitting on a gate and sings mad songs. The brāhmaṇa's wife asks him: When would I get a son? Oh king! what is the price of garlic in the mine of salt, etc.

– Sāyaṇa on *MīSū* 1.1.32

The Mīmāṁsakas' response to the above is formulated by Jaimini as in the above *sūtra*. Śabara explains this by saying that even such apparently senseless statements in the Veda are not actually meaningless because technically they are Arthavāda statements meant to eulogize the significance of rituals. It indirectly means that when even the non-living herbs performed the sacrifice, then not to talk of the learned brāhmaṇas. It is just like saying that in the late evening even animals do not walk, what to talk of erudite scholars. Apparently, there does not seem any connection between these two statements but actually it intends to prohibit loitering in the late evening for various reasons (*Śābarabhāṣya* on *MīSū* 1.1.32).

Moreover, all Vedic statements are mutually interrelated and primarily meant to be injunctive in nature; the injunction, in fact, has three aspects: (a) the goal, (b) the means, and (c) the method. It is why as soon as the word *jyotiṣṭoma* is uttered, the injunction "ought" has to be supplied for the sake of expectancy. Thereafter, the question of (a) means arises and the *soma* is stated to be the means. Then the (b) goal of this exercise is sought and *svarga* is given as an answer to it. Lastly (c) the method for performance of *jyotiṣṭoma* is inquired about and the reply is provided accordingly. In this way, the whole injunctive process is so well-knit and logically ordered that the opponents' view regarding its senselessness stands refuted and the authenticity of the Veda stands vindicated (*Śābarabhāṣya* on *MīSū* 1.1.32).

Sāyaṇa, while explaining the above *sūtra*, has stated further that the learned logicians follow a dictum *yatparaḥ śabdaḥ sa śabdārthaḥ* which means that the word should be interpreted in the sense in which it is employed and not in the sense it appears to be employed. Accordingly, all Vedic statements are to be interpreted in the injunctive sense only and not otherwise. Of course, some of them are directly injunctive in nature while others are in the form of Arthavāda and have to be taken only in a eulogistic sense (Sāyaṇa in the *Ṛgbhābhū*).

Hence the objection raised by the opponents regarding the *apauruṣeyatva* of the Veda stands refuted. Here, Sāyaṇa has shown the fallaciousness of the opponents' argument on another account also. He has taken the following reading of Jaimini's *sūtra*:

> *kṛte cāviyogaḥ syāt karmaṇaḥ samatvāt* ।

According to him, the word *cakāra* in this *sūtra* is used to prove the defectiveness of the inference put in by the *pūrva-pakṣa* (quoted above) as follows:

> *vedavākyaṁ pauruṣeyaṁ*
> *vākyatvāt*
> *kartranupalambhatvāt* ।

v. It is also worth mentioning here that another objection has been anticipated by Sāyaṇa in this regard in his *Ṛgbhāṣyabhūmikā*, which is from the side of Vedāntins and runs as follows.

Bādarāyaṇa, in his *Brahmasūtra*[14] has stated that *Brahman*, the omniscient Being is the origin of all scriptures. Interestingly, he has resolved this objection from the Mīmāṁsā standpoint by stating that even according to this *sūtra* of Vyāsa, no individual is held to be the author of the Vedas because *Brahman* is knowledge itself from the transcendental point of view. In fact, Bādarāyaṇa himself has upheld the eternity of the Veda at the empirical level also, when he says:

Ata eva ca nityatvam ।
– *Śāṅkarabhāṣya* on *BraSū* 1.1.29

Many Śruti and Smṛti statements, like the following two, also support the above thesis:

i. *vācā virūpanityayā* – *ṚV* VIII.75.6

ii. *anādinidhanā nityā vāgutsṛṣṭā svayambhuvā*
– *Mbh*, Śp 232-34

Therefore, on the basis of the above arguments quoted and refuted by Jaimini in his *Mīmāṁsāsūtra*, the Mīmāṁsakas have tried to prove that the Veda is impersonal, eternal and infallible:

pauruṣeyaṁ na vā vedavākyaṁ syāt pauruṣeyatā
kāṭhakādisamākhyānāt vākyatvāccānyavākyavat ।
samākhyānaṁ pravacanāt vākyatvam tu parāhṛtam
tatkartranupalambhena syāttato 'pauruṣeyatā ॥
– *Jaiminīyanyāyamālā* 1.1.8

XI

It is worth mentioning here that neither Jaimini and Śabara, nor Sāyaṇa, have taken note of the well-known Nyāya point of view, according to which the Veda is *apauruṣeya* because no ordinary *puruṣa* (being) is the author of the Veda but because God, the Omniscient Being, manifests the Veda at the beginning of each creation. In fact, Sāyaṇa himself begins his commentary on the

14 *śāstrayonitvāt* । – *BraSū* 1.1.3

Veda with the following invocatory verse based on a statement of the *Śatapatha Brāhmaṇa*:

> *yasya niḥśvasitaṁ vedā yo vedebhyo 'khilaṁ jagat* ।
> *nirmame tamahaṁ vande vidyātīrthamaheśvaram* ॥
> – *Ṛgbhābhū*, p. 1

It means that the Vedas predate the creation and that God creates the world according io the Vedic knowledge which is eternal, beginningless and endless. Even the very idea of creation belittles the significance of the Veda, so it is held that God did not create the Vedas but effortlessly revealed them. It is, therefore, that we hold them to be the divine manifestation of the eternal knowledge and not a creation anyway. Obviously, Sāyaṇa is here referring to God as the creator of the world but not as the creator of the Vedas, as the Nyāya holds.

On the other hand, Jayantabhaṭṭa, in his *Nyāyamañjarī* (pp. 573-81), has raised several objections against the Mīmāṁsā position in the form of *pūrvapakṣa* and has refuted them from the Nyāya point of view. It will be interesting to quote a portion of the debate as follows:

> *Nyāya*: Vedic sentential construction must presuppose an author because it is sentential construction, like any other sentential construction, found in a non-Vedic text.
>
> *Mīmāṁsā*: The Mīmāṁsakas may retort to the above by quoting a counterinference such as:
>
> > *vedādhyayanaṁ sarvaṁ guruadhyayanapūrvakam* ।
> > *vedādhyayanasāmānyādadhunādhyayanaṁ yathā* ॥[15]
>
> Vedic study as a whole, like all kinds of other studies, should follow the instructions of a teacher, since Vedic study is just like studying in contemporary times.
>
> *Nyāya*: The above suggestion is not relevant for proving the proposition because a similar statement can be made in case of the *Mahābhārata* also.

---

15 *Ślokavārttika*, Vākyādhikaraṇam, 366.

Mīmāṁsā: No, because in case of the *Mahābhārata*, it is unanimously known that it was composed by Vyāsa.

Nyāya: Even in the case of the Veda, it is well known that it was composed by Prajāpati.

Mīmāṁsā: Actually, the Vedic reference to Prajāpati is not meant to convey God as the creator of the Veda since nobody has come across the author of the Vedas.

Nyāya: Then the *Mahābhārata*'s reference to Vyāsa also does not denote that he is its author, since nobody has actually seen him.

Mīmāṁsā: The Vedas are such an important text that had they been composed by an author, he would not have been forgotten by the generations of Vedic students. Moreover, there is no beginning of creation at all, since the world, too, is eternal.

Nyāya: If a sentential construction could come into existence without an author then a piece of cloth could as well be produced out of threads without a weaver.

Mīmāṁsā: No, because the Vedas are an extraordinary text.

Nyāya: That is why they should have been composed by some extraordinary author instead of being taken as an authorless composition. Just as extraordinary products, like mountains, are created by somebody much superior than the producer of pots, even so they are to be taken as created by some such agency.

Mīmāṁsā: Nobody remembers the author of the Vedas.

Nyāya: *Anumāna* and *śāstra* both can prove that an extraordinary person composed them. Hence, it is logical to hold that the same God who created the world also created the Vedas because the composition of the Vedas requires knowledge of the whole world. Moreover, the same God who composed one of the Vedas should be taken to have composed all the four, since the four Vedas teach things interconnected.

In this way, Jayanta has reduced the Mīmāṁsā argument of impersonal authorship of the Veda to the divine origin of the Veda. Even the Yoga philosophy subscribes to this view with the only difference that it holds God also as an extraordinary *puruṣa*. Therefore, according to Yoga, Veda is *pauruṣeya*, because it is manifested by God, a *puruṣaviśeṣa*[16] while according to Nyāya, it is *apauruṣeya* because no ordinary individual, but God, has created it.

XII

In the light of the above, it may be stated that mostly all the schools of Indian philosophy agree on the self-validity and supreme authority of the Vedas. However, broadly speaking, the following three views (Chaturvedi 1972: 45) are available in Indian tradition regarding the origin of it:

a. The first view, propounded by Jaimini and elaborated by his followers is that the Veda is self-revelatory, nobody, not even God, has created it. Therefore, it is *apauruṣeya* in the strictest sense of the term.

b. God created the Vedas. Hence, the Vedas are in the form of God himself. This view is upheld by the Nyāya–Vaiśeṣika and Yoga schools of Indian philosophy.

c. The great seers, called *ṛṣis*, were granted Vedic knowledge by the grace of God after they practised severe austerities. Therefore, they codified this knowledge in language and the Vedas were revealed to the humanity.

Out of the above, the first view has been discussed at length in the foregoing pages while the second one has been hinted at in brief. As far as the third view is concerned, we find traces of it in the Vedic sources themselves where the *ṛṣis* are mentioned as the *mantrakṛtāḥ*.[17] In fact, even in this view the seers are not held

---

16 *kleśakarmavipākāśayairaparāmṛṣṭaḥ puruṣaviśeṣa īśvaraḥ* । – *YS* 1.24

17 *ṛṣe mantrakṛtāṁ stomaiḥ* … । – *ṚV* IX.114.2

siśurvā aṅgirasāṁ mantrakṛtāṁ mantrakṛdāsīt । – *TāṇḍyaBrā* 13.3.24

yām ṛṣayo mantrakṛto manīṣiṇaḥ anvaicchan devastapasā śrameṇa ।
tāṁ daivīṁ vācaṁ haviṣā yajāmahe sā no dadhātu sukṛtasya loke ॥

→

to be the creators of Vedic knowledge but are believed to be the instructors or interpreters of Vedic verses (Sarasvati 1997: 36-38). Various Mīmāṁsā scholars have explained that *mantras* being eternal cannot be created – they are either seen or employed in rituals by the seers[18] who have received God's grace and divine insights due to their hard penances and have manifested them for the welfare of the humanity. That is why they are venerated and stated to be the seers of the *mantras*:

nama ṛṣibhyo mantrakṛdbhyo mantrapatibhyaḥ । – *TĀ* 4.4.14

The Veda is undoubtedly divine knowledge and divine language which can only be transmitted through certain extraordinarily gifted persons called *ṛṣis*. The same fact has been expressed by Yāska in his *Nirukta* at more than one places:

i. *sākṣātkṛtadharmāṇa ṛṣayo babhūvuḥ* । – *Nirukta* 1.1
ii. In the beginning of Daivatakāṇḍa, Yāska explicitly mentions that the *ṛṣis* are the composers of the Vedic verse:

yatkāma ṛṣiryasyām devatāyāmārthapatyamicchanstutiṁ prayuṅkte taddaivatasya mantro bhavati । – *Nirukta* 7.1

– *TaiBrā* 2.7.7

māham ṛṣīn mantrakṛto mantrapatīn parādām । – *TĀ* 4.1.14

mantrakṛto vṛṇīte । – *Āpastamba Śrautasūtra* 24.5.6

18 *ṛṣiratīndriyadraṣṭā mantrakṛt karoti dhātustvatra darśanārthaḥ* ।
– Sāyaṇa in his *Bhāṣya* on *AitBrā* 6.1

śiśurvā āṅgiraso mantrakṛtāṁ mantrakṛdāsīd ityatra mantrakṛcchabdaḥ prayoktari prayuktaḥ । - Kumārila in *Tantravārttika*, quoted in Sarasvati 1997: 38

mantrakṛditi vyutpattirgarīyasī vedāpauruṣeyatva bhangat ।
kintu mantrān kurvanti prayogavidhina iṣṭalābhāya prayuñjata iti mantrakṛtaḥ ।
– Govinda Shastri in his commentary on *Raghuvaṁśa* 5.4
– Qutoed in Sarasvati 1997: 39

The deity of the verse is decided according to the intention of the seer who invokes a particular deity with a certain desire.

iii. Obviously, here is a clear statement indicating the personal intention of the seer, which is reiterated elsewhere too:

evamuccāvacairabhiprāyairr̥ṣīṇāṁ mantradr̥ṣṭayo bhavanti । –*Nirukta* 7.3

In this way, the insights of seers are based upon their higher or lower intentions.

On the basis of above and many more such internal evidences, it can be assumed that the Indian tradition, while accepting the divinity of Vedic knowledge, does not ignore the human aspect of its manifestation and propagation. In other words, the *r̥ṣi*s derive some extraordinary powers due to God's grace only after practising austerities and are gifted with the immediate perception of the reality. Their *r̥ṣitva* is rooted in the fact that they could directly perceive the truth of knowledge.[19]

Deserving of such Supreme knowledge, the *r̥ṣi*s do not conserve it for selfish interest, rather they transmit it for the posterity and the tradition goes on continually.[20]

It is therefore that the Veda is held to be *śruti* (knowledge) acquired by the disciple through oral transmission, directly from the mouth of the preceptors, no less than the seers themselves. In brief, the *r̥ṣi*s visualized the Vedic verses and exposed them; they did not compose them.

XIII

It is noteworthy that Francis Clooney, in his book *Thinking*

---

19 *r̥ṣir darśanāt, śtomān dadarśa iti aupamanyavaḥ, tad yad etān tapasyamānān brahma svayambhu abhyānarṣat tad r̥ṣīnāmr̥ṣitvam* । – *Nirukta* 2.3

20 *yo vai jñatonūchānaḥ sa r̥ṣiḥ* । – *ŚatBrā* 4.3.9

Ritually (1990), has given a new twist to this whole discussion. In his view, *Mīmāṁsāsūtras* 1-5 and 24-25 have dealt with the nature of *dharma* and the ordinary language respectively. *Sūtra* 27 attempts to extend this possibility to Vedic language also as if it was also an ordinary composition, which it is not.

> *Ṛṣis* are thus introduced, obliquely, as a threat to the original authority of the Vedic injunctions. Their function is not being described in a positive fashion, they're introduced only to make clear what their role is not.
>
> Because the Veda and Vedic sacrifice as communicative of *dharma* depend on an underlying relationship of word, purpose and action, it is always a given, continually actualized system that precedes any particular element involved in it now. The *ṛṣis* themselves are among these posterior elements, since they are merely "enlisted" to pronounce the Vedic words and hand them down, to make sure the text is known and able to be regularly translated into action. The words are not expressions of human wisdom and are not to be interpreted as statements of human values and goals.
>
> The importance of human factor is recognized and human beings are used to uphold and further the Vedic tradition. It is conceded that the *ṛṣis* are intimately connected with the texts that bear their names, but the connection is defended in a way that minimizes it. *Ṛṣis* expound the Veda, but their speech is not creative; there is nothing behind it but the ever-existent relationship of word–purpose–action, which can utilize any and all human agents as tools.
>
> It is here that the Mīmāṁsā doctrine of *apauruṣeyatva* begins to take shape, although without the kind of formal, technical defence that in turn requires further defence and explanation. *Apauruṣeyatva* is used here simply to dismiss the possibility that the *ṛṣis* might have a creative or authorial function in regard to the text. Jaimini's position seems to be that they are secondary, peripheral, whatever their insights or personal qualities might be. That they speak and teach is required and

> recognized, the remainder of their experiences and abilities is simply irrelevant. –Clooney 1990: 167-68

Evidently, the above statement is totally unfounded, since it seems to suggest as if Indian tradition in general and Mīmāṁsā system in particular propounded the concept of veda-*apauruṣeyatva* to deny the *ṛṣi*s their right of authorship. In contrast, the Indian view of Veda-*apauruṣeyatva* seeks to uphold the sanctity and authenticity of Veda on the one hand, but grants an exalted and unparallelled position to the *ṛṣi*s, the original seers of Vedic verses on the other. Clooney himself has elsewhere explained the authorlessness of the Veda according to Indian tradition from another angle and stated:

> The idea of authorlessness in ancient India can be analysed from a variety of perspectives. For instance, one could look at the grammar of classical Sanskrit itself, on which most Indian theological and philosophical texts were composed. Sanskrit does not understand the structure of a sentence to be that of subject/predicate, but rather that of a verb qualified by various relationships, including the agent and instrument, place, etc. The "subject" of the sentence is, grammatically speaking, only apparent. Edwin Gerow has explored at length the relationship between certain grammatical structures in the Sanskrit language and philosophical structures in Vedānta philosophy in particular. His observations on the impersonal structure of Sanskrit are pertinent for a comprehensive understanding of the notion of authorlessness. – 1987: 673

In view of the above, it is clear that the idea of veda-*apauruṣeyatva* is so pervasive in Indian thought that it cannot and should not be studied in isolation.

XIV

To sum up, it may be said that it is in the above and other specifically traditional Indian perspectives that the concept of Veda-*apauruṣeyatva* has to be properly understood and explained.

As far as the Mīmāṁsā perspective is concerned, it has to be emphasized that the primary aim of Mīmāṁsakas is to uphold the Veda and its authority. The Veda is defined by them as a collection of *vidhi* and *niṣedha*, the other aspects of it being subsidiary. Hence, when the Mīmāṁsakas approach the question of Veda-*apauruṣeyatva*, they intend to highlight the imperativeness which can be well protected if it is of impersonal origin. In other words, to convey the self-validity of Vedic injunctions, the Mīmāṁsakas resorted to the doctrine of eternity of word and defended the idea of Veda-*apauruṣeyatva*. It is against this background that the Mīmāṁsā view has to be comprehended.

In brief, the Mīmāṁsakas emphasize that the Vedic knowledge is Eternal, not produced by anyone, not even by God. The Eternal Vedic knowledge was, of course, perceived by the *ṛṣi*s and they imparted it to posterity; they first channelized its expression. Hence, it is not proper to propound that the Mīmāṁsā ignores the human aspect of knowledge. Rather, it restores the Vedic testimony to its supreme status through the concept of *veda-apauruṣeyatva*:

> From all this, we conclude that the Vedas are not the work of a Personal Author and being thus free from any defect due to such authorship, the Vedas must be regarded as the only source of knowledge (relating to *dharma*) which is infallible in its self-sufficient sufficient Validity. – Jha 1988: 162-63

To conclude, in the words of the Veda itself:

> *apakrāman pauruṣeyād vṛṇāno daivyaṁ vachaḥ* ।
> *praṇītīrabhyāvartasva viśvebhiḥ sakhibhiḥ saha* ॥ – *AV* 1.105.1
>
> Moving away from the words of human beings, choosing the divine speech, conduct yourself according to the good guidance with all your friends!

Appendix

Vedic Studies in Germany

saṁjñānaṁ naḥ svebhiḥ saṁjñānamaraṇebhiḥ ।
saṁjñānamaśvinā yuvamihāsmāsu niyacchatam ॥ – *AV* 7.52.1

Let us have concord with our own people, and concord with people who are strangers to us; Oh Dual Devas! you both create between us, and the strangers a unity of hearts and minds!

* * *

If history is to teach us anything, it must teach us that there is continuity which binds together the present and the past, the East and the West.

THE above statement of Max Müller, which was made in the "Last Essay" of his famous book *India: What Can It Teach Us*? is no less topical now than it was then. This appeal to the mankind for strong intellectual ties, uniting the known and the unknown, is as old as the Vedas – the verse from the *Atharvaveda* quoted above is a testimony to the fact. It is really a matter of immense gratification that the eternal and universal message of Vedic lore has been a source of sincere academic pursuit for the German scholars for more than past 200 years or even more.

The present paper is just a modest tribute to the zeal and commitment of German Indologists for their pioneering and untiring efforts towards bringing to light the ancient treasures of Indian wisdom. Their erudition, both philologic as well as philosophic, as also their contribution to Sanskrit language, literature and culture is simply unimaginable and immeasurable. It is, therefore, virtually impossible to give an exhaustive and thorough account of the enormous amount of service rendered by German scholars in the field of Vedic studies. However, an effort is being made here to represent a sketchy and selective outline of some of the most significant achievements in this regard compiled from various resources.[1]

II

Ordinarily, it is observed that the relations between two countries are rooted in the political considerations or economic equations, leading, in turn, to cultural exchanges. But it is remarkable in the case of Indo-German relations that they have developed the other way round. It was due to the keen interest in the intellectual quest of India evinced by German scholars during the last two centuries that the mutual exchanges between the two great countries began. The Germans had no share in the material profits which the colonial powers received from their Indian possessions, but the very fact enabled them to direct their attention to the spiritual treasures of India. The same is succinctly stated by a German poet Heinrich Heine (1797–1856) in his letter (1821) addressed to August Wilhelm Schlegel as follows:

---

[1] I must express my gratitude to late Professor Vachaspati Upadhyaya, the then Vice-Chancellor, Shri Lal Bahadur Shastri Rashtriya Sanskrit Vidyapeeth, New Delhi and Secretary, Maharshi Sandipani Rashtriya Vedavidya Pratishthan, Ujjain for entrusting this task to me. I thank Professor Lokesh Chandra, former President, Indian Council for Cultural Relations, New Delhi and Professor Gaya Charan Tripathi, former Head, Kalakosha Division, Indira Gandhi National Centre for the Arts, New Delhi as also his colleagues, Dr Vijay Shankar Shukla and Dr Vidya Prasad Mishra for facilitating procurement of some valuable resource-material for this paper.

> As to the study of Sanskrit itself, time alone will tell how useful it may be. Year after year, Portugese, Dutchmen and Englishmen have been dragging home the treasures of India in their big ships; we Germans have been mere onlookers. Yet the spiritual treasures of India shall not escape us.

Again, Heine has rightly observed in his world-famous book of songs, *Sonnettenkranz* that the Germans set up "factories in the universities for recovering the priceless intellectual treasures of the rich country lying on the banks of the Ganges".

In his introductory note to the chapter on Germany included in his *Sanskrit and Allied Indological Studies in Europe*, V. Raghavan (1956) has also highlighted the above idea in following words:

> Though the credit of discovering Sanskrit for the West goes to England and though it was at the feet of French pioneers that the first German Sanskritists like Bopp and Schlegel sat, Germany had taken to Sanskrit studies with such enthusiasm and disinterested love, that outside India, one can say without exaggeration, that it has been a second home of Sanskrit. Before the war, there were fourteen full chairs for Sanskrit at German universities, which is something that could not be said of even India; even after the war, there are no less than ten full professorships and some more Sanskrit departments of the second or third order. Max Müller and Deussen had captured the imagination of India and Bonn had played the role of something like a Benares to entire Europe. To give an account of German contribution to Sanskrit would be to write the history of Sanskrit Studies in modern times.

After going through a brief history of Indology in Germany, one can easily comprehend the breadth and depth in the truth conveyed by such statements as follows:

> After becoming a seat of Indology in 1818, the city of Bonn was fittingly dubbed: The German Benares on the Rhine. ... Such nicknames, which in all likelihood originated in student circles, frequently express a great deal of love and

> admiration. In this the nickname of the German Benares has fully succeeded.
>
> – Leifer 1971: 125

III

The tradition of Vedic studies in German Indology dates back to the beginning of nineteenth century when W. Colebrook's essay was first written (1905), although he was of the opinion that the Veda need not be translated, as it was hardly worth reading. It is also true that the earliest Western Sanskritists were more interested in the study of Sanskrit language and had rather neglected Vedic literature. However, it must be admitted:

> The Veda and more particularly the oldest and from many points of view the most important of Vedic texts, the *Ṛgveda*, had remained outside the sphere of the pioneer generation of Western Indologists. Its existence was dimly known, but it was yet unaccessible. In India, on the other hand, although the Veda has always been recognized as the unfallible source, the foundation and backbone of Hindu religion, yet in actual practice, what was understood by Veda or Śruti, were almost exclusively the Upaniṣads and apart from some *mantra*s indispensable in ritual, actual knowledge of the Saṁhitās, particularly of the *Ṛgveda Saṁhitā*, had become restricted to a narrow circle of *śrotriya*s and the role of the Veda in the religious and spiritual life of India in no way corresponded to the fundamental importance attached to it in theory.
>
> – Alsdorf 1964: 24

But once the area of Vedic studies picked up, the scholars in the West recognized the inherent worth of Vedic knowledge and started producing several fundamental works.

German scholar Friedrich Rosen (1805-37) must be credited for the first ever publication of a part of *Ṛgveda Saṁhitā* (first book). It was published after Rosen's death in 1838 in an imperfect state. The text and the Latin translation of the first book were complete, of the notes only a fourth part were in a finished state. This edition was reprinted by the Johnson Reprint Corporation, New York and London in 1968. Rosen studied Sanskrit at Berlin with Franz Bopp (1791–1867) and wrote his thesis in 1826 on "Specimen of the Chief Sanskrit Roots". It was followed a year later by a book *Sanskrit Roots* which is based on root classifications of Sanskrit grammarians. In 1827, Rosen went to Paris and in the same year, was invited to fill the chair of oriental languages at the University College of London. It was there that he got to study the rich treasures of Sanskrit manuscripts. Rosen never lost sight of his plan to produce something monumental in Sanskrit scholarship. He, therefore, devoted his spare time to preparing the text edition and Latin translation of the *Ṛgveda*. He thought that the character and genius of Indian language and literature could only be understood by tracing them back to the earliest periods, to which the Vedas belong and he conceived the plan to edit and translate the *Ṛgveda*. In 1830, he issued his *Riguedae Specimen*, in which he published seven hymns. He made use of two *Ṛgveda* manuscripts and he had Sāyaṇa's commentary at his disposal. He found Pāṇini's grammar and Yāska's etymology useful for the explanation of difficult words. He meant to write a preface on the life and religion of early Vedic period but could not do so due to his early death in 1837.

Thus, after the preliminary attempts at the *Ṛgveda* studies by Friedrich Rosen, it was left to Rudolph von Roth (1821-95) and to Friedrich Max Müller (1823–1900) both encouraged by the famous French scholar Eugene Burnouf, to realize the true importance of India's most ancient treasured texts, the Vedas. Max Müller's widely known and great contribution to Vedic studies provided the necessary textual basis for further researches while Roth's work, though less spectacular in amount, was no less important (Stietencorn 1969: 7). In 1846, three years before the first volume of Max Müller's edition appeared in the press, Roth had published an important book entitled *On the Literature and History of the Veda*. This book contained three treatises, viz.:

1. on the hymns of the Veda,
2. on the oldest Veda grammar or the Prātiśākhyasūtras, and
3. on historical events in the *Ṛgveda*: Vasiṣṭha's fight with Viśvāmitra.

Macdonell has called this an epoch-making work which became the starting point of Vedic research in Germany. It must also be mentioned here that in contrast to W. Colebrook's view quoted above, Roth was of the opinion that the study of Vedas would be of greatest value for Oriental history. Roth also propounded that the Vedic hymns mentioning wars were the older ones while those related to peaceful sacrifices belonged to a later period.

Roth's book was the first attempt to approach the history of ancient India with critical methods of the West and he was the first to glean historical data from the Vedic hymns. This is also to be recognized that in the course of his Vedic interpretation, Roth attached less value to Sāyaṇa and other Indian commentators who lived centuries after the hymns were composed, since he believed that there was no continuous tradition of exegesis from Vedic to medieval times. He, however, found Yāska's explanations of difficult Vedic passages very useful and, therefore, in 1852, he also brought out an edition of *Nirukta* with valuable elucidations (Stache-Rosen 1981: 62).

The most significant step towards Indic studies in Germany was perhaps the publication of seven huge folio volumes of *St. Petersburg Dictionary* prepared by Otto von Böhtlingk (1815–1904) and Rudolph von Roth in a short span of twenty-three years between 1852 and 1875. The first volume appeared in 1855, the seventh in 1875. It has been reprinted and an English translation was also prepared and published in India. Today, even after one and a half century, the work remains unsurpassed and an entirely invaluable tool for Vedic studies.

Roth undertook the task of dealing with the Vedic period and most of the words from the Vedic Literature in *St. Petersburg Dictionary* are from his pen only. Roth was the first to handle the lexicography of the Veda and so much of his time and labour was spent in indexing and comparing parallel passages to ascertain meanings. He was afraid that future researches in the field would make his share in the dictionary antiquated. But this did not happen till date. To appreciate the full value of this work, it should be mentioned that Roth had to find out the meaning of many obscure Vedic words for the first time. In doing this, he rejected the testimony of the medieval commentaries and devoting himself exclusively to the original texts, tried to let them speak for themselves. The results of his labours were, and still are, admirable and the fact that Vedic studies acquired so quickly a firm basis from which to proceed was mainly due to Rudolph von Roth. Thus

> Roth's contribution to Vedic research was second to none, not even to the first edition of the *Ṛgveda* that was to immortalize more than anything else the name of the great Max Müller.
>
> – Alsdorf 1964: 24

Besides the two above-mentioned significant publications, Roth, together with W.D. Whitney, edited the *Atharvaveda Saṁhitā*, which was published from Berlin in 1856. The work began by Roth and Whitney was continued by their students Morris Bloomfield and Richard Garbe (1857–1927) both of whom edited the Kashmirian *Atharvaveda* (Paippalāda branch). The text was reproduced in 544 plates by chromo-photography from the manuscript available in the University Library in Tübingen, in three volumes. It is worth mentioning here that Roth was perhaps the first Vedic scholar who realized that the *Atharvaveda* was younger than the *Ṛgveda* on account of its language.

Roth brought out metrical translations of typical Vedic hymns titled *Seventy Hymns of the Rigveda,* together with his two pupils Karl F. Geldner (1856–1910) and A. Kaegi. He also contributed several valuable articles to various journals. A few of the most important of his articles treat "Brahma and the Brahmans" (vol. I) of the German Oriental Society (ZDMG); "The Highest Gods of the Aryan Nations" (vol. VI); "Soma" (vol. XXXV); "The Habitat of the Soma Plant" (vol. XVII); "The Myth of Soma and the Eagle" (vol. XXXVI); "Learned Tradition in Antiquity, Especially in India" (vol. XXI) and "The Orthography of the Veda" (vol. XLVIII).

As stated above, many of Roth's pupils also worked in the field of Vedic studies. A few among them were well-known Sanskritists and besides collaborating with him, they worked independently too. Geldner's translation of the *Ṛgveda* is held to be a standard work even today. His was only the last of three complete translations of the *Ṛgveda* into German. The other two renderings began to appear in the same year, 1876. One of these was prepared by Hermann Grassmann (1809-77), a well-known mathematician who undertook the study of the Veda as mental recreation. Grassmann also prepared a *Dictionary of the Rigveda* which is an indispensable tool for Vedic researchers even today. The other German translation of the *Ṛgveda* was published independently by Alfred Ludwig (1832–1911), it contained copious notes and therefore proved to be quite useful for Vedic studies in the following period.

IV

Friedrich Max Müller is one of the greatest and best known Vedic scholars of Germany who held that the *Ṛgveda* is the most ancient book of the Aryan family. Max Müller's contribution to Vedic studies is almost astonishing. It is not without reason that Max Müller was called the "Veda Vyāsa of Kali Yuga" by Radhakanta Dev, one of the orthodox Hindu leaders of the last century.

Max Müller was destined to immortalize himself by publishing the first ever complete text of the *Ṛgveda* and other Vedic texts. He was just twenty-three years old when he went to Paris and attended E. Burnouf's classes on the *Ṛgveda*: "a new world was opened to me", Max Müller later wrote in his autobiography. After that, he decided to prepare and publish the complete edition of the *Ṛgveda* accompanied with the commentary of Sāyaṇa. But the greatest difficulty before him was to raise the enormous amount of money required for printing of this voluminous text. In 1846, Max Müller went to London where the East India Company agreed to bear the expenses of this ambitious project. The first volume was published in 1849 when Max Müller was only 26 years of age.

> The Honourable East India Company was at that time struggling hard against those who wanted that it should be abolished and the government of India taken over by the Crown, as was actually done a few years later in 1858. The directors of the company sanctioned the money for the publication of the *Ṛgveda* and the upkeep of the editor because here was an excellent opportunity to show the world that the Company was not exclusively bent on profit-making and the exploitation of India but that it was a generous patron of learning and culture.
>
> The first volume of Max Müller's edition appeared in 1849, the 6th and last in 1874; the row of bulky quarto volumes has been likened to a row of Indian elephants. This printed *Ṛgveda* caused a tremendous sensation in India. – Alsdorf 1964: 25

Since the first ever publication of the *Ṛgveda* was a literary-scientific event, some orthodox circles tried to ban it, pretending that a *mleccha* had written it, put their sacred texts for the first time in print and tried to interpret them, but its undeniable superiority over all MSS got established in a short while and after the publication of the sixth volume,

> Max Müller's work as well as his contribution as editor (he had got among others, Aufrecht, Brunnhofer, Eggeling, Thibaut and Winternitz to collaborate with him) were acclaimed. In India itself, he won support from an unexpected quarter. A circle of brāhmaṇas around Mūl a Śaṅkara, better known by his monk's name of Dayananda Saraswati and his followers founded a reformed community which they called Ārya Samāj or Community of the Lofty-minded. This Community was founded in 1875, one year after the appearance of Müller's "sixth volume". After having been criticized for so long, the Anglo-German scholar from Oxford was now accorded the honorary title of *Moksha Mula* (Root of Salvation), which is recognized by all Indians to this day. And Max Müller truly was the root which nurtured this new community founded for the purpose of purifying and reviving their religion. Dayananda read Max Müller correctly; he asked for a return to the plain and simple word. – Leifer 1971: 152

Max Müller's *Ṛgveda* edition was published at a time when in India, under the impact of Western influences, the movement of Hindu revivalism was just beginning and this made the significance of what he had done immensely greater. He, as it were, helped to give that movement a more solid basis and to furnish it with an effective weapon.

> Perhaps it is not too much to say that without Max Müller's edition of the *Ṛgveda*, Dayanand Saraswati's war cry "Back to the Veda" would not have been raised or at least not raised in the way it was. Dayanand founded the Ārya Samāj in 1875, exactly one year after the completion of Max Müller's *Ṛgveda* and he particularly insisted in going back not to the Upaniṣads or other late Vedic texts but to the *Ṛgveda* as the oldest and most authoritative document of Aryan religion. It may also be added here that apart from Vedic studies the work done by Western and that is to say primarily by German scholars, was not without significance for religious movements in India and even for the national movement, for, when these Western

> Indologists unearthed the literary treasures of India, making them accessible to the whole world and bestowing high praise upon them and when they recovered India's forgotten ancient history from newly deciphered inscriptions and coins, they strengthened India's self-respect, made Indians proud of their own culture and their glorious past, and helped them to shake off inferiority complexes, in short they helped the Indian genius to reassert itself against the spiritual onslaught of the West. – Alsdorf 1964: 26

More significantly, it should also not be forgotten that Max Müller's contribution to Vedic studies would not have been recognized in the traditional circles of India, had social reformers and enlightened citizens of India like Dayananda not accepted and appreciated the same in unequivocal terms.

Besides the first edition of complete *Ṛgveda* text with Sāyaṇa's commentary, Max Müller's chief work in the field of history of religion is the publication of a series of volumes under "The Sacred Books of the East". The series comprised no less than fifty-one volumes affording ample insight into the Oriental philosophy. In fact, Max Müller had instigated this work at the International Congress of Orientalists in 1874. He himself contributed the translation of the principal Upaniṣads, Vedic Hymns and the Dhammapada. Max Müller also published a *History of Ancient Sanskrit Literature* and the *Six Systems of Indian Philosophy.* In addition to this he delivered several lectures on Indological subjects and these lectures were also published under various headings such as *Chips from a German Workshop* (four volumes), *Lectures on the Science of Language* (fourteen editions), *Science of Language* (two volumes) and *India: What It Can Teach Us?* His *Autobiography: A Fragment* was published in 1901.

Thus, just glancing through the details of Max Müller's writings, the mind indeed bogs at the capacity for work of a man who was so truly dedicated to his avocation, that no words can pay a befitting tribute to his vast and everlasting contribution to Indology in general and Vedic studies in particular. Still, the following words of an Indian scholar are worth quoting:

> Of all contacts with the West, the most fruitful for India was the contacts with the German Orientalists, in the last century. India benefited a good deal by this. A new outlook on life sprang up in the place of the old one, which had become fossilized for centuries. It was just like a cool, refreshing breeze blowing in a stuffy room. Among those great savants who had contributed so much for this new outlook, none deserves our thanks more than the German scholar Max Müller. – Pant 1956

V

German scholars have also worked on the other three Vedas. Of them, the *Sāmaveda* was the first to be completely edited and translated into German. Theodor Benfey (1809-81) got it printed as early as 1848. After that the text of *Śukla Yajurveda* was published in 1852-59 by Albrecht Weber (1825–1901). Leopold von Schroeder (1851–1921) first prepared the edition of *Kṛṣṇa Yajurveda Maitrāyaṇīya Saṁhitā* in two volumes (1881-86) and then of the *Kāṭhaka Saṁhitā* in four volumes (1900-1910). As already mentioned, the text of the *Atharvaveda* was edited by Rudolph von Roth and W.D. Whitney in 1855-56 and its translation by Theodor Aufrecht (1821–1907) and Albrecht Weber appeared from 1850 onwards in several volumes of the latter's *Indische Studien*, but was not complete. Besides them, Julius Grill (1840–1918?) also translated 100 songs from the *Atharvaveda*.

Vedic studies in Germany were not only centred on the editing of texts and their translations, but many German scholars were also focusing on much more detailed research on topics related to Vedic literature. Hermann Oldenberg (1854–1920) wrote an important work on the *Religion of the Veda* and his two volumes of exegetical notes on the *Ṛgveda* are also a veritable mine of information. Besides this, Alfred Hillebrandt (1853–1927) published his challenging *Vedic Mythology* in two volumes and

Heinrich Zimmer (1890–1943) wrote his *Life in Ancient India* wherein he has discussed the social and cultural aspects of everyday life in Vedic India.

Thereafter Richard Pischel (1849–1908) published his three volumes entitled *Vedic Studies* in 1889, 1897 and 1901 in collaboration with K. Geldner. Pischel was of the opinion that the Vedas could be understood only by persons who have a profound knowledge of Indian thought of later periods and he regarded the Indian commentators as indispensable.

Moreover, there are several editions, translations and research works on the Brāhmaṇa texts wherein noted German scholars such as Martin Haug (1827-76), Hans Oertel (1868–1952), Sten Konow (1867–1948), a Norwegian scholar who often wrote in German, have made their mark. Julius Eggeling (1842–1918), Willem Caland, a Dutch scholar who wrote mostly in German (1859–1932), and Wilhelm Rau are also worth mentioning in this regard. Among the German scholars who have worked on the Upaniṣads, Johannes Hertel (1872–1955), H. Eduard Roer (1805-66), Paul Deussen (1845–1919) and Herman Jacobi (1850–1937) are significant. It shows that the tradition of Vedic studies in Germany has continued from the time of the first edition of the *R̥gveda* and later scholars like Paul Thieme, Walter Wilst and Karl Hoffmann have sustained interest in this field.

VI

In more recent times, several German scholars have made Vedic gods subjects of their monographs: Although Heinrich Lüder's (1869–1943) major work on the Vedic deity Varuṇa remained incomplete till the time of his death, yet his worthy pupil Ludwig Alsdorf has edited in two volumes those parts of the manuscript (Göttingen 1951-59), which had escaped the vicissitudes of war and were available. Paul Thieme has worked on Mitra and Aryaman, New Haven, CT, 1957. H.P. Schmidt on Br̥haspati and Indra, Wiesbaden, 1968. Further, the problem of the age of Veda has also caught the attention of later scholars and no consensus has been arrived at so far. Accordingly, W. Wuest of Muenchen has discussed *History of Style and Chronology of the Veda* and his study has been published from Leipzig, 1926. Besides, Paul Thieme's *Studies in the Etymology and Interpretation of the Rigveda* has been published from Halle, in 1949.

To conclude, it must be emphasized again that the above brief delineation is in no way perfect and systematic since there will still be many more names as well as works which might have escaped the attention of the compiler. This small write-up is just meant to give a glimpse of the rich and vast, continuous and far-reaching contribution of German scholars to the field of Vedic studies. If this article is able to generate any amount of interest in the minds of young Indian scholars to undertake a comprehensive, detailed account of Vedic studies in Germany, then it will really be a rewarding exercise and a fitting tribute to the toiling spirit of German Indologists.

Bibliography

Primary Sources

Aitareya Brāhmaṇa with the Commentary of Sāyaṇa, 2 vols, Pune: Anandashram, 1891.

Aitareya Upaniṣad (AitaUp), Eight Upaniṣads with the Commentary of Śaṅkarācārya, vol. II, tr. Swāmī Gambhīrānanda, 12th impression, Delhi: Publication Department, 2000.

Amarakośa of Amarasiṁha, Hindi tr. Brahmananda Tripathi, Varanasi: Chowkhamba Surabharati, 1992 (4th edn).

Āpastamba Śrautasūtra, ed. Narasimhachar, Mysore: Government Oriental Library, 1944.

Aṣṭādhyāyī of Pāṇini, vols. I-II, English tr. Srisa Chandra Vasu, Benares, 1898.

Āśvalāyana Gṛhyasūtra, ed. V.G. Apte, Pune: Anandashram Press, 1936.

Atharvaveda (AV) with English tr. Svami Satya Prakash Sarasvati and Udaya Vir Viraj, New Delhi: Veda Pratishthan, 1996 (repr. 2009).

Atharvaveda Saṁhitā, ed. Satya Prakash Sarasvati and Satyakam Vidyalankar, vols I-IV, 1996, New Delhi: Veda Pratishthan.

Bhaktisūtra see under Śāṇḍilya.

Brahmasūtra Bhāṣya of Śaṅkarācārya, Eng tr. Swāmī Gambhīrānanda, (6th impression) Calcutta: Advaita Ashrama, 1996.

Bṛhadāraṇyaka Upaniṣad, see *Aitareya Upaniṣad* above.

Bṛhaddevatā of Śaunaka, ed. A.A. Macdonell, Delhi: Motilal Banarsidass, (2nd impression), 1965.

Chāndogya Upaniṣad, 10th edn, Gorakhpur: Geeta Press, Saṁvat 2058.

Gopatha Brāhmaṇa of the Atharvaveda (*GoBrā*) in the original Sanskrit, ed. Rajendralal Mitra and Harachandra Vidyabhushan, Calcutta: Asiatic Society, 1870-72.

Jaiminīya or Talavakāra Upaniṣad Brāhmaṇa (*JaiUp*), the Text, Translation and Notes, ed. Hanns Oertel, New Haven: American Oriental Society, 1894.

Jaiminīya Upaniṣad Brāhmaṇa (The) or *Talvakāra Upaniṣad Brāhmaṇa*: Devanāgarī text with indexes in Roman script prepared from the edition of Hanns Oertel by Paṇḍit Rāmadeva with an Introduction of the History of Sāmaveda Literature by Bhagavaddatta, Lahore, 1921.

Jaiminīya-nyāyamālā, Pune: Anandashrama Press, 1946.

Kaṭha Upanisad (*KaṭhUp*), *Eight Upaniṣads with the Commentary of Śaṅkarācārya*, vol. II, tr. Swāmī Gambhīrānanda, Kolkata: Advaita Ashrama (12th impression), 2000.

Kātyāyana's *Vārttika* on Pāṇinī's *Aṣṭādhyāyī* (see *Aṣṭādhyāyī above*).

Kauṣītaki Brāhmaṇa Upanishad, ed. E.B. Cowell, Calcutta: Asiatic Society of Bengal, 1861.

Lakṣaṇasaṁgraha, ed. Gaurishankara, Jamelpur: Manabharidevi, Puttigram, 1996.

Maitrāyaṇī Saṁhitā of *Yajurveda*, ed. S.D. Satavalekar, Pardi: Svādhyāyamaṇḍala, 1998 (vs).

Manusmṛti (*MS*), ed. Surendra Kumar and Rajvir, Delhi: Arsha Sahitya Prachar Trust, 1999.

Mīmaṁsāsūtras of Jaimini, English tr. N.V. Thadani, Delhi: Bharatiya Kala Prakashan, 2007.

Muṇḍaka Upaniṣad, see *Kaṭha Upaniṣad* above.

Nighaṇṭu and the Nirukta by Lakshman Sarup, Delhi: Motilal Banarsidass, 2002 (repr.).

Nyāyakośa, Bhimacharya Jhalkikar, Pune: Bhandarkar Oriental Research Institute, 1978.

Nyāyamañjarī, Jayanta Bhaṭṭa, 2 vols, ed. K.S. Varadacharya, Mysore: The Oriental Research Institute, 1969.

Nyāyavārttikatātparyaṭīkā of Vācaspati Miśra, ed. Anantlal Thakur, New Delhi: Indian Council of Philosophical Research, 1996.

Parāśara-Mādhavīya of Mādhavācārya, ed. Vāmana Śāstrī Islampurkar, Bombay Sanskrit Series, Bombay: Government Central Book Depot, 1893.

Pāraskara Gṛhyasūtra, ed. Mahadeva Gangadhar Bakre, Delhi: Munshiram Manoharlal, 1982.

Ṛgbhāṣyabhūmikā (*Ṛgbhābhū*) of Sāyaṇācārya, ed. Haridatt Shastri, Varanasi: Vishwavidyalaya Prakashan, 1972.

Ṛgveda (*ṚV*) with English tr. Svami Satya Prakash Sarasvati and Satyakam Vidyalankar, New Delhi: Veda Pratishthan, 1996 (repr. 2009).

Ṛgveda Saṁhitā, ed. Satya Prakash Sarasvati and Satyakam Vidyalankar, vols I-XIII, New Delhi: Veda Pratishthan, 1977-87.

Ṛgveda Saṁhitā, ed. Śrīpāda Damodar Satvalekar, Pāraḍi (Surat): Svādhyāya Maṇḍala, 1957.

Śābara Bhāṣya, 3 volumes, English tr. Ganganatha Jha, Baroda: Oriental Institute, 1933.

Śabdakalpadruma, Raja Radhakanta Dev, 5 vols, Delhi: Nag Publishers, 2018.

Sāmaveda (*SV*) with English tr. Svami Satya Prakash Sarasvati and Satyakam Vidyalankara, New Delhi: Veda Pratishthan, 1995.

Sāmaveda Saṁhitā, ed. Satya Prakash Sarasvati and Satyakam Vidyalankar, vols I-II, New Delhi: Veda Pratishthan, 1991-95.

Śaṇḍilya Bhaktisūtras, translated into English, Tridandi Sri Bhakti Prajñāna Yati, Madras: Sree Gaudiya Math, 1991.

Śāṅkhāyana Āraṇyaka (*ŚāṅĀr*), ed. A.B. Keith, New Delhi: Oriental Books, 1975.

Śāṅkhāyana Brāhmaṇa, ed. R.R.G.G. Ojha, Pune: Anandashram Printing Press, 1977.

Sanskrit Studies in GDR, Part II: *Bibliography*, ed. Centre of Sanskrit Studies in the GDR, Berlin, 1978.

Sarva-Darśana-Saṁgraha of Mādhavācārya or Review of the Different Systems of Hindu Philosophy Eng. tr. E.B. Cowell and A.E. Gough, London: Kegan Paul, 1894 (reprinted with fresh typeset in 2016 by D.K. Printworld, New Delhi).

Śatapatha Brāhmaṇa (*ŚatBrā*), according to the text of the Mādhyandina School, Eng. tr. Julius Eggeling, Delhi: Motilal Banarsidass, 1978.

Śatapaṭha Brāhmaṇa of White Yajurveda in the Mādhyandina Recension, ed. A. Chinnaswami Shastri and Pattabhirama Shastri, Varanasi: Chaukhambha Prakashan, 2014 (repr.).

Ślokavārttika of Kumārila, English tr. Ganganatha Jha, 3 vols, Delhi: Sri Satguru Publication, 1983 (2nd edn).

Śrīmad Bhagavadgītā with the commentary *Padayojanā* of Śrī Rāmacandrācārya Sarasvatī, edited and published by S. Revathy, Chennai, 2005.

Taittirīya Āraṇyaka with the Commentary of Bhaṭṭa Bhāskara Miśra, ed. A. Mahadeva Sastri, 2 vols, Bibliotheca Sanskrita, nos 26-27, Mysore, Government Oriental Library Series, 1900.

Taittirīya Brāhmaṇa (*TaiBrā*) with the Commentary of Bhaṭṭa Bhāskara Miśra, ed. A. Mahadeva Sastri, 4 vols, Delhi: Motilal Banarsidass, 1985 (repr.).

Tāṇḍya Mahābrāhmaṇa with the commentary of Sāyaṇācārya, Calcutta: Asiatic Society of Bengal, 1870.

Vācaspatyam, (6 vols.), Taranatha Tarkavacaspati Bhattacharya, Varanasi: Chowkhamba Sanskrit Series, 1990.

Vājasaneyī Saṁhitā of *Yajurveda*, ed. Vasudev Laxman Sastri Pansikar, Bombay, 1929.

Vālmīki Rāmāyaṇa (vols.I-II), Gorakhpur: Gita Press, Saṁvat 2072.

Yājñavalkya Smṛti, with the commentary by Aparārka, Pune: Anandasram Press, 1903.

Yajurveda (*YV*) with English tr. Svami Satya Prakash Sarasvati and Udaya Vir Viraj, New Delhi: Veda Pratishthan, 1996 (repr. 2009).

Yajurveda Saṁhitā, ed. Satya Prakash Sarasvati and Satyakam Vidyālaṅkara (vols I-III), New Delhi: Veda Pratishthan, 1989-96.

Yogasūtra of Patañjali with the commentary of Vyāsa, Delhi: Motilal Banarsidass, 1996.

Secondary Sources

Abhayadeva, 2006, "Nighaṇṭu-Nirukta meṅ Vāṅnāma", in *Veda as Word*, ed. ShashiPrabha Kumar, pp. 165-72, New Delhi: Special Centre for Sanskrit Studies, JNU and D.K. Printworld.

Agrawala, V.S., 1963, *The Thousand Syllablled Speech*, vol. I, Varanasi: Prithivi Prakashan.

———, 1983, *Urujyoti*, Sonepat: Ramlal Kapur Trust.

Aguilar, H., 1976, *The Sacrifice in the R̥gveda*, Delhi: Bharatiya Vidya Prakashan.

Aklujkar, Ashok, 2001, "The Paṇḍits from a Piṇḍa-Brahmāṇḍa Point of View", in *The Pandit*, ed. Axel Michaels, New Delhi: Manohar.

Alsdorf, Ludwig, 1964, "Indian Studies in Germany", in *Indian Studies Abroad*, New Delhi: Indian Council of Cultural Relations and Asia Publishing House, London.

Altekar, A.S., 1956, *The Position of Women in Hindu Civilization*, Varanasi: Motilal Bararsidass.

Anirvan, Shrimat, 2001, "Vedic Exegesis", in *Cultural Heritage of India*, vol. I, Calcutta: Ramkrishna Mission Institute of Culture.

Apte, Balashastri Hardas (n.d.), *Glimpses of the Vedic Nation*, e-book, Madras: Sri Kamakoti Publishing House.

Aurobindo, Sri, 1985, *Archives and Research*, December.

———, 1998, *Secret of the Veda*, Pondicherry: Sri Aurobindo Ashram.

Bader, Clarisse, 1965, *Women in Ancient India*, tr. Mary E.R. Martin, Varanasi: Chaukhamba.

Balasubramaniam, R., 1996, *Primal Spirituality of the Vedas*, Project of History of Indian Philosophy and Science, New Delhi: Indian Council of Philosophical Research.

Bhargava, Dayanand, 2006, "Vedic Mantra-Vijñāna", in *Veda as Word*, ed. ShashiPrabha Kumar, pp. 65-70, New Delhi: D.K. Printworld.

Bhattacharya, N.N., 1990, *A Glossary of Indian Religious Terms and Cencepts*, New Delhi: Manohar.

Bloomfield, M., 1972, *Religion of the Vedas*, Delhi: Indological Book House.

Bose, A.C., 1966, *Hymns from the Vedas*, Bombay: Bharatiya Vidya Bhavan.

———, (1954 1960, 1999), *The Call of the Vedas*, Bombay: Bharatiya Vidya Bhavan.

Chaturvedi, Girdhar Sharma, 1972, *Vaidik Vijñāna aura Bhāratīya Saṁskṛti*, (Hindi) Patna: Bihar Rashtrabhasha Parishad.

Chaubey, B.B., 1970, *Treatment of Nature in the Rigveda*, Hoshiarpur: Vedic Sahitya Sadan.

Clooney, F.X., 1987, "Why the Veda Has No Author: Language as Ritual in Early Mīmāṁsā and Post-modern Theology", *Journal of the American Academy of Religion*, 55(4): 659-84.

———, 1990, *Thinking Ritually*, Vienna: Publications of the de Nobili Research Library.

Coburn, Thomas B., 1984, "Scripture in India: Towards a Typology of the Word in Hindu Life", *Journal of the American Academy of Religion*, 52(3): 435-59.

Coomaraswamy, Ananda K., 2000, "Vedic Exemplarism", in *Perception of the Vedas*, ed. Vidyanivas Misra, pp. 355-74, New Delhi: Indira Gandhi National Centre for the Arts.

Coward, Harold, 1992, *Sacred Word and Sacred Text*, Delhi: Sri Satguru Publications.

Cromwell, S. Crawford, 1974, *Evolution of Hindu Ethical Ideals*, Calcutta: Firma KLM.

Dandekar, R.N., 1978, *Vedic Bibliography*, vol. I (2nd edn, 1986), vol. II (repr. 1978), Poona: Bhandarkar Oriental Reserch Institute.

Das, Priyavrata, 2012, *Glimpses of the Yajurveda*, 2nd edn, Bhubaneswar: Vaidik Anusandhan Pratisthan.

Das, Santosh Kumar, 1986, *The Education System of the Ancient Hindus*, Delhi: Gian Publishing House.

Deussen, Paul, 1908, *Philosophy of the Upanisads*, Edinburgh: T & T Clark.

Emeneau, M.B., 1967, *A Union List of Printed Indic Texts and Translations*, (repr.), New York: American Oriental Society.

Fox, Nick J., 1997, "Is There Life After Death?: Texts, Frames and Differends", in *Foucault, Health and Medicine*, ed. Alan Petersen and Robin Bunton, pp. 31-50, London: Routledge.

Gonda, Jan, 1963, "The Indian Mantra", *Oriens*, 16: 242-97.

———, 1975, *Vedic Literature: A History of Indian Literature*, vol. 1, Part I, Wiesbaden: Otto Harrassowitz.

Heimann, Betty, 1937, *Indian and Western Philosophy*, London: George Allen and Unwin (reprinted by D.K. Printworld, New Delhi, 2018).

Jha, Baccha, 1988, *Śāstradīpikā*, Varanasi: Krishnadas Academy.

Jha, Ganganath, 1964, *Pūrvamīmāṁsā in Its Sources*, Varanasi: Banaras Hindu University.

Joshi, Kireet (ed.), 1988, *The Good Teacher and the Good Pupil*, Auroville: Auroville Foundations.

Kane, P.V., 1941, *History of Dharmaśāstra: Ancient and Medieval Religious and Civil Law*, vol. II, parts I and II, Poona: Bhandarkar Oriental Research Institute.

———, 1973, *History of Dharmaśāstra*, vol. IV, 2nd edn, Poona: Bhandarkar Oriental Research Institute.

Kaviraj, Gopinath, 2009, *Bhāratīya Saṁskṛti aur Sādhanā* (Hindi), part II, Patna: Bihar Rashtrabhasha Parishad.

Keith, A.B., 1925, *The Religion and the Philosophy of the Vedas and Upaniṣads*, Massachusetts: Harvard Oriental Series.

Krishnamurti, J., 2013, "Is What You Call Conflict ?", in Speaking Tree, *Times of India*, 10 June, abridged from his first dialogue in Rome, 1986 (*courtesy*: KFI).

Kumar, ShashiPrabha (ed.), 2006a, *Veda as Word*, New Delhi: Special Centre for Sanskrit Studies, Jawaharlal Nehru University and D.K. Printworld.

———, 2006b, "The Concept of Veda-Apauruṣeyatva", in *Pūrvamīmāṁsā from an Interdisciplinary Point of View*, ed. K.T. Pandurangi, vol. II, part 6, pp. 235-251, PHISPC, New Delhi: Centre for Studies in Civilization.

———, (ed.), 2005, *Salf, Society and Value: Reflections on Indian Philosophical Thaught*, Delhi: Vidyanidhi Prakashan.

———, 2005a, "Ethical Concepts in the Vedas", in *Self, Society and Value: Reflections on Indian Philosophical Thought*, ed. ShashiPrabha Kumar, pp. 26-33, Delhi: Vidyanidhi Prakashan.

———, 2005b, "Guru-Siṣya Relationship in Vedic Education", in *Self Society and Value: Reflections on Indian Thought*, ed. ShashiPrabha Kumar, pp. 90-107, Delhi: Vidyanidhi Prakashan.

———, 2005c, "Vedic Yajña: From Ritual to Spiritual", in *Self, Society and Value: Reflection on Indian philosophical Thought*, ed. ShashiPrabha Kumar, pp. 59-75, Delhi: Vidyanidhi Prakashan, (Author, provide page range).

———, 2003, "Obligations Towards Others: The Indian Perspective", in *Breaking the Barriers: Essays in Asian and Comparative Philosophy*, ed. Frank Hoffman and G. Mishra, pp. 219-26, Fremont, USA: Asian Humanities Press.

———, 1999, *Facets of Indian Philosophical Thought*, Delhi: Vidyanidhi Prakashan.

———, 1999a, "Indian Feminism and Vedic Thought", in *Facets of Indian Philosophical Thought*, ed. ShashiPrabha Kumar, pp. 25-43, Delhi: Vidyanidhi Prakashan.

———, 1999b, "Ecology and Conservation in the Bhūmisūkta of Atharvaveda", in *Facets of Indian Philosophical Thought*, ed. ShashiPrabha Kumar, pp. 56-69, Delhi: Vidyanidhi Prakashan.

———, 1999c, "Vedic Philosophy of Education", in *Facets of Indian Philosophic Thought*, ed. ShashiPrabha Kumar, pp. 11-24, Delhi: Vidyanidhi Prakashan.

———, 1998a, "Indian Feminism in Vedic Perspective", *Journal of Studies on Ancient India*, 1(2-4): 141-52.

———, 1998b, "Vaidik Sarasvati: Viduṣī Nārī ke Rūpa Meiṅ", in *Vaidika Anuśīlana*, (Hindi), pp.136-48, Delhi: Vidyanidhi Prakashan.

Leifer, Walter, 1971, *India and the Germans,* Bombay: Shakuntala Publishing House.

Lupton, Deborah, 1994, *Medicine as Culture: Illness, Disease and the Body in Western Societies*, London: Sage Publications.

Macdonell, A.A., 1971, *A History of Sanskrit Literature*, Delhi: Munshi Ram Manohar Lal.

———, 2002, *Vedic Mythology* (repr.), Delhi: Motilal Banarsidass.

Macdonell, A.A. and A.B. Keith, 1962, *Vedic Index*, vol. 2 (Hindi tr. Ramkumar Rai), Varanasi: Chowkhamaba Vidyabhawan.

Mee, Jean Le, 1975, *Hymns from the Ṛig-Veda*, New York: Alfred A. Knopf and Random House, Toronto, Canada.

Mishra, Vidya Nivas, 2000, *Perception of the Vedas*, ed. Ananda K. Coomaraswamy, New Delhi: Indira Gandhi National Centre for the Arts.

———, 2004, "Ṛta in Veda", in *Ṛta: The Cosmic Order*, ed. Madhu Khanna, New Delhi: Indira Gandhi National Centre for the Arts and D.K. Printworld.

Monier-Williams, Monier, 2005, *A Sanskrit–English Dictionary*, Delhi: Sharada Publishing House.

———, 2003, *English–Sanskrit Dictionary,* New Delhi: Munshiram Manoharalal.

———, 1966, *Sanskrit–English Dictionary*, Varanasi: Indica Books.

Mookerji, R.K., 1947, *Ancient Indian Education* (repr.), Delhi: Macmillan.

Moore, Charles (ed.), 2008 (rpr.), *The Indian Mind,* Delhi: Motilal Banarsidass.

Müller, Max, 1971, *Six Systems of Indian Philosophy*, Varanasi: Chowkhamba Sanskrit Series Office, fourth edn (1st published from London, 1919; retypeset edn published in 2024 by D.K. Printworld, New Delhi).

Müller, Max, 1883, *India What Can It Teach Us,* New York: Funk & Wagnalls Publishers.

Mumford, Lewis, 1956, *The Transformations of Man*, New York: Harper and Brothers.

Narahari, H.G., 1944, *Atman in the Pre-Upaniṣadic Vedic Literature*, Madras: University of Madras.

Nikhilananda, Swami, 1967, "The Realistic Aspect of Indian Spirituality", in *Indian Mind*, Hawai'i: University of Hawai'i Press.

Noelle, W., 1963, *Impact of Indian Thought on German Poets and Philosophers*, Etah: The World Jain Mission.

O'Flaherty, W.D., 2000, *The Ṛig Veda: An Anthology*, London: Penguin Books.

Padoux, André, 1992, *Vāc: The Concept of the Word*, tr. Jacues Gontier, Delhi: Sri Satguru Publication.

Pandey, R.P., 1995, "The Vision of the Vedic Seer", in *Hindu Spirituality*, ed. Krishna Sivaraman, Delhi: Motilal Banarsidass.

Panikkar, Raimundo, 2001, *The Vedic Experience Mantramañjarī* (repr.), Delhi: Motilal Banarsidass.

Pant, A.V.S., 1956, *Voice of Ahimsa* (October).

Plott, J.C., 1974, *A Philosophy of Devotion*, Delhi: Motilal Banarsidass.

Prabhavananda, Swami, 1962, *The Spiritual Heritage of India*, London: George Allen & Unwin.

Radhakrishnan, S., 1953, *Principal Upanisads*, London: George Allen & Unwin.

———, 1956, *Indian Philosophy*, vol. 1 (X[th] Impression), London: George Allen & Unwin.

———, 2007, *Indian Philosophy*, vol. 1, 16th impression, New Delhi: Oxford University Press.

Raghavan, V., 1956a, *The Indian Heritage*, Bangalore: The Indian Institute of Culture.

———, 1956b, *Sanskrit and Allied Indological Studies in Europe*, Madras: University of Madras.

Raja, K. Kunjunni, 1963, *Indian Theories of Meaning*, Madras: Adyar Library and Research Centre.

Raju, P.T., 1982, "The Concept of the Spiritual in Indian Thought", in *Spirit, Being, and Self*, New Delhi: South Asian Publishers.

Rao Shastri, Shakuntala, 1969, *Women in the Vedic Age*, Bombay: Bharatiya Vidya Bhavan.

Renou, Louis, 1931, *Bibliographic Vedique,* Paris: Paris Librarie of Amerique et d'orient.

———, 1957, *Vedic India,* Classical India, volume three, Calcutta: Susil Gupta (India) Pvt.Ltd.

Saraswati, Dayananda, 2001, *Svamantavyamantavyaprakaśa*, 422-27, appended in *Satyārthaprakāśa*, Delhi: Arsha Sahitya Prachara Trust.

———, 2001a, *Satyārthaprakāśa*, Samullāsa I: Īśvaranāma Vyākhyā, Delhi: Arsha Sahitya Prachara Trust.

———, 2008, *R̥gvedādibhāṣyabhūmikā, Vedaviṣayavicāraḥ*, Delhi: Arsha Sahitya Prachara Trust (first published 1993).

Sarasvati, Vidyananda 1997, *Veda-Mimāṁsā* (Hindi), Delhi: Vijaykumar Govindram Hansanand.

Satavalekar, n.d., *Vaidik Vyākhyānamālā* (Hindi), Pardi: Swadhyaya Mandal.

Schweitzer, Albert, 1960, *Indian Thought and Its Development*, Boston: Beacon Press.

Sharma, Acharya Shriram, 2003, *Eternity of Sound and the Science of Mantras* (*Sabda Brahm*: *Mantra Vijñāna*), Haridwar: Yugantar Chetna Press.

Sharma, Baldev Raj, 1972, *The Concept of Ātman in the Principal Upaniṣads*, Delhi: Dinesh Publications.

Sharma, I.C., 1991, *Ethical Philosophies of India*, 2nd edn, Ghaziabad: International Publishing, Dubai.

Sharma, Munshiram, 1979, *Bhakti kā Vikāsa* (Hindi), Varanasi: Chaukhamba Vidyabhavan.

Sharma, Pandit Shriram (Acharya), 2003, *Eternity of Sound and the Science of Mantras* (*Śabda Brahma: Mantra Vijñāna*), Haridwar: Yugantar Chetana Press.

Singh, Balbir, 1984, *Hindu Ethics*, New Delhi: Arnold-Heinemann.

Sivaraman, Krishna (ed.), 1995, *Hindu Spirituality: Vedas Through Vedanta*, Delhi: Motilal Banarsidass.

Staal, Frits, 1979, "Oriental Ideas on the Origin of Language", *Journal of the American Oriental Society*, 99.

Stache-Rosen, Valentina, 1981, *German Indologists: Dialogue*, New Delhi: Max Müller Bhawan.

Stietencorn, H.V., 1969, *German Indology: Past and Present*, Bombay: Shakuntala Publishing House.

Sundarraj, M., 1994, *Ṛgvedic Studies*, Madras: International Society for the Investigation of Ancient Civilization.

Upadhyaya, B.S., 1974, *Women in Ṛgveda*, New Delhi: S. Chand Publishers.

Vedalankara, Ram Nath, 2042 (Vikram Saṁvat), *Vaidika Nārī* (Hindi), New Delhi: Samarpana Shodha Sansthana.

———, 1991, *Vaidika Madhuvṛṣṭi* (Hindi), Delhi: Govindram Hasanand.

———, 1976, *Vedoṅ kī Varṇana-Śailiyāṅ* (Hindi), Haridwar: Gurukul Kangri Vishwavidyalaya.

Vedamitra, 1964, *Education in Ancient India*, Delhi: Arya Book Depot.

Yajña-saṁskṛti, 1983, *Videha-vāṇī* II (Hindi), pp. 174-77, Ajmer: Veda Sansthan.

Woodroffe, John, 1950, *The Serpent Power*, Madras: Ganesh & Co.

Wujastyk, Dominik, 2009, "Interpreting the Image of the Human Body in Premodern India", *International Journal of Hindu Studies*, 13(2): 189-228.

Index